**ROCKETMAN**

**NEW AMERICAN LIBRARY**

# ROCKET MAN

**ASTRONAUT PETE CONRAD'S INCREDIBLE RIDE TO THE MOON AND BEYOND**

Nancy Conrad and Howard A. Klausner

Introduction by Buzz Aldrin

New American Library
Published by New American Library, a division of
Penguin Group (USA) Inc., 375 Hudson Street,
New York, New York 10014, USA
Penguin Group (Canada), 10 Alcorn Avenue, Toronto,
Ontario M4V 3B2, Canada (a division of Pearson Penguin Canada Inc.)
Penguin Books Ltd., 80 Strand, London WC2R 0RL, England
Penguin Ireland, 25 St. Stephen's Green, Dublin 2,
Ireland (a division of Penguin Books Ltd.)
Penguin Group (Australia), 250 Camberwell Road, Camberwell, Victoria 3124,
Australia (a division of Pearson Australia Group Pty. Ltd.)
Penguin Books India Pvt. Ltd., 11 Community Centre, Panchsheel Park,
New Delhi - 110 017, India
Penguin Group (NZ), cnr Airborne and Rosedale Roads, Albany,
Auckland 1310, New Zealand (a division of Pearson New Zealand Ltd.)
Penguin Books (South Africa) (Pty.) Ltd., 24 Sturdee Avenue,
Rosebank, Johannesburg 2196, South Africa

Penguin Books Ltd., Registered Offices: 80 Strand, London WC2R 0RL, England

First published by New American Library, a division of Penguin Group (USA) Inc.

First Printing, May 2005
10  9  8  7  6  5  4  3  2  1

NEW AMERICAN LIBRARY and logo are trademarks of Penguin Group (USA) Inc.

LIBRARY OF CONGRESS CATALOGING-IN-PUBLICATION DATA:

Conrad, Nancy.
　　Rocketman : astronaut Pete Conrad's incredible ride to the moon and beyond / Nancy Conrad and
Howard A. Klausner.
　　　p.　cm.
　　ISBN 0-451-21509-5 (hardcover : alk. paper)
　　1. Conrad, Pete, 1930–1999.　2. Astronauts—United States—Biography.　I. Klausner, Howard.
II. Title.
TL789.85.C657C66　2005
629.45'0092—dc22　　　　2004030189

Set in Fairfield
Designed by Ginger Legato

Printed in the United States of America

In memory of Pete Conrad
and dedicated to the child in all of us
who has experienced the exhilaration of
overcoming a challenge
and winning

He was the third man to walk on the Moon.
He was the first to dance on it.

He was the Rocketman.

# INTRODUCTION

**I** have two memories that stand above all others when I think of Pete Conrad. I should qualify that by noting the fact that Pete and I were friends and colleagues for nearly forty years. Like me, Pete flew in NASA's Gemini Program. He also walked on the Moon, four months after I did in 1969. Both of us invested much of our post-NASA time, energy, and resources opening up space to the general public, not just a fortunate few. Truth told, I could probably summon up a thousand Pete Conrad memories, if pressed. But my two favorites pretty much sum up this lightning rod of a man all by themselves.

And neither is what you'd probably think.

The first took place in the mid-nineties, when Pete and I found ourselves together in Los Angeles at an anniversary party celebrating an historic milestone. It wasn't terribly unusual for us to be at such an event—astronauts from our era are fortunate enough to have calendars full of such dates every year, many of them black-tie affairs, very stately and properly dignified.

This one was slightly different.

My wonderful wife, Lois Aldrin, and Nancy Conrad share a deep and abiding love for the rock band Pink Floyd, and when the band's record company decided to celebrate the twentieth anniversary of their milestone album, *The Dark Side of the Moon,* the ladies made darn sure they got an invite—by dragging two old guys who happened to have *walked* on the Moon as their dates. I probably don't need to note the fact that neither Pete nor I was terribly familiar with Pink Floyd, or this particular album. As a matter of fact, I recall more than a few grumbles and groans during the forty-five-minute drive to the gala about the two of us having to go to this thing in the first place.

"Relax," said Lois and Nancy, turning up the CD player, playing this music we would be honoring tonight. "You boys are going to have a ball."

As usual, they were right.

Now, if you don't know this about Pete, you're about to. He was, by far, the merriest prankster I ever met, simply unable to resist a good joke or yanking the chain of someone who took himself just a bit too seriously. We proceeded down the red carpet into the hall, fully aware that nobody in this crowd recognized us and that they were probably wondering how two guys born in 1930 managed to get a ticket. (Not to mention, *why.*) Our lovely wives were having a ball, so we got over ourselves.

Eventually, someone from one of those entertainment shows vaguely recognized us, or his boss did, and they fired up the TV lights and got a sound bite out of us. At the conclusion, the correspondent, who probably was in diapers when *Apollo 11* and *12* flew, smirked at Pete and asked, "So. What do you *really* think of *Dark Side of the Moon*?"

"Well, there is no dark side of the Moon, for starters." Pete smiled back.

"Oh, really? Then what do you call that?" The young man pointed rather snidely to a poster of the album's cover on the wall.

"Oh, I'm sure it's a great record. It's just misnamed. There is no dark side of the Moon; there's just the other side. The light shines on it too. We just don't see it when it does."

The poor guy was confused, and not entirely convinced. He, like most people, including Mr. Floyd, I guess, was under the mistaken impression that the Moon does not rotate and that there is a dark side, on which the sun's light never shines. Not so. And the guy certainly didn't seem to care for having his understanding of our solar system shaken up in front of his cameraman. But Pete being Pete, he patted the guy on the shoulder reassuringly. "Trust me. I've been there."

The evening ended with the crowd lying on beanbag chairs, staring up at a laser demonstration on the ceiling as the misnamed album played at a volume that I am certain is the limit of human sound tolerance. I looked over at the only other sixty-four-year-old in the room, and there was Pete, staring right back at me with the same amazed, excited, and just plain exuberant expression I'd seen at least a thousand times.

"Buzz, isn't this just *super*?!"

There are a number of astronaut tomes out there; scores of histories and analyses of the achievements of the men and women of the space program, with all the detail that an engineering or history student could ever want. This book is not that.

This book is the story of a man—a man who embodied the very spirit behind that space program. Charles "Pete" Conrad was a great pilot, a gifted engineer, a problem solver, and a natural-born leader. But it was that *gee whiz!* face, the wide-eyed, openmouthed curiosity and delight at lasers crisscrossing over his head to music, all the while with a brain thinking up a hundred new ideas simultaneously that he couldn't wait to share with someone . . . that was the spirit of all of us then. And that spirit put the two of us on the Moon.

That was Pete. That was my friend. And this amazing ride is his story.

If it were up to me to encapsulate Pete Conrad's place in history, i.e., his role along with all of us who were and are fortunate enough to be part of the NASA team, it would simply be *getting people into space*.

Pete and I agreed first and foremost that the Apollo Moon landings were humanity's first baby steps off this planet and onto another. The achievement remains, in my view, the most significant one in human history. But if that achievement is to be relegated to the status, say, of reaching the summit of

Mount Everest just because it is there, or breaking some sort of record simply to determine that it can be done, then that achievement was largely in vain.

Historians point out that there would have been no Apollo program, no American Moon landing in 1969, had there not been a Cold War and subsequent space race between the United States and the Soviet Union. True that may be, but for those of us tasked with actually getting people there and home again, the proverbial picture was a lot bigger than a "race." For all of us at NASA in those early years, the real mission was opening the door to space itself, for all humankind. And for many of us, like Pete and myself, it became our life's work.

A permanent human presence in space is inevitable. Whether we accomplish President Bush's challenge to establish a lunar base and Mars landing by 2020, or it takes much longer to establish this presence, history itself tells us that at some point, humanity will be forced to venture beyond the occasional orbital shuttle flight or visit to the International Space Station. Pete and I both believed that the Apollo and Skylab programs were the first steps in this venturing forth.

But they were indeed baby steps. And we haven't taken any new ones in a long time.

There are many compelling arguments to go boldly forth into space, and just as many against. It is expensive, it is dangerous, and space is largely unknown . . . now. But just as surely as we will someday run out of fossil fuels and be forced to make drastic changes in the production and consumption of our energy, there will come a time when the ability to leave this planet will be as necessary as crossing the ocean was to the Europeans in the Middle Ages, or leaving the coastal settlements to cross the Appalachians became for the early American colonists.

Then, as now, the key to that is in profit, not governments. True, governments were the ones who laid the groundwork, financing those first exploratory forays across the Atlantic and Pacific, then colonizing distant lands. And it was certainly the United States government—the taxpayers—who created and funded NASA, performing the exact same function in getting us to space.

But now that we've achieved this first round of goals in space, the very fair and necessary question remains: Now what? Is it even possible to open up space the same way the Europeans opened up the Atlantic and North America five hundred years ago? Obviously, the answer is no. Not yet. But eventually, this same pattern will emerge. Private citizens will venture into space. And profit will be their primary motivator.

Pete and I spent our careers working on this very thing, and I continue to do so today. Walking on the Moon was just that first step, and one of the things I loved most about this man was that he was far more interested in talking about the future than about an admittedly pretty terrific accomplishment we had in common. For more than thirty-five years, I can't remember a single conversation with Pete that didn't eventually roll around to rockets, cheaper and easier ways to get them into orbit, and how to reuse them and get people back to the Moon and beyond. And he always, always had that *gee whiz!* expression when it did.

Each of us believed that the private sector was the next logical place for space travel. Pete started four companies with that specific vision in mind. Indeed, he and I were among the first space entrepreneurs. His vision was more along the lines of a space airline or an orbital FedEx, as this book details. His favorite illustrations were getting "raspberries to Rome" in forty-five minutes, or an executive from her Chicago office to Tokyo in under an hour—all using a Single Stage to Orbit rocket.

I share the same vision, with a slightly broader application: space tourism. But not just going for a ride—how about staying in an orbiting space hotel? Purchasing a seat on a regular orbital sightseeing run to the Moon or Mars? The technology and know-how for this exists today. All that's required is the infrastructure. If that sounds overly optimistic business-wise, consider that the global outlay for mere terrestrial tourism is nearly four trillion dollars!

Pete used to say at the end of any flight, in or out of our atmosphere, "It's all about the ride." I can only imagine his happy, *gee whiz!* laugh, watching Burt Rutan capture the X-Prize in September of 2004, putting the first private vehicle into space twice in two weeks. And Richard Branson's launching of Virgin Galactic. Two private-sector businessmen venturing forth into space. Taking the next steps. Venturing forth.

But I promised you a second memory. This one took place more than a year after Pete died, at Johnson Space Center in Houston.

NASA had decided to dedicate a section of land at JSC to the memory of the astronauts who have departed this life, whether from old age, accident, or illness or in the line of duty. For each astronaut, a tree is planted, and there is of course a ceremony when a new one is added to the grove. As you can imagine, the ceremonies are fairly reflective, sometimes somber affairs.

When we dedicated Pete's tree, his beloved friend and *Apollo 12* crewmate Al Bean decided that Pete should be the one determining the tone of the day. When he took the podium, Al "channeled" the spirit of our departed comrade, which is itself a bit of a departure at a NASA ceremony. I don't recall anyone ever laughing out loud at one of these things before or since, but we surely did this day. And Pete would have had it no other way.

"Pete" had just one message to transmit from across the universal divide through Al, and it was for NASA administrator George Abbey. He thought it would be just a fine idea to light those trees at Christmastime. And reminding us all that his motto had always been "If you can't be good, be colorful," he further suggested . . . well, no, he *insisted* . . . that all those lights be white—except his.

And if you visit Johnson Space Center during the holidays, you will be pleased to note that NASA kept its promise to Pete Conrad. For among all the brilliant white, shining trees, reminding us of the lives and spirits of the men and women who have flown into space and then moved on from this life, only one shines with red and green bulbs.

And this is as it should be.

Enjoy the ride.

Buzz Aldrin
Los Angeles, California
February 3, 2005

# PROLOGUE

It wasn't a very lucrative job, sweeping up the hangar, mowing the lawn, fueling up and washing down single-engine airplanes at Paoli Airfield just off the Main Line in Philadelphia. It wasn't terribly exciting, either. If it weren't for the sound of a Tri-Motor passing through or an occasional touch-and-go, it could be as downright tedious as any other gig a sixteen-year-old could find in the hot-as-hell Pennsylvania summer of 1946. Actually, it was worse than that, because the planes were so close, and all Charles "Peter" Conrad could do was watch. And listen. And dream.

Yeah, but swinging a sling blade next to the dirt parking lot still beat jerking sodas or delivering newspapers. Summer for Peter Conrad was the same as most teenage summers, really, then or now. Work, baseball, a movie or a jitterbug with a pretty little thing once every blue moon. Just so long as it wasn't a cotillion. Peter loved to dance, but by sixteen there wasn't a force of nature strong enough to drag him back to that living hell.

It was pretty much down to one thing for Peter Conrad. Summer was all about the ride. He'd trade it all, any damn day of the week, for a ride.

Every now and then, Mr. Turner would take him up in the Piper, vents open, wind and motor so loud it didn't matter if Peter Conrad wanted to scream in teenage agony or joy. Nobody could hear him but that wind.

And Lord, what a day it was, two thousand feet over Muncie Valley, when old man Turner gave him the stick, and the bird was his. The boy's hand closed around it, and felt the vibration of the center of his universe. And like Moses himself before the burning bush, Peter Conrad heard his calling, and saw the rest of his life open up before his eyes.

**T**hat was *last* Saturday. His feet were planted firmly back on the ground today in the ninety-five-degree, 90-percent-humidity day. All by himself, in the unnatural quiet of a deserted airfield. No roaring Tri-Motors today, just flies, cicadas, bees, and the *swish* of his blade. The place was as dead as Saint David's Cemetery at midnight, and here stood the world's greatest aviator of the future, the boy who'd shot down a thousand Messerschmitts in his mind, chest-deep in weeds, swinging away, sweating and cussing his young ass off.

Time to smoke one of the Chesterfields he'd stolen from his older sister Patty. Sixteen was a little young to smoke, but truthfully, in the forties, it would have been odd if a hearty, strapping young man didn't. No surgeon general's warning on those packs; Glenn Miller had smoked them, hell, even Jimmy Stewart. If old man Turner saw him, the only thing that would matter to him was that Peter was taking a break from the weeds.

*The hell with it.* Peter sat down on a rock and lit up. Just half a drag—his young lungs couldn't yet take a grown-up hit of an unfiltered cigarette. He went deep into his thoughts—thoughts that shouldn't have gone so deep. Not yet.

The few bucks he was making shouldn't have mattered to a boy who started life in a three-story manor home they jokingly called the "Roadside Cottage," but they did now. He'd watched, not fully understanding, as the last of the staff left the place—just before the family moved from the cottage to somebody's empty three-bedroom carriage house in Saint David's, with Peter's uncle paying the rent. Father had moved out, with Mother's encouragement.

Sixteen was old enough now to understand that Charles Conrad Sr. was a soft heart who cried at the movies because it was the only place he could: crying at the family's fortune slipping like water through his hands, crying because he couldn't make a decision or make a stand like his wife. Crying because he couldn't face a day without a drink.

Without a lot of drinks.

Peter didn't cry. Mother wouldn't have stood for it; Father would have crumbled. So he just stayed in his room, tinkered with an Erector set, read *Popular Mechanics*, and listened like a musical connoisseur to the roar of his Indian motorcycle, up on blocks in the dirt-floored garage, throttling her up. He was too busy, moving too fast to cry.

If there was a God, thought the boy, He had a wide-open highway in His heaven, no speed limit, and definitely no age limit. He could take that iron monster out and let her roar anytime he damn well pleased.

There wasn't any mother and father on the Indian. No puny-ass carriage house, no disappearing fortune or crying father, or D in English when Peter would stomp it down a gear to redline her on a straightaway, and feel the rumbling between his legs, wind and motor filling his ears with the only sounds worthy of God's heaven. . . .

He stopped mid-drag. A sputtering motor—'27 Sopwith biplane, no doubt about it. Circling the field, a hundred feet, tops. Restart, and another sputter.

*Holy shit, this guy's in trouble.*

Peter sprinted for the flight line. There wasn't a soul in sight—including the Sopwith. *Where the hell is he?*

Another sputter, a gunning of the throttle, a big cough, and the silent shadow of a biplane over his head. This guy was out of gas, flying perpendicular to the runway, dropping like a stone. Nothing Peter could do but watch, and it wouldn't be pretty. The Sopwith banked a hard left, dead-stick, using the last airspeed he had, catching a puff of lazy wind. But the pilot was out of runway, nothing but trees where he was headed. He'd have to whip a one-eighty fast, too fast for that clunky old bird. The way he was dropping, he'd probably catch the two left wings and cartwheel her down the dirt field. Forty feet of altitude just wasn't enough. She wasn't moving fast enough to pull that turn.

*But damn if the sumbitch isn't gonna try.*

On instinct, Peter started running toward the landing strip like there was something—*anything*—he could do but watch. And watch he did, as the pilot yanked that little dead-stick biplane around. Peter swore that wingtip threw a wisp of dirt as it kissed the ground; then somehow the bird righted herself just as gravity won the day. Bounce, bounce, and she rolled to a gentle stop, not a hundred feet from the boy, as if it were any other landing on any other flight.

Peter Conrad moved wide-eyed toward the Sopwith like Dorothy approaching the Wizard of Oz himself. The pilot calmly flipped up his goggles and climbed down off the right wing step.

He looked like Apollo; six feet and then some, covered in leather top to bottom. Pencil-thin mustache, scarf thrown around him like a movie star. Matter of fact, he looked a lot like Clark Gable as he unbuckled the strap on that leather helmet. For all Peter knew, he *was* Gable. Or some World War II P-51 ace out for a spin this afternoon.

The pilot threw his hands on his hips as if this field and all the world belonged to him, and him alone. Surveying the flight line like Ike before D-day, he took out his own Chesterfield, firing it up with a shiny lighter. And he fixed his eyes on Peter.

"Say, there, boy."

"Yes, sir?"

"Mind if I ask you a question?"

"No, sir."

Another drag, another left-and-right survey. "Just where in hell am I, anyway?"

"Paoli Field." Pause. "Just off the Main Line." Another pause. "Philadelphia . . . ?"

"Philadelphia. Right." He took a deep drag. "So, west would be . . . ?"

"That way."

"Right." The pilot nodded, satisfied, and tossed the Chesterfield aside. "How about filling her up?"

"Yes, sir!"

And with that, the best airman Peter Conrad's young eyes had ever seen strode like a man to the back side of the hangar to gear down and take himself a monster leak.

And the boy knew that very moment that come hell or high water, by God, he was gonna grow up and be that man someday.

BOOK ONE

# DEPARTURE

# ONE

**February 12, 1996**
**Denver Centennial Airport**
**3:04 a.m. Local Time**

"Jeez, Paul, look out!"

"I got it, I got it!"

Learjets don't turn too well on the ground going one knot. This particular Lear, a 35 christened *Cablevision Tool*, lurched to its left, missing a parked Super Viking by a gnat's whisker just twenty feet into its roll out of the hangar.

It was all the sixty-five-year-old Pete Conrad could do not to laugh out loud as he belted himself into the rear left seat. "I could actually *use* a belt," the ex-astronaut joked to himself.

He actually hated the term *ex-astronaut*. He'd heard it easily a thousand times in the twenty-three years since he'd retired from NASA, but never so much as the last few weeks, coming from about half of the assembled throng here in the hangar at oh-dark-thirty. News cameras, PR people, friends, and family were here to send off Pete and three other pilots with cheers and waves as the Lear pointed toward the brand-spanking-new runway of this brand-spanking-new billion-dollar airport. They were having a go at the round-the-world speed record: 24,000 miles in under fifty hours in a business-class jet. And fifty feet out of the chocks, the damn thing nearly ended, their plane almost crunching into the side of another jet parked deferentially out of their way.

"Whoaaa . . ." mouthed the twenty-five-year-old fourth pilot, Dan Miller, looking over at Pete, wide-eyed.

"Just remember," Pete said reassuringly, winking. "If you can't be good, be colorful."

Behind the smile, the ex-astronaut was something less than relaxed, anticipating the full-power release coming up in about three minutes—in the hands of Paul Thayer, who in his day was one of the world's finest fighter pilots. But this wasn't his day. Paul was not prepared, not proficient in this aircraft, and not a young man anymore. Yet here the guy was in front of *USA Today,* the *Denver Post,* CNN and Channel 9 Denver, piloting them out of here into God knew what lay ahead.

Then who *should* be on the stick? Mark Calkins, the chief pilot of Daniels Communications? With his twenty-four hundred hours flying front left in this very aircraft, it was safe to say Mark knew it almost as well as he knew his wife, Deb.

How about the wet-behind-the-ears Miller to Conrad's right, just hired as the company's number two pilot, in the right place at the right time when Bill Daniels came up with this crazy idea?

Right place, right time. That was a familiar tune to the man who'd ridden the rocket. The kid was good. On the practice runs and in the sim, Pete saw in Miller a little of the old Pax River test pilot he'd once been. Not terribly experienced, constantly playing an imaginary drum set like he'd been drinking Red Bull all day, the guy was a born stick and rudder man.

Maybe it was right that it was the seventy-six-year-old World War II ace who'd done a round-the-worlder three years before. Paul Thayer was hell in a P-51 in 1945, and deserved the title of war hero.

But fifty years was still fifty years.

It didn't matter now. Pete had just made damn sure it wouldn't be *Pete* in the spotlight. After thirty-something years there he'd gotten used to it, but never much cared for it. This one wasn't about him. Hell, none of 'em were, and he'd be the first and loudest one to tell you that.

Yeah, he let them throw his name out in every press release and every news report running up to this takeoff, because it helped. This wasn't an attention-getting stunt by a billionaire businessman craving the spotlight, like climbing some mountain he had no business being on, or standing at the tiller of his zillion-dollar yacht, counting on the hired guns to do the heavy lifting on deck.

This flight wasn't about Bill Daniels and his money either. Hell, Daniels was a first-class combat pilot himself, and he wasn't even on board! So why? What could the billionaire possibly get out of all this if he wasn't even along for the ride?

Daniels had read Paul Thayer's journal of his round-the-world attempt in '93 (Thayer spent most of the two months checking out the world's best golf courses at each stop), and got an idea. Bill would take a shot at the speed record, employ the Metro State College Aviation Program in Denver, whom Bill sponsored, to act as a virtual mission control, and simulate the flight in real time with student pilots. And pledge up a few hundred grand to another passion, Junior Achievement, if they broke the mark. He'd use his company bird, another in his serial love affair with the Learjet; his pilot; and his old pal Pete Conrad, whose every NASA launch he'd attended, front row center. The flight itself would cost just shy of a half million, once the long-distance modifications and prep and fuel and possible payments to get out of any local stickiness abroad were factored in.

There was a lot at stake here, and Pete knew that. So he went about the three-month training and run-up with the dead seriousness he had carried into his *Gemini* flights. And *Apollo*. And *Skylab*. And he let his famous name attract more publicity, giving the same interview fifty times in the last week, playing the sound-bite game with the best of them.

*Hey, Pete, why you doing this?*

"Records are meant to be broken. It's this one's time."

*Isn't this a little tame, Pete, compared to walking on the Moon?*

"Aw, hell. Been there. Done that."

It worked like a charm. So the best stick and rudder man who ever strapped on a Navy plane—that coming from Al Shepard, who sure as hell didn't say that about anybody *else* but Al Shepard—just closed his eyes, sighed, and remembered what he was doing here in the first place, even if it was in the left rear seat, powerless.

This was for the record. For his friend. For the kids. But what it was really for was the ride.

Always the ride.

**M**ark Calkins, sitting in the copilot's seat, wasn't given to panic attacks. Flying the bush in Alaska for four years in a Cessna so loaded it wouldn't stay straight and level, trying to get it around a mountain you knew was out there somewhere in a complete whiteout, with no radio or anybody to talk to anyway . . . well, that sort of thing built character, or *cojones,* anyway. As complex and temperamental as the Lear could be, it wasn't quite the test *that* was.

As Bill's chief pilot, vice president of the air division of Daniels Communications, and devoted lifelong admirer, Mark had flown this flight already a thousand times on paper, in his head, and in the simulator. Flight plans, clearances, fuel tanks, weight restrictions, weather forecasts—Mark had lived and breathed every foot of this 24,000 miles in the three months he was given to prep for it. Had to be the February jet stream, if they were to have a shot at breaking Brooke Knapp's mark from '83. Mark thought he was prepared for anything . . . anything but a full-power takeoff from a guy who wasn't up to it.

Paul Thayer was a damn good man, and had been a damn good pilot in his day. But he'd only just gotten rerated, and barely at that. He was clearly uncomfortable in this aircraft. His check-rides and simulator time had been so iffy, Dan Miller would not sit up front with him. But Thayer was Bill's friend, and a war hero. This whole idea started with him. So there he was, sitting front left, wrestling Bill's Lear back to the center of the taxiway.

And Mark Calkins, in command, wished to hell it were him or the ex-astronaut making this takeoff instead.

**Runway 17 Left**
**3:07 a.m.**

Checklist done, taxi complete. Cleared for takeoff and all the way to the Atlantic coast, the Lear turned onto the active runway and held short. Clocks on board, in the tower, and in the Metro State Flight Center were poised to start the instant the wheels left the ground. Thayer ran the engines up to full. The aluminum tube they'd be sitting in for two days and nights shuddered in response, ready to explode down the runway.

Pete darted his eyes back and forth, studying the body language of the front-seaters. Thayer was tense, his movements uncertain. Even after the weeks of run-up, he was clearly unpracticed.

Mark was more tense, staring straight ahead, his left hand moving instinctively toward the throttle, his right on the copilot's wheel—just in case. For Conrad, the sight had the same effect as a blinking red warning light.

"Okay. Here we go." Thayer released the brakes, and the Lear burst out of its hydraulic hold like a jaguar released back into the wild, and started immediately hard left!

"Paul, the nosewheel steering isn't engaged!" Mark shouted. The airplane screamed for the frosted weeds.

> Conrad: "Oh, shit."
> Calkins: "Let me have her."
> Thayer: "I've got it."
> Calkins: "Let me *have* her, dammit!"

Mark's practiced hands took over, flicked three switches in a flash. The Lear righted herself just as she hit eighty knots; straight as an arrow thundering down Runway 17 Left, she'd be at 140 in eight seconds.

"Rotate!" Mark called. And he responded to his own command, pulling back on the stick, throwing Learjet N10BD's nose into the dark Denver sky, and starting the clock on their race around the globe.

All from the copilot's seat.

To his left, the war hero stared steely out the windshield, his pride bruised. He wouldn't utter another word for nearly half a world.

Back right, Miller munched a protein bar, drumming with the rock band in his head.

Back left, the ex-astronaut who flew two *Gemini* missions, commanded a flawless Moon flight, and saved *Skylab* from falling out of the sky—and the best Navy stick and rudder man ever, with eleven thousand flight hours . . .

. . . exhaled, and laughed silently at the irony—after twenty million miles of high-performance aircraft flight, to die in the backseat of a damn business jet crammed full of jet fuel and Junior Achievement friendship posters and protein bars on some crazy-ass run at a round-the-world speed record. Sixty-five-year-old Commander, USN (Retired) astronaut Charles "Pete" Conrad muttered the lines to his kid's favorite Talking Heads record fifteen years ago:

"'Well . . . how did I get here?'"

# TWO

"**B**lue dyer" was a well-respected and well-paying trade in seventeenth-century Europe. They didn't call it *royal* blue for nothing. Those in the Rhine River Valley who weren't royalty certainly wanted to be, and dressing for success was as important then as it is now.

This was the trade Thones Kunders was born to: dyeing coats and cloaks and dresses and blankets and any other wool items you could think of using the same family business model that was killing the local competition: doing it better for slightly less, going after the local burgher and shopkeeper market, who far outnumbered royalty anyway.

Thones couldn't care less about being blue dyer to the stars. Didn't much care for the ruling class, either. He was a high-volume man who just did it better than the other guys. So at twenty-five, as much as one could say about a nonaristocrat in 1683, the world of what is now southern Germany and Austria was his.

But Thones possessed a bit more than a skilled pair of hands and a knack for business. The DNA also included what we might today call a wild hair. The call of the wild. The eye of the dreamer. It's common to all us Homo sapiens, but most grow past it and accept with grace and dignity the relatively mundane lot given us.

Not so Thones. The prospect of five hundred acres of virgin soil in a dark and mysterious place of ghost stories and fairy tales, in this *North America*—sold to him for ten pounds sterling by William Penn himself—and a brand-new beautiful bride as ready for something new as anyone . . . well, it was just too good to pass up. Too exciting just to sit on the deed five thousand miles away and let it grow into a nice real estate investment to sell at a profit to some enterprising English joint stock company a few years out, having never even seen it. Thones and his wife, Katherine, heard the call. And they answered.

They booked passage aboard the vessel *Concord* in July of 1683, stopped once in England, then took the long haul across the Atlantic for their brave new world.

Thones staked off his land alongside a gaggle of other Quakers and Dutch Reformists, and in 1689 was granted a charter along with ten other prominent town fathers, establishing Germantown, Pennsylvania.

And here beginneth the American experience of the Kunders family, who became the Cunreds, branching off into the Cunards and the Conards, and finally the line Conrad in the early 1800s.

Clothes and money. The Conrads knew and made both—plenty. Fine linens, work clothes, army uniforms, investment banking, real estate development. The clan stayed successful, establishing itself as a first family in and around Philadelphia, remaining there as the twentieth century came roaring in.

**A** 1923 Wayne, Pennsylvania, newspaper article warned off all ". . . get-rich schemers, custodians of 'sucker lists,' bond salesmen, and *particularly* wedding brokers" from bothering rich old widower Pearson Conrad when he very publicly received half of the million-dollar estate upon the passing of his brother, W.B., another success story in the long line of Conrad linen merchants. The old guy just wanted everyone to leave him the hell alone, and was furious with his local paper for running the story in the first place, unleashing a blistering letter to the editor, which of course that editor declined to print.

Pearson Conrad's youngest son, Charles, laughed it off with the rest of the evening paper's readers, seeing Dad's sudden inheritance as just more of the old Conrad luck, if not birthright. Charles was no snob, but you didn't have to be a genius to see the pattern. The Conrad family had never known anything *but* affluence.

The adventurer/dreamer/wild-hair gene had come boiling to the surface on Pearson's side of the clan, rendering up his son Charles as a football player, lifeguard, and captain in the balloon corps in the Great War. He took the same pluck of his ancestor Thones in training to sail back across the Atlantic and lob bricks and bombs on his Germanic cousins from a thousand feet up in a flimsy, unstable, and very unreliable "combat" balloon. The balloon guys even trained with real bullets whining by them, which downed and killed a few crews along the way. But the war ended, and Charles's wild-hair gene got put away, to quietly wait for its next carrier.

Life seemed to drift by comfortably, predictably, and a bit dully for the adult Charles in 1920s Philadelphia. He'd married himself a beauty out of Newark in 1921, the stately and elegant Frances De Rappelage Vinson, and brought her to the Main Line to settle down into the family tradition of making money in real estate and investment banking. And so it went. Three years and two lovely daughters later, Charles had settled into a predictable, but enviable routine: early up and out, mornings in the office, lunch in town, maybe return to the office (and maybe not), the club in the afternoon, dinner in the dining room with Frances only—never with the children, who would be served by staff in their rooms—brandy and cigar and the *Wall Street Journal* in the evening, maybe a step down to Martini's, the local speakeasy a block and a half away. A quiet, dignified life drifting by on Waterloo Avenue in Devon, on the Main Line of Philadelphia.

Until June 2, 1930, anyway.

\* \* \*

Pennsylvania Hospital in Philadelphia is damn proud that they've been providing maternity care longer than any other hospital in America. Opened in
1793, it was expected when ground was broken that they would be the premier medical facility for the newly named capital of the newly independent
United States. Even though the capital was moved to Washington D.C., it
was still a hell of a good place to have a baby 140 years later, when it was
time for Frances Conrad to deliver. She'd had Patricia and Barbara here in
'23 and '26 respectively. The third, and still unnamed Conrad baby, as of the
morning of June 2, would call Pennsylvania Hospital his or her landing site
as well.

It was an old building. Most newborns could easily be heard in the room
next door, with the loud ones heard halfway down the floor. When Frances
pushed out her eight pounds of brand-new Conrad a little after four in the
afternoon, the *entire* floor, as well as the ones above and below, were made
fully aware. Smoking calmly in the waiting room as the most senior of the
expectant fathers there, Charles got his first hint that the predictable qui-
etude he'd come to know on Waterloo Avenue was at an end. He knew
without being told that the indignant roar spilling forth was coming from a
boy. And by the sound of him, the wild hair seemed to have found a new
home.

The boy sure was healthy. Those weren't the cries of a sickly child. He
wouldn't need his sisters' assistance in their chosen welcome-home
costumes—Bobbie as doctor, Patty as her trusted nurse. And neither he nor
Frances would need the standard three days in the hospital either. After two
she called it a wrap, and sent for Morris the chauffeur.

Straight, proper, and well versed in etiquette, Frances Vinson Conrad
possessed a healthy respect for tradition, unless that tradition just made no
sense. Then pity the fool who tried to impose his will upon her. Protofemi-
nist? Absolutely not. Strong individual who just happened to be a woman?
That was Frances. And thus her stance when it came to naming the third and
final Conrad child. The discussion had been front and center these past nine
months, and was at times spirited.

Since 1930 was decades before ultrasounds and amniotic checks,
Simon—the bartender at Martini's—was as apt to predict the sex of the child
as the chief of staff at Pennsylvania. With two girls already, Charles was

clearly hoping for a boy to "round things out a bit." He had decided already what he would be called.

"Charles Junior," he declared. "No middle name."

Frances's immediate reply is lost to history, but the fact that the boy Conrad will be forever remembered as "Pete" marks a pretty clear winner in the delivery room standoff.

"There is already a Charles in the house, Charles."

"His grandfather was Charles."

"Never met him."

"I would like a junior, Frances."

"Why?"

"Tradition."

It was a silly tradition to her, despite her well-bred, old-world pedigree. It was tradition for tradition's sake and nothing more. In her very logical mind, there was one Charles Conrad; why did they need another?

*Think of the practical. . . .*

"Charles! Telephone!" Which one? Every time the phone rang, that would be the response. Waste of time, breath, and energy.

*The personal?*

The boy was going to be himself, not live in the shadow of some legacy just to carry on a name. "Junior" might mean something at the end of a signature on the club roster or a dividend check, but it was something altogether different in a game of tackle football or walking home from school past bigger, meaner boys. *"Juuunior,"* she could just hear them chanting, as they piled on top of him. And it wouldn't be a term of endearment.

No. Junior was out.

But ever the diplomat, and never the capricious wielder of her considerable personal power, Frances understood the value of compromise. She found a satisfactory middle ground just as the hospital clerk made her round to the room.

"Charles—no middle name—Conrad," Charles harrumphed, nodding in triumph.

"But he will be called *Peter*," she finished.

Why Peter? She liked the sound of it. And at forty-eight hours old, Charles "Peter" Conrad received the first in a lifelong series of destiny-making influences from confident, determined, and strong women.

* * *

"This is fun! Do it again!" the two-year-old voice would shout over and over, to the momentary panic of everyone within earshot—panic due to the lack of visual contact with the future pilot. With five acres of mature elms and oaks and maples on rolling hills, the boy could be anywhere.

Perhaps he was in the tree swing he'd leaped out of fifty times already, trying to beat gravity, and losing like the rest of us—with a very drawn-out and indignant wail.

Maybe he was roaring about in the Air Mail pedal car, which, in theory, should keep him on the driveway within eyesight and earshot, only he always seemed to slip away to some new and secret destination known only to him.

Young Peter loved to wander through the hedge when he heard the old black gardener mowing the neighbor's yard with the tractor mower. More than once the old guy had brought Peter back with a terrified but relieved smile, having spotted the boy at the last possible second. And just as many times he had plopped Peter onto his lap and let him steer.

Even at his mother's funeral half a century later, the old-timers in Devon still talked about when four-year-old Peter Conrad figured out the ignition switch and gearshift on the enormous family Chrysler, and backed it right out onto the main road. Just like "Jingle Bells"—laughing all the way.

The boy just loved things that moved, the louder and bigger, the better. The second-biggest memory of his young life was getting to climb inside the engine of a mighty General Electric locomotive down at the rail yard, the engineer letting him hold the switch as he guided her onto a coupling.

The biggest? Going for a nickel ride on Father's lap at the 1935 Devon Horse Show—in the backseat of an open-cockpit Stearman biplane.

It wasn't a quiet household anymore. Not that Bobbie and Patty were mousy and overly prim and proper; they just figured out the boundaries quickly. Peter, however, was a force to be reckoned with, in volume and intensity, and didn't recognize boundaries just yet. Heads flew off of statues, leaded crystal broke, Erector-set triumphs of mechanical engineering came crashing down from the third floor, appliances came apart and never quite worked right again. And the boy's constant kinetic energy fed his sisters' potential energy, until the whole damn thing hit a critical mass worthy of Los

Alamos, sending the household into a rollicking twelve-hour force-ten gale of kid noise.

Charles wasn't home much in the thirties, needless to say.

Three children, as rambunctious as three children will be, tearing through the house they called the Roadside Cottage, on Waterloo Avenue. Just an average family in an average household, except for one tiny detail: The Conrads were rich, in a time most people were broke.

You don't feel rich if it's all you've ever known. Three floors, six bedrooms, five perfect acres on the Main Line with a nanny, a staff to cook and clean, and a chauffeur to drive for you were simply the way of Bobbie, Patty, and Peter's world. If you didn't know poor, how could you possibly know rich?

The three kids thundering through the Roadside Cottage had no way of understanding the economic straits in which the country was drowning, or that the Conrad family would be in those same straits in the not-too-distant future.

The thirties were difficult years in Philadelphia, as they were across the nation. As old and proud as Boston, the city kept its stately pomp and circumstance as the stock market and the American economy collapsed like a house of cards around them.

Renowned for its working-class roots, the railroad, and the rabid sports fans, Philadelphia was, in fact, where the vast majority of East Coast investment banking and stock trading took place outside the Big Apple. When the dollar dropped to a tenth of its previous value, the pictures coming out of Philly looked like they did from most American cities: banks closing, soup lines, blue-chip stock certificates used to start trash-can fires. You didn't have to be a Nobel economist to know the proverbial shit had hit the proverbial fan.

A lot of the boys at the club panicked outright. Some lost it all; some whose wealth was all margin accounts never had it to begin with. Charles Conrad watched as the saying he would repeat over and over to Peter played itself out in those trying days: *Circumstances don't make a man; they reveal him.*

The Conrads took it on the chin. Investments Charles had carefully managed for ten years were suddenly worth pennies on the dollar. He'd kept cash reserves of nearly a hundred thousand dollars—a spectacular sum in the thirties—but it all but evaporated into thin air, called by the bank and his brokerage to cover his own margin accounts. He owned a building full of tenants who couldn't make their monthly lease payments, while his mortgage remained due and payable on the first. . . .

While Mother read in the first-floor library, Bobbie and Patty tied up the telephone line talking with their boyfriends on the second floor. Peter took apart clocks and radios and lamps on the third, inventing lever-and-pulley systems to have his orange juice delivered to him in the morning as he got dressed for school.

And Father poured another drink in his study, while he crunched numbers, juggled accounts, and faced a darkening Depression head-on.

Keeping it together as best he could.

# THREE

It was never demanded, nor even stated, that young Peter would follow in his father's footsteps. It was simply assumed: Haverford School, Yale, Officers' Training, the service, then settle into a profession or business, preferably here on the Main Line. Of course, Peter would make up his own mind after school, but for those years there was never a question that he would prep at the venerable old Haverford School.

In 1884 the Pennsylvania Railroad laid fifteen miles of track heading westward, and the tiny outposts along the way were turned overnight into middle-class suburbs, led by the middle managers and lower-level executives that the railroad "suggested" move to the country, setting the precedent for the bedroom communities to come. And for young executives having young families, and of reasonable enough means to afford a college preparatory school for their sons, the Haverford School was chartered. It grew right along with the Main Line suburbs. Even the names of the towns changed to something more respectable. Tiny Louella, where the campus would sit, became Wayne, named after the Revolutionary War general.

*Scholarship, leadership, citizenship, and high standards of character and conduct* were the carved-in-stone watchwords and mission of the grand school. Haverford had been educating leaders for over fifty years by the time Peter entered grade school in 1936. Proud of its standards and traditions, Haverford was simply the place for an upwardly mobile, motivated boy to go in the Philadelphia area. And if tradition is a reasonably accurate predictor of things to come, then the 1939 Haverford Christmas Tableaux was truly something to behold.

On the Main Line's tradition meter, The Tableaux was rated somewhere between the pope's Christmas Eve Service and the lighting of the White House Christmas tree. Stately and somber, it was meant to invoke the most transcendent reflections of the true meaning of Christmas.

Fourth grader Peter Conrad was tapped for a featured role in the pageant . . . as the Holy Mother herself, the Virgin Mary. To put it mildly, he was not pleased with the honor. *Totally pissed off* would be more accurate.

*The Virgin Mary? Okay, it's the Shakespeare thing. There aren't any girls to play the female parts, but* the Virgin Mary? *Let me be the female sheep or the innkeeper's wife or something,* anything, thought the nine-year-old Peter Conrad, *but front and center, where all my friends are gonna see and give me shit till I'm dead,* as the Virgin Mary!

Alas, the fair hair, the baby face, and the slight stature of Master Conrad made him the natural choice for the part. For six straight nights, Peter had to sit stock-still, looking "wistful" in the art department's manger, holding one of Patty's long-discarded dolls in swaddling clothes, itching his rear end off in a ridiculous hooded wool bathrobe, perched atop a bale of hay he was sure had been sampled already by a number of the local livestock, while Freddy Fenorick snickered at him under his fake beard, holding down the fort in the much-coveted role of Joseph.

Freddy Fenorick was a pain-in-the-ass kid. When Conrad caught an episode of *Leave It to Beaver* years later, and saw the character of Eddie Haskell, he swore up and down he was based on Freddy Fenorick, fourth grader at the Haverford School for boys, standing like Jesus's daddy himself next to Peter, passing gas as frequently as he possibly could, trying to break Peter's "wistful" look.

The performance nights were bad enough. But the following days at school were unbearable, as the "Virgin Mary" had to endure the intolerable cruelty of his grade-school colleagues, who hadn't yet transcended to the higher consciousness surrounding our dear Savior's birth. Not at recess anyway.

On the sixth and final night, the exhausted Virgin Mary had had about all he could take. Even Freddy had lost some of his edge. As a matter of fact, he'd lost a lot of it. Christmas cookies and boiled custard from the all-sing that afternoon were taking their toll, and Freddy was wilting under the sweaty fake beard and hot lights of closing night, when all of the area's finest donned their holiday colors and braved the cold to pay homage to the stately traditions of Christmas on the Main Line.

As Peter itched, and fidgeted, and stared straight ahead with all the serenity a bored and furious fourth grader could muster, Joseph suddenly vomited all over the Virgin Mary in the Haverford School auditorium in one violent heave.

The reaction was swift and predictable—gasps throughout the packed hall; teachers rushing to the aid of Freddy; the Wise Men, goats, and cows scattering in a unified chorus of, "Oooh, *gross!*" And a chain-reaction puke or two.

The Virgin Mary quickly extricated himself from his itchy, puke-soaked bathrobe and, in his underwear, cussed and punched the lights out of Freddy before the horrified audience below.

So much for tradition.

# FOUR

**Learjet N10BD**
**1254 Zulu**
**45,000 feet, crossing the Florida coast**
**527 knots**

**F**reddy Fenorick. How long had it been since he'd thought of Freddy? Pete opened his eyes slowly from a catnap, laughing at the memory of his theatrical debut.

The theater was in the old jet driver's blood, actually. Father had even backed a Broadway show in the twenties. It was so grand: the production, the acting, the costumes. Especially the costumes. The wild man in Charles loved it all, and he'd passed that love on to his boy.

Costumes later became uniforms, and in sixty-five years, the boy had worn a ton of them: flight suits, Navy blues, space suits, deep-sea-diver rigs, Nomex race-car-driver suit, cowboy gear, even biker leathers. Hell, twenty years ago Conrad didn't hesitate a blink before trading his *Gemini* flight jacket for the world's top-rated Spanish matador's jacket. The bullfighter understood: You can't play the part without the uniform. That red-and-gold jacket was framed and hanging in his living room right now. It made him smile every time he walked through that door.

Today, February 12, 1996, Pete Conrad was wearing a NASA-blue Speed-vision flight suit, along with the rest of the crew, lying on top of a sleeping bag in the only "bunk" in this crowded, reconfigured Learjet, four hours southeast of Denver. He grabbed a headset next to the snoring Dan Miller, and bid Captain Calkins a good morning.

"Where the hell are we, anyway?"

"Doesn't look familiar? You launched right under us four times."

Pete smiled, glancing out at the familiar sight of Cape Canaveral. But he let the opening to hold court with his memoirs pass. "How's our time, Mark?"

"Fair. We had a great tailwind till an hour ago; then it hauled around on our nose. We gotta make a decision, Pete: Ponce or Saint Kitts."

"What's the fuel?"

"Not critical. A thousand pounds on the ground at Saint Kitts."

"It's a hell of a long way across the pond to Africa. Unless the wind's just howling behind us, we'll be on vapors by the time we're feet dry. We need every mile we can get behind us. We'd better go for Saint Kitts."

"Yeah . . ." Mark replied thoughtfully from the right front. He was still driving, Paul Thayer in the pilot's seat was nose-deep in a paperback, still smarting from the takeoff debacle. He hadn't even looked at Mark since they'd been airborne. "The only thing is, all those kids in Ponce. This is such a big deal to them. Half the island's at the field right now."

This flight *was* a big deal to people they'd never met, and never would again. Kids mostly.

With eight stops around the world, fueling and customs turnarounds had to be planned down to the second if they were going to have a chance to break the record. Even with a healthy midwinter jet stream that was *supposed* to be on their tail, there was no margin for error. Not a minute to burn. Every turn had to be thirty minutes or less, or they'd be behind the eight ball the whole way.

But like any high-profile event—especially one with a Moon-walking as-tronaut aboard—one of only twelve humans to ever sanely and accurately call themselves that—it was a very *public* event. There would be politicians, city fathers, fat cats, airplane buffs, and the local Junior Achievement kids standing eagerly at the fence with posters to exchange, hoping to shake the hand of the captain and maybe even the astronaut. . . .

Achievement and records were great, but not at the expense of people. Nobody understood that better than Pete Conrad. These were people. Kids. With feelings, and hopes, and dreams, and pride. Thirty years in the public eye either turned you into a royal egomaniacal asshole, or made you aware— every day of your life—how blessed and lucky you really were. It was never stated, but always understood—it wasn't so much a record-breaking business jet the crowds wanted to see. It was the astronaut. That was as much a factor in this flight as wind, weight, and fuel.

"Mark, my boy, this one's your call."

Calkins agonized. The people in Ponce were so stoked even to be a *part* of this flight. Mark had exchanged thirty or forty faxes and phone calls with them, and they had a backup fuel truck waiting behind the two Mark has requested (and two was a *lot* to request on a tiny island). The governor would even be there with the tower guys to make sure their airspace would be clear. Any other flight not in emergency status would be ordered to hold their approach or takeoff so these guys could have a clear run.

But three hundred miles was three hundred miles. And with light winds forecast, and the very limit of this already overweight jet's range ahead of them—over the Atlantic, no less! Ponce, lovefest though it would be, was always an alternate site anyway, a just-in-case if their fuel was critical. It wasn't. But if they set down now it would be—three hundred miles from the African coast. A lousy place for a water landing and a swim.

They needed the miles.

"Saint Kitts it is."

It was a good decision. Pete nodded, and closed his eyes for a little catnap, knowing he was up front across the pond.


"**P**ete. Pete!" Captain Calkins had hold of his foot, shaking it urgently. "The HF radio's dead."

"Are you sure?"

"I can't raise Miami or New York."

"Oh, shit."

The normal operating radios in air traffic corridors are VHF, or very high frequency. It's quiet, doesn't have a lot of static, and, with a range of about three hundred miles, it's more than adequate over any chunk of land with a modern traffic-control network.

But the Atlantic doesn't qualify for that description. Then they had Africa. The Middle East. Asia. Russia. Siberia, then the Bering Strait before they'd be anywhere near a VHF ping from the modern, advanced aviation communications network in the good ol' USA.

The good ol' "we give a shit what happens to you guys" USA.

Communication is not a luxury in the aviation business. It's damn near as critical as it is in spaceflight. Guidance, traffic, weather, clearances, distress calls . . . going VHF-only on this flight was somewhere between stupid and outright suicidal. It was the only time in the accelerated run-up to this mission that Conrad had to pull rank. There would be an HF radio, and there would be a backup. Whether it seemed redundant or not, space was not a consideration, and cost was immaterial—they were expensive as hell to buy or rent. But they would have both, or this flight wasn't leaving the ground. Not with him on it.

Still, backup or not, the situation confronting them now *was* critical. They had a spare, sure, but the HF radio is not a plug-it-in-the-cigarette-lighter unit. The thing was mounted in about as inaccessible a place as possible right now—behind one of two in-cabin fuel tanks crowding them all together in the forward section with more than a ton of gear.

Small detail here: HF radios interact with highly charged ions from the atmosphere, and have been known to throw a spark or two. A spark in a pressurized, oxygen-enriched aluminum fuselage with thirteen hundred pounds of highly flammable jet fuel in there with you . . .

Well, there were better things, that was for damn sure.

And the space between the HF mounting bracket on the back of the 200-gallon tank and the rear bulkhead was about four inches. The crawl space to get there after climbing over all the gear was about twelve.

And here they were, whistling along at over five hundred knots, with the last specks of sand for 3,300 miles coming up in twenty-four minutes.

And they were deaf and dumb as a post.

# FIVE

It was one of the greatest nights of the boy's life, near midnight out in the garage when the tiny little tubes glowed orange. The damn thing worked! The ten-year-old *Popular Mechanics* addict had scavenged parts from a busted RCA, a transformer from a Lionel O Gauge train set, and some spare wire from Morris's kit, and connected them all together.

Morris was the Conrad family's utility infielder—driver, handyman, and one of the kids' best pals. With a mechanics' hands and tinkerers' minds, Morris and Peter were truly kindred spirits, whether fixing lamps and washers or changing the oil in the car. Peter adored him. Truth be told, he spent a lot more of his childhood hours with Morris than with Father. Now here they were, in the middle of a Saturday night, hunched over the workbench lit by a single forty-watt bulb, touching copper connectors as gingerly as brain surgeons. . . .

Suddenly, through the hiss and pop of that cardboard speaker, came the sounds of WSM, Radio 65's Grand Ole Opry, right out of Nashville, seven hundred miles away.

The young boy and the old boy yelled like they'd just won a ball game, staring wide-eyed at the glow of electricity in the tubes bringing them music from nearly a quarter-way across the country. There was another world outside the Main Line, a place where cowboys and cowgirls strummed guitars and sang songs about heartaches and troubles and real life, and Peter could touch those wires together and listen to them every Saturday night. Especially when those heartaches and troubles would belong to him.

Financially, the house of Conrad was in trouble—deep trouble. Charles had kept a cool head in the economic hurricane of the thirties, but the shell game was catching up with him. The Conrads of Waterloo Avenue might have presented the picture of the good life, but by 1942, there just wasn't enough money to sustain that picture.

The family didn't eat together. The kids ate in their rooms, served by Lulu. Mother and Father ate in the dining room downstairs. It had always been that way. But the double doors that were once open were now closed. Hushed tones replaced the happy banter of everyday life. The occasional laugh at the day's news or the local gossip was nowhere to be found now.

There are variations on the theme. Sometimes it's a genuine disaster of one kind or another. Or maybe it's the blue blood who's lived for years—hell, sometimes *generations*—on a family name alone. Then one day the old boy blows his brains out at his polished mahogany desk, and it turns out the family hasn't had a dime for years. Maybe it's the gambler who got lucky, and just didn't have the sense to hang onto it.

Charles was neither of those. The Conrads weren't blue bloods, but they sure weren't peasantry, either. Charles had a gambler's instinct inside. Any good investor has to have that. A gambler knows he's going to lose almost as many hands as he wins; the game is to stay just one up.

Charles was not the blow-his-brains-out type, or the cry-in-his-beer sap who'd tell anybody who'd listen what a rotten hand he'd been dealt. He was an after-dinner regular at Martini's, same as always. There weren't too many nights when the now-legal drinking establishment wasn't packed with folks fighting the same fight as Charles Conrad in the 1930s and early 1940s. He kept 'em laughing with a story or a joke. They needed that as much as they needed the drink, just to know they weren't alone in this.

Only at the movies did the mask come off, in a dark theater full of strangers and friends, watching Shirley Temple, Judy Garland, Hepburn and Tracy. Every Saturday Charles took Peter to the Devon picture show. Then it was twice a week, sometimes with Peter, sometimes by himself. Sometimes three. It didn't matter if they changed the feature or not.

Peter would glance out of the corner of his eye at Father, whose shoulders were shaking, trying to hold something inside. All that the outside world could see was a tiny sniffle, a quick wipe of the eye. But twelve-year-old Peter was old enough to spot despair, anger, shame, and fear. He just wasn't old enough to understand why.

Or that the shoulders of half the men in the theater were shaking too.


In the money business they call it the spiral. Just like water in the toilet, it all starts to swirl around and around, faster and faster, heading down the drain. So went the third and final fortune managed by Charles Conrad. With nothing to hold on to, he swirled around like that water until the fall of '43; then the bottom dropped out once and for all.

The staff went first. Only Lulu stayed on for no pay—as long as she could. Morris shook Peter's hand, telling him not to cry even as he fought his own tears.

The nicer artwork was next, then the Persian rugs, statues, and furnishings. Then the club membership. The car. Both Bobbie and Patty had graduated high school and started nursing school. There was a war on; that would continue. But Haverford? Would it go, too?

Boy Conrad—*legacy* Conrad—was growing into big little man on campus. An underclassman, Peter was short as short gets, but he could skate. And tackle. And anchor the dirt behind home plate like a big leaguer, slugging a terrific .350 batting average. The varsity days ahead looked great for Peter Conrad and Haverford athletics.

More than that, the kid was funnier than hell. Having survived Freddy Fenorick's hurling in the fourth-grade Christmas pageant, he was more often than not the lead in the middle school productions, and was showing up in the upper school shows now, stealing them more than once.

But his grades were falling. Math and science may have been a snap for the boy who loved moving parts and connecting wires and helping Morris tune a carburetor. But middle school at Haverford was and is about *reading*: Hawthorne, Tennyson, Chaucer. And history. And Latin. There weren't any moving parts there.

It was a small town. People knew one another's business. The whispers of the Main Line reached the ivy-covered walls of Haverford, and the troubles in the Roadside Cottage were known. It would have been a surprise had Peter's grades *not* fallen. This was a boy going home after athletics every night to a crumbling family fortune. How did that *not* leave a mark somewhere? Peter was carrying the weight of the world on his little shoulders right now. But it would pass, he told himself.

Only it wouldn't.

It got worse.

# SIX

*S*low *reader* was what they used to call it. Occasionally some nose-up, elbow-patches Ivy League type would even leave off the *reader* part. At Haverford, a school that lived and died by its standards, reality could occasionally be ruthless. There was no grading curve, no being saved in the classroom by brilliance on the field. Even the legacy thing went only so far. Ds and Fs in English and history could not be offset by As in athletics and drama, not even in math and science. Failing at half of the core curriculum was still failing. That was and is the reality of a college prep school. Cruel though it may be, it's a necessary weeding-out process. One couldn't fake it through Haverford.

The boy just might be "slow." Maybe he was just lazy. Whatever the reason, it was always just about seventh grade when it caught up to the failing students. They could fake it till then.

What wasn't understood anywhere in 1943 was what transpired between the printed page and the information processor under the blond hair of Peter Conrad. Two crystal-blue eyes acted as gatekeepers, controlling the information flow. Those were eyes that could see at twenty feet what you and I see at ten, eyes that could see the stitches of a fastball speeding at seventy-five miles an hour as it sailed the sixty feet, six inches from Bobby Taylor's hand into Peter's catcher's mitt; eyes that, a decade later, could spot the very wire his fighter jet would catch on a rolling aircraft carrier—from more than a mile out.

But right now those eyes sent Peter's brain information that became garbled on the way. Lowercase Rs and Ss faced backward. The letter C came out E. And half the time those eyes could not—*would* not—follow a sentence left to right for more than four or five words. Instead they penetrated downward into the page itself, finding and focusing on flaws in the typesetting barely visible to any without a magnifying glass.

Peter Conrad was suffering from acute dyslexia. It was a learning disability that didn't even have a name in those days, outside of obscure ophthalmic journals, and even there it was widely dismissed by doctors and teachers alike as theoretical at best. It wasn't theoretical to Peter. It was a brick wall. And all the demerits and extra homework and study halls and lectures from Mother and Father wouldn't even make a dent in it. It was just something he'd have to work through.

So the boy with the crumbling family fortune, the one the other boys snickered at when it was his time to read aloud from *The Iliad*, the one who clutched his temples with skull-crushing headaches at his desk at night, endured his professors' smart-ass comments about being lazy, and lousy marks every grading period.

And that boy got angry.


**T**he last days of the Roadside Cottage on Waterloo Avenue were a blur. Still too young to fully understand why, Peter watched as the fixtures of his first twelve years were carted off. He listened as the hushed tones downstairs became hisses, then shouts, then slamming doors. Father was leaving the house earlier, then staying later at Martini's. He went to more movies, with and without Peter, sometimes in the middle of the workday. And then it was time to leave. One Saturday Frances's brother, Edgerton, arranged for a truck to gather the remainder of the Conrad possessions and drive them across Devon, in full view of the entire Main Line—to the burg of Saint David's and a tiny three-bedroom carriage house, where Edge paid the rent and figured out what the hell to do next.

"Uncle Edge" was a Wall Streeter. He liked Charles well enough, although he had always been a tad uneasy about Charles marrying his sister. Truth is, Charles Conrad's downward spiral didn't surprise Edge all that much. Even with some spectacular successes in real estate and investments, Charles just never gave off the sense of stability in the long term. He couldn't hide the wild hair underneath that bespoke suit, club membership, and oak-paneled office.

There was a side to Uncle Edge that would have left Charles to fend for himself. He made this bed; let him lie in it. But blood was blood. And disapproving or not, Edge was not letting his sister's family slip through the cracks. He gritted his teeth and did the right thing. He wrote a check or two, called in a few markers, and found them this one-story rental in a nice neighborhood, but there was no mistaking it for the Roadside Cottage on Waterloo Avenue. He even footed the bill to keep Peter in Haverford.

And in the blink of an eye, the Conrads had gone from the manor house in Devon to the carriage house in Saint David's.


Charles's only sister Ethel's son David had an Indian motorcycle—candy-apple red tank and trim, and 400ccs of rolled and pressed Pittsburgh iron. Son of a bitch, that thing roared like the god-awfulest creature that ever rolled or crawled out of the primordial ooze. She spewed smoke out the back like she was on fire, too. It leaked oil, the carburetor had to be torn down and rebuilt every hundred miles or so, and the clutch slipped. For little cousin Peter, it was love at first sight.

David was a straight-A-er who could speak Latin, do calculus like Einstein, and write like Fitzgerald. But David couldn't look at one of those pain-in-the-ass achievement test questions with a drawing of eight interlocked gears and tell you which way the last one was turning. He might have understood the science behind the carburetor, but he couldn't adjust one if his life depended on it. And David hated skinning his knuckles and getting oil all over himself.

But his younger cousin didn't mind it a bit. Peter loved the smell of gasoline, internal combustion engines were about as complex to him as breathing, and messing around with gears and pulleys and belts was as close to religion as he ever got.

David was a sweet spirit of a boy. At seventeen he was well able to fathom what was happening to his younger cousin. The bike didn't much fit him, really. Oh, he liked riding it well enough—when the damn thing ran. But it never seemed to want to. And every time that kid came over, all *he* wanted to do was mess with it.

Without a second thought David knew what would get Peter through the darkest days of his young life: an oil-leaking, smoke-belching, clutch-slipping Indian, which he gave to his cousin when he went off to Yale. It was the first thing placed on, and the last to roll off, the moving van that took the Conrads to their newly downsized life.


**T**he headmaster's office at Haverford School is about as friendly and inviting as it sounds. It had the usual old-book, oaken smell and the feel of higher learning, overlooking the commons below. But unless you were the headmaster, relaxing with a cup of tea and translating some obscure Cantonese text for fun, it was about as inviting as something out of Kafka.

"Mrs. Conrad, do come in," Leslie Severinghaus said as he hurried from his desk to meet Frances. She entered with her usual dignity, a polite smile, and little more. "Tea?"

"No, thank you."

"Things are well, I trust? How are you finding Saint David's?"

"It's lovely."

Pause.

"Yes, well . . ."

Hers was a regal presence, calm and composed, and Severinghaus was suddenly uneasy. For the first time since taking the helm in 1937, the headmaster felt as if he were suddenly on the other side of his own desk.

"I . . . thought we might have a chance to talk about Peter."

She nodded slowly.

"He is struggling here, as you may know."

"Yes, we are aware of that."

He shifted uncomfortably in his seat. The meeting was barely a minute old, and it was unraveling already. "He is a very good boy; I want to emphasize that right off the bat. There's not a soul here who does not adore your son."

"But . . ."

"But . . . he is below passing average in all but two subjects for the fourth straight quarter. He's being tutored, given extra study hall, even homework contracts . . . that he is not honoring. And you're bound to have noticed he has become a fixture in Saturday demerit hall."

"Yes. I've noticed."

He waited, but she offered up nothing more.

These meetings didn't go like this. Students and parents alike usually walked in this room like condemned prisoners at times like these, hat in hand, babbling appeals and apologies, and the headmaster would occasionally, like a good king at Christmastime, grant their supplication. Mrs. Conrad was not acting her part.

"Well . . . I was curious whether you and Mr. Conrad had had a chance to discuss this matter with the boy."

"It's come up. We are concerned."

Severinghaus didn't know whether to laugh or get mad. Mostly he was utterly taken with this woman. He'd never seen such a poker face. Surely she knew that *he* knew about the family's financial problems. Like he wouldn't notice that the tuition checks bore someone else's name?

But Frances Conrad was the Rock of Gibraltar. Her terse answers weren't disrespectful; the woman wasn't defending the boy's behavior or performance. She was simply the picture of dignity, calm, and grace. And Leslie Severinghaus suddenly felt a peg or two lower.

"Mrs. Conrad, I don't like delivering news like this, but this simply cannot continue. A quarter here and there, that's understandable. But we have to face facts. The boy is not making the grade. And it won't get any easier. You're bound to know we have a waiting list a hundred deep who would kill to be here."

She nodded slightly, averting her eyes. Waiting for the closer.

"I wonder if Haverford really is the place for this boy to . . . fully thrive."

"Mr. Severinghaus, you are undoubtedly aware that my husband's business has suffered catastrophic losses lately. It has clearly been a strain on us all, but things are settling down. I can promise you that this is the last such meeting you will need to call."

My god, the headmaster was in awe of this woman. No tears, no babbling explanation, no pulling out the "legacy" cannon. She didn't even react to the "wonder if Haverford is the place for the boy" bombshell, and that one always got a reaction. One of the Vanderbilts got so weak-kneed at that one, he bought a new building. And his kid only had a C–! *That Charles Conrad,* he couldn't help but think. *He did all right landing this one.*

"Well, then. I'm glad we had this little chat. I look forward to Peter's getting back on track. Please give my best to Mr. Conrad."

"I will. Thank you for having me in."

And as regally as she entered, Frances gathered her scarf, shook his hand, and glided out.


Lord, what a headache. Peter had been at his desk for two hours conjugating verbs. Latin verbs. More accurately, they were conjugating *him.*

Oh, the meeting with Mother and Father had been a doozy. Grounded for a month, chained to this desk. Forbidden to ride the Indian. Now here he was on a perfect Sunday afternoon, sitting inside, staring at words he would never remember, trying in vain to block out some sappy-ass lovesick ballad coming out of Patty's room for the hundredth time today. She was home for the weekend, nursing her own heart, broken by some fraternity boy in Philly.

*The hell with it.* He slammed the books aside and fled for the only refuge he had in the tornado that was his life right now—the garage.

The first thing Peter had done with the Indian was break down the clutch assembly and refit her with a shorter cable. She worked like a dream now. He wasn't legal to drive it on the streets yet, and one of the 4-F cops who should have been off fighting the Nazis was fighting him instead. Twice he'd gotten nailed bombing around town; the last time the cop had brought him home, reading Mother and Father the riot act. Next time would be jail.

So Peter would ride the thing around the garage, around and around and around, wearing the dirt floor into a smooth track, driving anybody in earshot as bonkers as he was going with that record on Patty's phonograph.

*Screw the track, and screw the 4-F cop,* he thought as he kicked the starter and the old girl roared to life like a suddenly awakened bear. Peter Conrad was going for a ride.

The Indian was not a smooth ride. The thing vibrated as she snarled along, her shocks and struts about as forgiving as that surly cop out there. It didn't matter. Fat tires and a big motor—that was all he wanted today. He lit a Lucky, stomped her into first gear, and popped that rebuilt clutch, looking every bit the juvenile delinquent Brando would in *The Wild One.*

Smoke. Gas. Exhaust. A barely muffled engine, and the wall of wind noise. There wasn't any conjugating this thing as he hit fourth, no moving van from the manor house to the carriage house. Hell, no. Just Peter and this screaming monster and a gallon of gas. He downshifted into a curve, leaned easily toward the pavement, brought her out, and pulled the throttle for everything she was worth, heading west.

Doctor? Lawyer? Banker? Forget it. Peter was in his own downward spiral at Haverford, and he knew it. He'd be lucky to get a job pumping gas or changing oil at the rate he was going.

Like that was so damn bad? Nothing made him happier than this right here: kicking around the garage, tearing this thing down and putting her back together better than she ever was, and letting her fly. Hell, at least he *could* fix a motor. What was *Father* going to do?

Him and the old man . . . He laughed bitterly. At the exact same place. Hanging on while the whole world spiraled, trying to pull them down.

The speedometer was still busted. But he knew sixty when he felt it. And it felt good. He waved to no one as he shot by the tiny Paoli Airfield. Maybe he'd work there. Fix planes. Gas 'em up, paint the hangars. Maybe he could trade for flying lessons.

Now wouldn't that be a kick in the pants.


**H**e could not believe it. Two hours later, *Bobbie was still listening to the same goddamn song!* Peter gritted his teeth, going one more round with the Latin verbs. Like it would make a difference anyway. Mother and Father's voices joined this sissy crooner's in his head . . .

Mother: "Peter, you will buckle down and do the work."

Father: "Remember, son: The Conrads are a legacy at Haverford."

Mother: "School, chores, studies. That's Peter Conrad's life until these marks improve."

Suddenly . . . silence. No more music. Peter shook his head violently, try-ing to knock loose the demon in his brain, the one fighting him with the same verb he'd been staring at for ten minutes straight, giving him a mind-bending headache.

Wait a minute. *The first four letters of this gibberish are the same as that one. And the suffix is . . .*

"Tenderly. I love you tenderly. . . ."

Like a raging wind, he slung the book aside, flew from his desk, out his own door and through Patty's, ripped the platter from the phonograph, and with a primal cry of victory, smashed the piece-of-shit song over his sister's lovesick skull.

# SEVEN

**R**ain. Not a gentle summer shower, but sheets of water. Peter sprinted from his buddy's car to the front door, laughing, as he was soaked to the bone before he fell inside.

"Take your shoes off!" Patty yelled from the kitchen. Home for the summer, she was back in her role as big sister. She'd always barked orders at Peter, but he never minded. Patty was equal parts teacher, protector, and purveyor of dirty jokes to her baby brother.

Peeling off his soggy Keds, he glanced at the hall table, and froze when he saw it. The mail had come. Patty had tossed the stack on the table as she hurried to change for her date tonight. The return address leaped out at him like a glowing chunk of Kryptonite from the Superman comics. And he knew: It was bad news, and it was bad news for *him*.

He moved slowly toward it. It was from the Haverford School. Addressed coldly, formally to Mr. and Mrs. Conrad, it wasn't from a mass mailing. It was too early for athletic schedules and the school calendar to arrive. And his grades had come a month before with about the same amount of joy as a telegram from the War Department.

The grades hadn't improved. They'd been sliding steadily since Father had moved out. The end-of-the-year exams were a complete disaster; they could scarcely have gone worse. The boy's eyes burned right through the envelope, as though he really were Superman, X-ray vision and all.

The Haverford School would not be inviting Charles "Peter" Conrad back for the '47–'48 school year.

He turned and ran toward the garage, his cocoon, his sanctuary. The rain stinging his cheeks, he was angry at Father all of a sudden.

It wasn't Charles who'd opened the world of the garage to Peter. Father was a stockbroker; his nails were always impeccably clean. If he wasn't at the office, he was in the sitting room, engrossed in the financial pages, or having gin and tonics at Martini's or the club—but only as a member's guest these last couple of years. He surely wasn't banging around in here.

No, it was Morris the chauffeur who had brought Peter into this holy place of tools and motors and gears. The smell of gasoline and fertilizer had the same intoxicating effect on Peter as apple pie out of the oven for other kids.

Some of the happiest moments of his life were spent in this room, and the bigger one over on Waterloo, with Morris's gnarled old hands and mechanic's brain right alongside the boy, as he watched every turn of the screwdriver, every pull on a spring.

But Morris was gone now. As was the town car. And all the family's money. And Father. And now, Haverford.

All that was left was the old Indian, sitting where the car used to be, wheels off, up on blocks, exhaust manifold carefully disassembled, laying on a drop cloth alongside the bike. Peter went to the workbench and checked on the carburetor he'd torn down last night, its pieces soaking in two coffee cans of solvent. One by one, he wiped them clean with a shop rag, starting the re-assembly.

The young hands were so expert, so practiced, it was as automatic as tying his shoe. His mind wasn't necessary for this task, so it drifted inevitably to the obvious, try as he might to push it aside.

*I'll never get into college. I'll be lucky to get into a trade school. Never get to fly . . .*

The hands slowly stopped. The eyes squeezed shut to force back the tears, but they couldn't. *He* couldn't. He gingerly laid the carburetor down and hung his head to cry.

Maybe it was ten seconds, maybe it was ten minutes, before his world recovered from this uncontrollable spin, and he returned to the here and now. He knew instantly that he wasn't alone. Turning slowly, he saw his mother standing in the doorway. By the look on her face, she had clearly opened and read the letter on the hallway table.

God, she was a beautiful woman, ice cool. Peter Conrad worshipped his mother, amazed at her strength, her iron will to get this family through this hell. Father was always the softy, doling out compliments and praise no matter what. But it was her praise he wanted most. The worst part about the letter would be explaining it to her.

Strong, Frances was. Warm, she was not. But it pierced her, seeing her only son in this moment. He was too young to know this much pain.

"Mother, I need to tell you—"

"I know, Peter." She stepped inside his sanctuary. He wiped his eyes, turning away to compose himself. She smiled sadly at the effort. "It's one of the things I love most about your father. He can cry."

*Unlike me,* was the unspoken conclusion to that thought.

"Mother, I'm so sorry. I just . . ."

"No, Peter. I'm sorry. I know how you've struggled. We've all been struggling."

"What's going to happen to us?"

She closed her eyes and took a deep breath. "Whatever it is, we'll be fine. We'll be fine."

"I can't keep my eyes on the page. I get a headache when I look at the words; they all just . . . run together."

She nodded blankly, not really understanding. His lip quivered, and the tears started again.

"Mother, am I . . . stupid?"

Her eyes glanced at the shining rebuilt carburetor on the workbench, tools carefully cleaned and laid out next to a schematic drawing of the engine he'd sent away for—the kind of drawing only an engineer understood. And her own lip quivered.

"I think not," she whispered.

And for the first and only time in his sixteen years—including the entire time of her declining marriage and the falling fortunes of the Conrad family—Peter Conrad saw tears in his mother's eyes. And like a baby, he ran for her arms.

He felt her body quaking as she pulled him to her, holding him tighter and tighter, silently bleeding off the pressure, the anger and frustration and heartache she'd stoically forced down these past years. And this cool, composed tower of strength lovingly caressed her boy's back, letting her emotions go, if only for a moment.

"We will start over. You will graduate high school, you will go to college, and do whatever you will—to your own heart's content."

She kissed the top of his head, released him, then turned and hurried back out to finish this cry all by herself.

# EIGHT

**February 12, 1996**
**Learjet N10BD**
**Approaching Saint Kitts**
**Twenty-six minutes to initial descent**

**M**ark Calkins looked anxiously out at the white beaches of Puerto Rico forty-five thousand feet below. At six hundred miles an hour, the Learjet sang its high-pitched song at maximum fuel and aerodynamic efficiency.

The song was accompanied by the grunts, groans, and myriad cusswords of Pete and Dan Miller, tearing apart what had once been a careful, methodical stowage and placement of a thousand pounds of aft cargo—a stowage Mark had planned down to the last detail, and executed with military precision the night before. Now it looked like a teenager's bedroom. Boxes, emergency gear, protein bars, bottles of water, paperwork, and spare parts were slung crazily about as Pete and Dan dug like rescuers in a collapsed coal mine. If they couldn't find the spare power coupling for that HF radio, the flight was over in Saint Kitts.

"Got it!" Pete crawled forward through the detritus to the cockpit. "Okay, Mark. Rip that baby out. Let's see if we can fix her." Mark opened a Swiss Army knife and pried off the face of the Cockpit Display Unit like a thief boosting a car stereo. Pete already had the spare CDU out of the box.

It didn't take an engineer to test it. Hook the positive and negative wires onto the leads. They'd know in ten seconds.

"Okay, Mark. Give it a try."

Mark keyed the microphone, initiating the automatic tuning sequence. *TX* (transmit) displayed. *Good, good.* All four men waited with gritted teeth for the next display. If it locked on a frequency, they were golden. If it flashed, they were screwed. Five more seconds . . .

The damn thing flashed. The response was predictable. Everybody swore vehemently, except Mark, a devout Christian. But he certainly thought every word of it. He looked desperately to Pete—one last ember of hope in these ashes.

"Pete. We do have that spare receiver exciter box."

"Yeah . . ." The issue wasn't survival; it was the record. They had to have that HF radio if they were going to cross the Atlantic. Not to mention the rest of the planet. Yes, they had a spare.

The issue was *time*. The time it would take to replace and install the thing. With the spare mounted behind the 110-gallon custom fuel tank, which was shoved all the way aft, it wasn't like changing a lightbulb. In front of the 110-gallon drum was the ninety-gallon tank, with a tiny crawl space that now resembled the obstacle course from hell with crap strewn all over the aircraft.

The only sane way to do it, of course, would be to disconnect the front tank, slide it all the way forward, slide the big tank forward of the emergency hatch, then pay an avionics specialist sixty-five bucks an hour to do the job while they went and had lunch, returned some phone calls, and caught a few winks in the Caribbean sunshine.

And good-bye, record on their first leg. Hello, looking like very public idiots. And making Bill Daniels—the finest guy to walk the planet—look doubly so for financing this fool ride in the first place.

Pete had had a mission or two aborted on him. Scrubbed flights. Hell, he even ran out of gas in a T-38 a mile short of Ellington Field in Houston, popped out, watched the bird go down and explode under him, then packed his chute and walked calmly to somebody's house to use the phone. Machines break. This sort of thing just happens.

But he couldn't bear the look on Mark's face. He'd worked so hard, was as devoted to Bill Daniels as if Bill were his own dad, and would rather fall out of this thing at 45,000 feet than fail him.

What the hell. They had to try. Mark needed to stay in the cockpit. Paul, the World War II ace, topped six feet; he'd never fit in that space. Pete, at five-six and 150 pounds, with no beer belly, had been a gymnast as a kid, and even at sixty-five was still every bit as agile. Dan was a little shorter and equally svelte. If they were as lucky as lucky got, they might be able to pull off a miracle.

"Come on, Dan. Let's give it a shot."

Boating people know the feeling. It's like lying on your belly to retrieve a dropped nut behind the prop shaft in a beer cooler–sized engine compartment, and screwing it back on the bolt, in complete darkness on a rolling sea. That would have been a walk in the park compared to this.

This was more like sliding into a space the precise width of your body, reaching with one fully extended arm, touching fingers with your helper on the other side, while shouting instructions to one another over two screaming turbofan engines about finding and changing out that screw in the first place, in the middle of a six hundred–mile-per-hour blackout.

Except these guys had to do a lot more than attach a nut and bolt in a cramped space. They had to disconnect and dismount one radio and install another in total darkness with a breathing and venting and popping drum full of highly explosive jet fuel against their cheek and abdomen.

And they had twelve minutes to get it done.

If it was cluttered before, the cabin of the Lear was utter chaos now. Pete and Dan had to dump everything in the tight space between the bulkheads and the fuel tanks into the main cabin, which was about a third of its normal size anyway.

There was only one tiny problem: The installer had torqued the nut onto the bolt of the mounting bracket. Finger-tight would have been just fine. And there was no way in hell Pete could get a wrench in there. He cussed a mighty blue streak, skinning his left thumb and forefinger to a bloody mess while getting that sucker undone. But he got it. And out popped the HF radio.

Now, in with the ten-thousand-dollar spare. If Pete dropped it, the game was over. Mark had begun the long descent, and the warm, moist Caribbean air started getting bumpy.

"Okay, Dan. I can get it onto the bolt, but I can't let go of it to screw the nut on. Can you get it?"

"Yeah, I think so."

Pete gently passed the radio over his head, from right hand to left, and slid it gently against the back wall of the tank. The plane hit a thermal and bounced hard.

"Damn it!" Conrad conked his head, and almost let the unit slip out of his hand. He jimmied and slid and jimmied and slid, looking for the bolt. . . . "Okay, got it! Screw away, my boy!"

"Aww, shit, Pete!" Pete didn't have to be told. He felt the nut slip out of Dan's fingers, roll across his hand, and fall to the deck.

"I'll hold the radio. Squat down; see if you can feel it on the floor."

A long wait, then: "I can't find it, Pete. It must have rolled over to you." Pete knew they had about three minutes till final descent, and Mark would have a hell of a time bringing her in without the radio. He couldn't do it safely at a strange field, and Paul clearly didn't know this aircraft. It was now or never.

"All right, you hold the radio on the bolt; let me see if I can get it." Pete eased himself down into a lying position and stretched his arm as far as it would reach, feeling along the floor. "Got it."

He was back up in a nanosecond, reached his bloody fingers back in there, and popped the nut back on, screwing her down finger-tight this time.

Both crawled like mountain goats over the junk to the cockpit. Saint Kitts was right off the aircraft's nose, and the tower undoubtedly was trying to raise the jet, assuming they had radar. "Go ahead, Mark. She's in. Give it a try," offered Pete anxiously, wiping sweat off his face.

Mark keyed the mike. TX. And the radio tried to tune itself: 10, 9, 8, 7, 6, 5 . . .

A hiss, a pop, and a high-pitched squeal of a long-distance transmission, then a locked frequency number and a Caribbean-accented controller's voice.

"Aircraft approaching Saint Kitts, please identify."

The guy might have almost heard the screams and high fives around the cabin.

"Goldenrock Approach, Learjet 10BD is with you, over. . . ."

# NINE

**C**hange is usually gradual. The catalyst for change, however, is almost always instantaneous. A lucky break, sudden realization, a catastrophe. For the dinosaurs it was probably a meteor slamming into their idyllic, cozy, warm little tropical planet. It may have taken a few million years, but it looks like that's what brought the Ice Age that did them in.

For humans, it's always a *decision* that brings change. Every time. Made *by* a person or *for* a person. In the case of Peter Conrad, it was a threefold combination. First his decision, then the Haverford School's, then his mother's.

Peter decided, in the infinite wisdom of a sixteen-year-old, that cutting English class and bombing through the campus quad on the Indian one bright May morning—shirtless, cigarette between his teeth—would be a fine way to welcome spring to Haverford. Three cardinal rules, worth about a hundred demerit hours, were broken in under twenty seconds. It's still a record.

It was this incident that finally brought about Haverford's decision that Peter would be going to school elsewhere the following fall.

It was Frances who decided where that elsewhere would be.


**"H**ands to work; hearts to God." These were the marching orders of the Shakers as they rose every morning in the Berkshire Mountains three hundred years ago, hacking out their home one tree, one rock at a time in the forest southeast of what is now Albany, near the Massachusetts–New York border.

If you visit the town of New Lebanon, home to the Mount Lebanon Shaker Village Monument, you can see those words materialized in the buildings: rough-hewn logs, planks, and bricks sitting on stone foundations, weathered, faded, then remodeled, but as sturdy and strong as the day of their first Sunday meeting.

Mount Lebanon Shaker Village is also the present-day home of the Darrow School, which opened its doors in 1932. Its student body was a curious mix in 1947 of the brilliant, the underachiever, and the misfit—alongside some "normal" boys, of course. The school boasts an impressive roster of high-achieving alumni.

Charles "Peter" Conrad Jr.'s application described him as five-six (*and a half, damn it!*), 125 pounds, having completed tenth grade. There was no mention made of his doomed run at eleventh grade in '46–'47; nor was it necessary. This wasn't the first restart Darrow had offered. And yes, he'd been signing his name with the "Jr." suffix for a while now.

Sports: football, baseball, hockey. Hobbies: crew, skiing, mechanics. Musical Talent: none. Smoking at home: yes.

No essay, thank God. Headmaster Lambert Heyniger, a stern, imposing fellow of good Shaker stock, initialed the ACCEPTED stamp himself.


**E**astern prep schools have traditionally prided themselves on being academic bastions, training generations of doctors, lawyers, businessmen, and other professionals. Prepping at a place like Haverford isn't a guarantee of going to Harvard or Yale or Princeton, but it sure doesn't hurt your chances.

Darrow was marching to a different prep school drum in 1947. Though the school was academically solid, the mission statement was a tad more on the personal side than the noble words that concluded Haverford's: ". . . high standards of character and conduct." Noble qualities though they are, Darrow chose the less austere ". . . inspiring a confidence for life."

If there was anything Peter needed at that moment, it was confidence. Arriving in New Lebanon from Haverford was as dramatic a move for him as uprooting from the Rhine River Valley and starting up Germantown, Pennsylvania, was for his forefather Thones Kunders.

Peter went from the suburbs to the woods, from polished marble to post and beam. And from musty library stacks to stacks of freshly corded firewood.

The change might not be so gradual after all.

# TEN

The flight log entry for August 22, 1947, is innocuous enough: *Piper J-3, Certificate #NC49567, Make of Engine, Cont. 65, flew local for 1.0 hours.* Pilot's remarks: *Light winds, 20 miles visibility.*

But the signature in the far right column belonged to the planet's newest certified pilot at 3:30 EST that day, having just completed his first solo airborne ride: Charles Conrad, Jr.

His responsibilities had grown in two summers working at Paoli Airfield. He'd graduated from pulling weeds to washing down planes, which led to gassing them up, then changing their oil or fixing a tire. Old man Turner would take Peter along once in a great while to deliver an airplane to Williamsport or Chester. He even let the boy fly awhile.

"Will you teach me to fly?"

"Can't, son. I'm not instructor rated."

"Do you know somebody who is?"

"Lots of 'em. None that'll do it for free, though."

And that was that, for a time. Peter went up whenever somebody would take him, and learned every damn nut and bolt and belt on the things. As always, he watched them take off and land. And take off and land. Hoping. Planning. Dreaming.

More than two years had gone by, and not one hour in the sky as a passenger counted for squat. Lots of dreams had long since faded away on a sweltering afternoon when he lay on his back on the heat-softened tarmac, fighting with a frozen bolt on a landing strut. The phone in the office started ringing again, for the fifth time. Nobody was there, Mr. Turner was God knew where, and Peter didn't feel like answering it anyway. But it kept ringing. And ringing. And ringing.

"All right, for God's sake!" The boy tossed a solvent-soaked rag aside and strode across the blacktop, snatching the phone off the hook. "Paoli Field, Conrad."

His bark was no match for the voice on the other end. It unleashed a tirade of profanity-laced insults from someone who would have no doubt rung the phone for twenty-four hours till somebody picked up. And curiously enough, the shouting voice was decidedly feminine.

"Hold on, stop. What can I do for you, ma'am?"

"Where is that son of a bitch Turner?"

"He's not here. Can I help you with something?"

"Yeah, you sure as hell can! Look up above you at the flight board."

"Lowell, Margaret. Piper J-3."

"Splendid. He can read."

"Cross-country with student, Paoli–Scranton–Williamsport–return."

"Does it say anything about a frozen choke?"

"Uh, no, ma'am . . ."

"Guess what? *It's got a goddamn frozen choke!* I just set down in the middle of a cornfield!"

"Oh, Mrs. Lowell, I am so sorry—"

"That's *Miss* Lowell, broom boy! Where the hell is Turner? Doesn't he check these things before sending them out?"

"Yes, ma'am, he does. Where are you?"

"Draw a line heading three-three-five, seventy-one-point-six miles. Right off Highway Nine. See that very pissed-off woman on the porch of some farmer who isn't even home? That's me!"

"I'm on my way."

A *tough broad* was how they would have described Margaret Lowell back in the days when you could get away with that. She dressed like a man, had a severe haircut, and was beautiful in that Rosie the Riveter sort of way. Her student was a woman of about the same age, who looked like a pretty housewife. Margaret stared in dismay—*irritated* dismay—as Peter roared up on the Indian.

"Conrad?"

"Yep."

"And you didn't bring my car because . . . ?"

"I'm not legal to drive it."

"You legal to drive *that?*"

"No, but at least it's mine." He flashed a gap-toothed grin.

"Do you seriously expect the three of us to ride back to Paoli on that?"

"No, ma'am. I'm gonna fix the choke. Where's the Piper?"

The entire operation took about twenty minutes. Margaret was agitated, would have picked her tirade up right where she left off if the boy didn't move like he did in the engine of the J-3, humming to himself, confident as a surgeon.

"The choke's fine." A little more tinkering and tightening. "The throttle spring popped, flooded her right out."

"Meaning . . . ?"

"Meaning this new one oughtta do the trick. Let's fire it up."

On the first contact, the engine roared to life. Peter listened, then nodded, satisfied. He gathered his tools, gave her the okay sign, and hopped back onto the Indian, buckling his leather helmet.

* * *

It was nearly dark when he rolled back into the parking lot at Paoli Field. Margaret was waiting for him alone, smoking a cigarette on the hood of her car.

"I didn't get a chance to thank you, Mr. Conrad."

"It's Peter. I'm sorry about the inconvenience. Good thing you knew how to land her dead-stick."

"How old are you?"

"Sixteen."

"That was a handy piece of work you did. That Piper never flew so smooth. Here's ten bucks."

"No, ma'am. No, thanks."

"Well, there must be something I can do."

Nothing provocative there, no lines for a sixteen-year-old boy to read between. She didn't seem the type anyway. But he did manage another grin at the fact that he had gone from "broom boy" to "Mr. Conrad" in one afternoon. And since she asked . . .

"How about teaching me to fly? I'll work out the rental with Mr. Turner. If you're not too expensive, I can save up between lessons and—"

"I'll teach you to fly, Peter."


It didn't take long. Margaret was a gifted instructor, having taught hundreds of women to fly in the WASP program during the war. And for a boy who'd spent the last three summers working at an airfield, tuning up planes, copping free rides whenever he could, and devouring every aviation magazine to be found, there wasn't that much to teach, frankly. To Peter Conrad, flying was as easy as driving the Indian. Aerodynamics and mechanics? Second nature. He understood how a plane actually flew better than she did. And he didn't just hear the Continental 65 motor; he *listened* to it. And felt it. It was only a matter of getting the hours.

On their seventh day together, student pilot Conrad taxied the Piper to the end of the runway, held short, and ran the engine up to full, doing his final check. Margaret reached between them and pulled the throttle back down to idle. Then she unbuckled her seat belt and opened the passenger door.

"Have a nice flight, Conrad." She hopped down, latched the door behind her, and strode toward the hangar without looking back. He waited just long enough for her to get clear of his prop wash, then ran the engine up to full again, releasing the brakes.

We remember our firsts with unmatched clarity. First day of school, first car, first kiss.

For a pilot, the first solo flight is stamped on the consciousness for the rest of his life. There's not a flier anywhere who can't give you a minute-by-minute, mile-by-mile account of that first time, not a detail left out.

Light winds, twenty miles visibility. One hour to Scranton and back, flying at 2,500 feet, airspeed of 65 mph. Fifty years and eleven thousand flying hours later, Pete Conrad could tell you the make and model of the cars rolling under him on Highway 6 as he climbed out, leaving Mother Earth for the first time alone, by his own hand.

This was that cataclysmic event for Peter, as path-altering for him as the meteor was for the dinosaurs—except with a much happier ending.

Dark days had become dark months, then dark years as Peter's reality had rapidly become heartache and failure.

Now suddenly those days disappeared like the ground below as he pulled the stick back to his lap. For this airborne hour, an inexperienced yet steady hand guided this ship. And the curtain lifted at long last.

The voice of doubt and shame was finally—*finally*—drowned out by the heavenly song of that Continental engine, bringing back the same joy and freedom he'd known swinging hour after hour in that tree swing back on Waterloo Avenue, wishing as hard as he could for the very moment he was living here at 2,500 feet.

This was Peter Conrad's flight. He could point that nose at any of the 360 notches on his ball compass. He could keep her straight and level, or bank her hard and dive toward the ground, yanking her back at the last possible second with the ease and grace of a Pennsylvania hawk.

So he did both. Again and again. And by the time the Piper's wheels touched the ground again, the flight plan for Charles Conrad Jr.'s life was filed.

\*　\*　\*

**H**e taxied the J-3 back to the hangar, and was out of the cockpit and sprinting toward Margaret before the prop was finished spinning. She laughed at his whoops and hollers, sitting at the picnic table with the woman he recognized as her student pilot the day of their first meeting.

He grabbed Margaret by the shoulders and planted a wet one right on the kisser, bear-hugging her before she could get a word out. The "student" leaped at Peter suddenly like a striking cobra, cocking her right fist to deliver a mighty blow to the side of his head. Margaret stopped her midswing.

"Peter, this is my . . . friend, Deborah."

With passing years and the attendant wisdom, he would come to realize what Margaret meant by *friend*. Not that it mattered one whit. Deborah could have broken his jaw, for all he cared. He wouldn't have felt it that day.

"You want to go again?" Margaret smiled as she signed the logbook. He was turning the prop back over in a matter of seconds.

He never saw Margaret Lowell again. But he never forgot one single detail of that flight on August 22, 1947. It summoned a broad smile every time he called it back up. And it wasn't because of the near-punch from Margaret's girlfriend. It was because for the rest of his life, Charles "Peter" Conrad would be referred to as . . . a pilot.

# ELEVEN

February 12, 1996
Learjet N10BD
1608 Zulu
Saint Kitts Airport

Joy had given way to focus and a practiced set of descent, approach, and landing procedures. Dan Miller was in the driver's seat, his movements competent, if hurried. He had a way to go to really master a bird like the Lear 35, but he set her down like a pro. Now the focus turned to the frantic ballet of refueling her, declaring customs, and getting departure clearance in under thirty minutes. The flight crew had talked about the ballet a thousand times over the last two months, even practiced pieces of it, but they had never rehearsed the entire production start to finish.

It's not as simple as pulling your car up to the local Chevron station, popping the lid, and throwing the nozzle in while you wash the windshield or go grab a soda. The Lear 35 has a fuel tank in each wing, and then there were the custom tanks riding with them in the cabin. Each had its own screw top, accessed only through the emergency escape hatch. There was a sequence that had to be followed, involving electric pumps to balance the load. The interior custom-tank refueling was far from trivial: A spill inside the cabin, no matter how small (like, *drops*) could easily leave vapors that would ignite with the first transmission of the newly installed HF radio, mounted on the back of the tank.

Add to this volatile mix a typically laid-back Caribbean island ground crew with a passable but ancient BP fuel truck, and a clueless and vaguely hostile tower, seeming to enjoy every maddening second of their delayed departure.

A thirty-minute turn was a fantasy, and these guys knew it. And this was the first of eight stops . . . ?

Pete Conrad leaned forward in the copilot's seat, struggling to communicate with the tower. With the engines whining, Dan eased her out onto the taxiway. The ground crew had done just fine, making up for their inexperience by hustling and smiling. Pete had had to bark at one of them for trying to muscle the nozzle into the interior of the jet, and spilling a drop or two, but complimented him as they finished, signing the back of his white shirt when asked.

But they were already at forty minutes, and still had no departure clearance.

"What did he say?" Pete's patience with the whole radio thing was a memory now.

"He said five more minutes."

"Five minutes?" Pete keyed the microphone, speaking pleasantly and deferentially, but not entirely hiding his irritation. "Goldenrock, Ten Bravo Delta. Request VFR departure; we will get clearance en route."

The response was garbled, but he was sure he'd heard the word *affirmative* in there somewhere.

"Hey, Mark, these guys knew we were coming, right?"

"Yeah, but they weren't too happy about our high-speed approach. I don't think they were too crazy about being an *alternate* site, either."

The radio squawked clearly now. "Learjet 10BD, hold short for departing traffic."

"Damn it!" Pete barked. It would be at least four minutes before the two American Eagle commuters rolling slowly toward the taxiway would be airborne.

Mark Calkins groaned in despair. Dan Miller drummed his kneecaps and clacked his teeth together. Paul Thayer stared silently out at the rusting relics of aviation's past parked in the weeds off the field. He'd probably flown some of those models forty years ago.

Conrad busied himself with the departure checklist again. He couldn't bear to watch as the American Eagle took off at a leisurely—*excruciatingly* leisurely—pace. "Left generator set to off; you don't have that engine lit; let's light it now. Pitot heats go, lights and strobes on, ignition on—" and he suddenly blurted into the radio, "Goldenrock, still looking for that clearance."

Another garbled response—last straw. The runway was now clear, the sky empty. "Crank it, Dan. We're out of here."

That was all the kid needed. He threw the throttle forward as the tower and other aircraft on the ground chattered on with no regard for them, the record, or any other damn thing, it seemed. Pete continued, not particularly listening for a response, "10BD to roll, please."

More garble and static, which might have been a takeoff clearance. It might not. Didn't matter anyway. Forty-six minutes from touchdown, behind schedule already, Ten Bravo Delta rotated skyward, belly full of fuel, and headed for Sal, Cape Verde, off the coast of Africa.

# TWELVE

**H**eadmaster Lambert Heyniger stood six-foot-seven, and tipped the scales north of three hundred. His voice was a deep, booming baritone, and a classically trained one at that. He never got a chance to use it at the Met, but boy, oh, boy, could it fill those Berkshire woods when he bellowed it across campus. And God help you if it was your name echoing around up there, as you were summoned forth.

Heyniger had a weakness for the most "challenging" of the cases. There was no such thing as a dull kid, just a bored one, as far as he was concerned. Peter's abysmal transcript from Haverford, "slow reader" and all—not to mention his growing motorcycle-rebel status—didn't even faze the man. After five stern, introductory "Welcome to our world, Master Conrad" minutes with the boy, Heyniger found himself fighting a smile.

This kid wasn't an idiot. He wasn't even a rebel. He was just a boy—a boy who needed to channel a Hoover Dam's worth of energy, curiosity, and moxie. And these woods were just the place to do that.

Besides, the boy had just learned to fly, as everyone knew inside of five minutes with him. Whatever darkness had been hanging over Peter Conrad in Wayne, Pennsylvania, was lifting fast by the time he showed up in New Lebanon, New York.

Darrow's approach was twofold: Put hands to work, literally, and open the doors to the student's natural abilities and passions. It was no cop-out, touchy-feely approach. Peter would have to repeat the eleventh grade. He would have to read Homer and Chaucer and study the Dred Scott decision and solve the same calculus problems he would have at Haverford.

But he'd also have to chop firewood. Cut trails. Plant new trees and build small houses for the less fortunate with the habitat crew. Take food to the needy at the holidays.

Suddenly there was a meaning to the whole thing. And a *destination*.

They didn't know what dyslexia was at Darrow, either. There was some postdoctoral reading on the subject out there, but only experimental approaches to it. By and large, society and even academia mostly looked on any diagnosed dysfunction as a crutch, and attacked the problem more with discipline than strategy.

Heyniger didn't have any magic bullets. All he could do was hold the bar high, keep encouraging, and remind the boy that there *was* a destination, a reason for this difficult but necessary process. Peter would get through this. He would excel. Or he wasn't going to get to fly; not to the places and in the planes he dreamed of flying, anyway.

He stared at the pages just as long as he had before, fighting the headaches like an enemy. Only this time he wasn't letting them win. If he had to stay up all night in his dormitory, after the mandatory two-hour evening study hall, then so be it. The hours he spent and the skills he was learning in the Piper weren't a distraction or a hobby; they were *fuel*. And a procedure.

To fly an airplane, there is a system—a series of preparations and tasks and operations that must be followed in the correct sequence in order to start the engine, roll it down the runway, achieve lift, fly, and bring it home. There was a system and checklist for how you talked on the radio. There was even a system for what to do when it all went to hell up there, which, every so often, it did.

Late one night in the Darrow library, as Peter studied for a final, the two separate wires of learning and flying touched. Orderly preparation, checklist, and procedure, repeat. If there was a system for flying, why couldn't there be a system for learning?

It could even work for reading. Text, dictionary, notebook. Text, dictionary, notebook.

It did work. Eight hours with *Hamlet* became four with *Macbeth,* then three with *Romeo and Juliet.* If he put on a costume and acted it out, which he would do with whatever spare Elizabethan-looking clothes he could cobble together from the drama class, he didn't care how long it took.

History? Just a series of stories, and the boy loved a good story.

Math and science? A walk in the park.

In the spring of 1948, for the first time since sixth grade, Charles Conrad, Jr., made the honor roll—barely squeaked onto it, but he made it. He danced all the way across campus to the dining hall, shouting it to anyone who would hear: "Honor roll, daddy! *Honor rollllll!*"

Was he so happy because he'd exorcised a demon? Because he'd vindicated himself, proving he wasn't a "slow reader" after all? Because he'd finally managed a deep and lasting restoration of a wounded self-esteem?

Yeah, sure.

The real reason for the cross-campus dance was that honor roll kids didn't have to go to evening study hall. Peter could now do his homework in his room (and listen to country music on the radio he'd made, hidden carefully under his bed).

In the blink of an eye, the "challenging" kid, the rebel, became the heart and soul of the old Shaker village: quarterback and captain of the Darrow football team, skating for the hockey team, behind the plate on the baseball squad, a fixture with the Darrow Players . . . hell, Peter Conrad was even the campus mailman!

Meanwhile, the logbook was getting filled up. Every weekend he wasn't in a team sport or at a school function, he'd take the train or find a ride back to the Main Line and Paoli Airfield. Or West Chester. He'd trade work for hours, but the days of sweeping and weed chopping were pretty much behind Peter now. He was tuning motors, machining parts, taking the birds up for shakedown flights.

It was as dramatic a turnaround as Lambert Heyniger had ever seen.

"Conrad, what do you plan to do when you leave these hallowed halls?"

"Fly, sir."

"I thought you were going to catch for the Yankees?"

"Fly, sir."

"What about the stage? The movies?"

"Fly, sir. I'm gonna fly."

Heyniger was a dyed-in-the-wool Princeton man. A favored son. Every year at least one Darrow boy enrolled there, sometimes as many as three. It was as much an accomplishment then as now. But favored son or not, Princeton has never been in the business of *doing* favors. You either have it or you don't.

Peter Conrad had just over a 3.2 grade point average. His college boards were decent, but not world-beaters. Repeating the eleventh grade would have probably been the deal breaker, except for the U.S. Navy. Before Heyniger called the admissions office, he called the commander of Naval ROTC at Princeton, someone he didn't know. The fellow didn't want to be sold. Just wanted a name, in that typical cryptic, military-intel way. He'd check Mr. Conrad out himself, and let him know if it was worth the boy's even applying.

It was a bright, sunny, perfect Philadelphia spring day when Darrow senior Peter Conrad managed to sneak home for the weekend. He'd flown takeoffs and landings most of the day, a couple of touch-and-gos. Now showered up and looking sharp for a prom that night, he was buying a mum at a flower shop when he spotted his former headmaster at Haverford, Mr. Severinghaus, strolling importantly with two equally esteemed pillars of the Main Line community—Haverford board members, probably.

Peter tossed the flower girl a buck and hurried across the street. He wouldn't miss this opportunity for all the tea in China.

"Mr. Severinghaus." The old man turned slowly. "It's Peter Conrad, sir." His shoulders raised instinctively, stretching that five-foot-six (*and a* half, *damn it!*) for every millimeter it was worth.

"Yes, yes. Mr. Conrad. How have things worked out for you at . . . ?" He trailed off, not remembering where Peter had landed after his dismissal. Or pretending not to remember. It was hard to tell.

"Darrow, sir."

"Darrow. Right. Fine place. The other men smiled, nodded, and harrumphed right along with the old man. "You had a good run, then?"

"Yes, sir, I made the honor roll. I was elected president of the senior class, and captain of the football team."

"Well, how about that?" He chuckled, patting Peter on the head like a third grader or a puppy. "Just shows what you can do when you put the old nose to the grindstone, eh?"

"Yes, sir, I guess it does."

More harrumphing and agreeing grunts. "And where will you be heading next year, lad? City College?"

"As a matter of fact, I'll be attending Princeton." Peter smiled. "On a full Navy scholarship." He savored the look on the old boy's face for the rest of his days, nodding to all three as he went his way. "Good evening to you all, sirs."

# THIRTEEN

**M**ore than three thousand young men applied for Naval Reserve Officer Training Corps scholarships to Princeton for the fall of 1949. Seventy-five were awarded; Peter Conrad was one of them. His best Devon buddy, Stockton Rush, also an early departer from Haverford due to academic and behavioral transgressions, had also reinvented himself, and showed up three dorm rooms down in Lockhart Hall. Both Stockton and Peter had already achieved a fair amount of celebrity, the intricate labyrinth of escape tunnels they'd constructed at Haverford the stuff of legend by now. It was actually one tunnel, but why let the facts get in the way of a great story? It was certainly a factor in those early departures. Peter and Stockton let the legend grow as it would.

Peter had been only there a month or so, and was studying at his desk in room 104, when outside the window, walking down the street, he saw the strangest man he had ever seen anywhere, galumphing along. He had one foot in the sidewalk, one in the gutter, slurping an ice-cream cone. The guy's hair was a rat's nest, chocolate was smeared all over his rodent-looking mustache, he hadn't shaved in days, and he was wearing a horrible beige sweater and muttering to himself.

"Look at this guy," Peter said as Stockton breezed into his room with two Cokes. "I don't think he's doing too good."

"You don't know who that is?"

"No . . ."

"Einstein."

*"That's* Albert Einstein?"

"Swear to God. And check it out"—Stockton laughed—"look at the book he's got."

"What do you expect him to carry, a football? He's Einstein."

"No, see the bookmarks? Roger Thorn told me they're his paychecks. He never remembers to cash them. Guy's got, like, a five hundred IQ, and he doesn't understand money."

"Or it just doesn't matter to him." Peter smiled, watching the world's smartest man continue on his way.


**P**eter and six others were the first declared majors in Princeton's inaugural Aeronautical Engineering program in 1949. The Guggenheims selected Princeton and Cal Tech as the two sites for their jet-propulsion labs, research centers designed to study this brand-new way to move airplanes through the sky. Talk about being at the right place at the right time. For a freshman who far preferred numbers and diagrams to words on a page, who lived and breathed every facet of aviation, this place was paradise.

And Peter was showing up on the ground floor. Jet engines had been operational for only ten years or so. Although Frank Whittle's prototype had flown in Britain in 1939, the Allies stuck with good old propellers throughout World War II. The Luftwaffe bolted them onto their fighters toward the end of the war, but in the heat of battle there wasn't a lot of engineering analysis going on. What kind of airframe could be designed and built that would withstand an exponential leap in thrust? Just what was an airplane capable of with one of these things strapped to it? What about two of them?

The bottom of Peter's class schedule card read, *Naval Science 101*. As if this new heaven could possibly get any better, it did so in this class every Monday, Wednesday, and Friday at three P.M.

He'd always loved knots. Father had never been much at it, but Morris had taught him a trucker's hitch by the time he was five years old, and every knot known to every sailor since the Phoenicians by ten. After the third class, the old-salt instructor sat down with the other students and let the wisecracking cadet teach him a few hitches.

This ROTC thing was just a kick in the pants! Drilling, marching, rifles on the firing range, sailing regattas. He was outside more than he was inside. Perfect. The Navy even gave him fifty bucks a month and paid his rental time in the Navion at the local airfield.

And he was getting a grade for it all? Could it possibly get any better than this?

Oh, yeah. It could definitely get better.


It was a cold, misty day for June when the battleship *Missouri* cast off from Norfolk, bound for Halifax, Nova Scotia. The last battleship commissioned by the U.S. Navy, the *Missouri* was three football fields long, and looked as new as the day she came down the ways of the Brooklyn Navy Yard on January 29, 1944. She had punished the Japanese fleet mercilessly that year, and in 1945, right there on the foredeck, MacArthur accepted Japan's surrender.

Even today, as she sits quietly as a museum in Pearl Harbor, it's impossible to step on board, and not feel *something*.

Conrad felt it. He and all the cadets on their first naval exercise fought like hell not to just stare openmouthed at the sheer size and might of this boat, and wonder how they'd gotten so lucky as to be here at all. He stood at the forward port rail, waving at no one in particular, feeling part of something a lot bigger than himself.

Cadets get a flavor of everything on that first cruise. Regardless of their chosen path, the Navy believes every officer needs to have working knowledge of every corner of these floating cities. So Peter found himself in front of the largest engines on Earth. He loaded magazines for the gunnery exercises. He worked the radio and radar, plotted course headings, and actually took the helm for a minute or two. He swabbed the deck and peeled potatoes as well.

It may have been mundane for the sailors who called this boat home, but for Conrad, the kick in the pants just kept getting kickier. It was impossible for these guys not to laugh at his gap-toothed permagrin, no matter how lousy the duty he pulled.

He was as concerned and worried as anyone when the ship was called home suddenly at the outbreak of the Korean War. But quietly, he was sorry to see the most eye-opening six weeks of his life come to an end.

# FOURTEEN

**B**ryn Mawr sophomore Jane DuBose was a tall, statuesque, olive-skinned society girl, and the most beautiful creature the twenty-one-year-old Peter had ever seen. The first thing Jane noticed about him was that he was shorter than she. The second thing? He didn't give a damn. That, plus a focus and life plan a lot clearer than the other college boys around here, and a raucous energy level that kept everyone around him laughing, made Peter Conrad a likely candidate for accompanying her on her own journey.

The uniform didn't hurt, either.

The next thing Jane knew, she was in an airplane just about every weekend of her life, going to the Jersey shore, back to Philly, maybe a dinner in Albany. It was just a tad more dynamic than the average collegiate dating experience.

Take, for instance, the midsummer run out to Pittsburgh. It was hot as hell in the Navion, a very aerodynamic, bubble-cockpit four-seater owned by the NROTC. By Conrad's sophomore year, it had practically become his personal plane, as he was flying it constantly.

Here they were, Peter and Jane and another couple, everybody sweating to beat the band. The vents just made it worse, blowing hot, sticky air through the cockpit. The men had long since removed their shirts. With everybody long-faced and miserable, Peter decided to spice things up a little. How about an unannounced barrel roll or two?

He didn't factor in two components of the equation, however. All four of them were smoking. Not unusual in 1950, it was practically de rigueur for the upwardly mobile intellectuals at Princeton and Bryn Mawr. Smoking in a nonpressurized airplane was as commonplace as it was in a car. Factor two: The ashtrays in the Navion hadn't been emptied in days. They were brimming over with butts and ashes when he stomped the rudder and threw the wheel at a hundred miles per hour.

Not only was he instantly flying blind in a gray cloud—the cabin was filled with howls of protest and profanity. The ashes that stuck to their sweaty skin became a black, syrupy paste by the time he shut the engine down at the hangar, enduring his passengers' fury while they hosed themselves off behind the building.

He was unable, as always, to stop laughing.

If Jane's beauty and charm and excellent breeding weren't enough for Cadet Conrad, there was always the Ranch. And as far as Jane's father was concerned, it was where the cadet would prove himself worthy of his little girl's hand.

Winn DuBose was the picture of the Texas gentleman rancher. He'd married himself a society girl, and Jane followed in her mother's footsteps. But Winn . . . that man was a cowboy, head to toe. And Uvalde, Texas, was as near to heaven as that cowboy got outside of a pine box. Winn owned sixteen hundred acres of scrub oak and dusty pasture, with fences that needed constant mending, horses to be shod, cattle to be branded, dipped, and vaccinated.

"Hell, boy, does it get any better than *this?*" he roared at Peter as they sad-dled up before the sun on the first morning of Peter's two weeks there.

Breakfast was at five. Nobody, not even the adoring Jane, could hold back a laugh when Peter stepped to the table, feeling instantly like he'd shown up at a pool party wearing white tie and tails. Shiny boots with spurs, tight-pressed brand-new jeans, a Gene Autry patterned flannel shirt with kerchief, and an expensive "cowboy hat" he'd bought from a haberdasher in Philly . . .

Meanwhile Winn was wearing faded, patched jeans, a stained and torn work shirt, and boots that looked like they came from the Army surplus store—the *Confederate* Army surplus store. Same with Jane's brother, Tom.

"Well, young man. Looks like you're ready to go," said a smiling Winn, en-joying the hell out of this, as any father of a beautiful daughter would.

"Yes, sir, I'm ready." The city slicker nodded. "I just need one more thing."

"What's that, son?"

"A big pile of shit to roll around in, break these duds in a little."

Thus began a forty-five-year love affair between Peter Conrad and the Ranch.

He'd ridden a horse or two, but they were trail nags or sleepaway-camp ponies. Nothing could have prepared the Main Line boy for a Texas bronc. He hit the ground his share that first day, but had it down by lunch. The boy could ride, Winn noted to himself. A little green, but he sure wasn't afraid of it.

Peter wrestled his first calf to the dirt, and took a hoof to the nose. Bleed-ing like a stuck hog, he whooped a rebel yell like he'd been doing this his whole life. He was happy to add a new stain to the shirt Tom had lent him. He could swing an ax better than Tom, even if he was half a foot shorter. And before that first week was out, he roped his first steer from the back of a gal-loping mount.

Best of all, as far as Winn was concerned, Peter knew who Roy Acuff was. And Hank Williams. He and Winn sang "Your Cold, Cold Heart" at the top of their lungs, a torture session to the horses, the defenseless prairie dogs, and Tom, who, once they started their third round of "Honky-Tonkin," found a section of fence on the far end of the sixteen hundred acres to work on.

"You know something, Pete?" Winn slapped him on the back as they hung their saddles in the tack room. "You're all right."

It's always a big day when you win over your girl's dad. But it was also the first time he could remember being called *Pete,* the name he'd carry for the rest of his life. And as perfect as it was, coming from the smoky, gravelly voice of this old cowboy on the Texas range, he wondered why he'd never considered it before.

Pete Conrad. Cowboy. Naval aviator.

He liked the sound of that.

BOOK TWO

# WINGS

# FIFTEEN

February 12, 1996
Learjet N1OBD
28,000 feet, descending
Approaching Sal, Cape Verde
2031 Zulu

*Jeez, this bird is smooth,* thought Pete. The Lear 35 is not known to be the easiest jet to fly, but in the hands of a guy who'd been flying for fifty years, she responded as advertised. Not a vibration in the wheel, hypersensitive to the touch; even pushing over into a steep descent in rough African coastal air, she still rode lean, lithe, and smooth at five hundred knots.

Pete had taken front left halfway across the Atlantic. The winds had been as forecast by Nancy Schnetz Jeppesen Dataplan, who'd plotted their entire worldwide route with them. They made up most of their lost time, and the flight was settling down into something near normal. Near normal, that is, for a business jet crammed with two extra fuel tanks and survival gear, redlining around the globe going for a record.

Communication was still a headache. It had not improved a whit since leaving the Caribbean. Clearance for airspace departure and handoff between Saint Kitts, San Juan, Puerto Rico, and tiny Piarco Island off the coast of Venezuela had been an utter debacle. There was confusion over the flight plans filed, which waypoints had been plotted, who authorized what altitude, and which vector was authorized across the Atlantic. And in the middle of this, the HF radio still didn't work worth a damn, and they'd long since passed VHF range. Static and garbled Caribbean- and Latin-accented English was as good as it got for two hours.

What did it matter, really? They had four full tanks of fuel, the wind at their backs in a zooming Lear, and more than a century's flying experience on board. Just *go*, right?

Wrong. Any disputed procedure from any traffic center throws the entire flight into protest hearing. The long arm of the FAA would reach out to them for any cited violation, and smack the fire out of them with a hefty fine. And the mark would become a permanent part of all their flight records. On top of that, the authorities in Paris might refuse to certify the record at all, no matter what their time.

Besides, it was just plain dangerous.

"Let us not forget boys," offered the former astronaut, trying to lighten this tense cabin a bit, "this is technically the Bermuda Triangle." He broke into the *Twilight Zone* theme, raising a laugh and singalong.

He rifled through his handbook, found a frequency, and dialed it into the HF, keying the mike. "Houston Control, this is Learjet Ten Bravo Delta; how do you read?"

"Ten Bravo Delta, this is Houston," the radio blared clear as crystal. "Go ahead."

"Roger, Houston . . ."

Mark Calkins wondered if he was the only one aboard thinking what he was thinking. Electromagnetic static, in the Bermuda Triangle, and here was one of the *Apollo* astronauts repeating the very words he'd uttered from the surface of the Moon twenty-seven years ago, "Roger, Houston."

*Doo-doo-doo-doo, doo-doo-doo-doo, doo-doo-doo-doo . . .*

### Saint Kitts to Sal
### 100 miles out

All quiet, save for the turbofans roaring at forty thousand rpms and the thunder of slicing through the sky at six hundred mph. Nobody was talking, anyway.

It was a short day; the sun was down behind them already. When they'd come in too fast back at Saint Kitts, owing to the HF radio fix and the general apathy of the tower, Dan Miller had had to do a full 360 degree turn to slow her down enough to land safely. They lost four minutes right there.

Pete wasn't going to do that. He started the descent early, as soon as any of the Cape Verde Islands was in sight. He began his descent as he had every descent since the Piper: with a checklist. He smiled at the digital displays in front of him, remembering the dials of flights past. Hell, when he started flying, *digital* meant something related to your fingers. Even his *Apollo 12* command module was mostly toggle switches; its onboard computer had the memory capacity of today's pocket calculators from Radio Shack.

But look at this display. Son of a bitch, this thing was beautiful. In the craziest of the Buck Rogers comics he'd read as a kid, they never would have dreamed of this bird.

"Windshield heat, on. Crossing three thousand."

"Hey, Pete," Dan Miller interrupted the ritual procedure, "can I ask you a question?"

"Sure, Dan."

"How long have you been flying?"

"About fifty years."

"Holy shit, man."

"Yeah, that's what I say."

"So which was your best day? First solo, or walking on the Moon?"

"Neither one." Pete twisted a knob or two, letting Dan puzzle over the pause. "First carrier landing."

# SIXTEEN

**P**ensacola is the first step in the naval aviator's journey after college. If naval science is a kick in the pants, Pensacola is a swift kick in the ass. By a Marine—a shouting, spitting, rattlesnake-tempered Marine drill instructor with steel-toed boots. And God help you if you showed up there expecting some deferential, future-officer treatment—as if these noncoms would maybe put you through some tough PT, but at the end of the day, they knew you were the elite.

Right.

You are a sniveling, drooling, spineless *candidate* with a humiliating little scab the barber gave you free of charge—your "Welcome to Pensacola" haircut.

And, oh, yeah: Two in three of you aren't gonna make it.

That's really the drill instructor's job—to break you. It's a lot better for you, and better for the military—certainly better for the taxpayers who fund those Mach 1 rides you're dreaming of—if you break here on the ground, and not as you come in too hot on a pitching, rolling aircraft carrier, catching a wingtip, splattering you and their very expensive bird from here to kingdom come.

Pete got his Princeton diploma on June 16, 1953. Twenty-four hours before, he'd received his ensign's commission. Twenty-four hours after, he was taking Jane off of Winn's arm, making her his wife.

Ten days after that, the honeymoon was as over as over gets. Sergeant Rattlesnake was screaming and spitting a quarter-inch from his face, emphasizing each point with every recruit's new name, *candidate.* Just daring Pete's skinny ass to drop either of the buckets of sand at the ends of those outstretched arms. It took Gethsemane-like willpower, the straining focus of a power seeming beyond Pete to transcend this hazing . . . and keep from bursting out laughing.

He didn't minimize the seriousness of it, didn't for a second doubt the drill instructor's sincerity when he promised he'd grind him into dog food in a heartbeat.

It was just so damn *great!* Those twenty-ten eyes were on the prize at the end of this twelve weeks of living hell, and the same guy who rebel-yelled when he got a calf's hoof to the nose didn't mind this either. *If this is what it takes to fly Navy, well, bring it on, Sarge.*

The flying was the easy part. Pete, the only cadet who showed up fully instrument-rated, was soloing in the SNJ trainer aircraft from the get-go. Watching those brand-new jets screaming overhead, he couldn't wait to climb into one, light it, and go.

If you'd asked the drill instructors, they'd tell you that three classes of individual showed up at Pensacola hoping to win those wings: the cocky, the kiss-ass, and the wiseguy. Truth be told, it took a little of all three to move through the ranks and strap on a jet. But one quality always came out dominant.

Pete Conrad was off the charts in the wiseguy column. Matter of fact, he came awfully close to "smart-ass" a lot of days, especially the hot and humid ones (which was *all* of them in the summer of '53). And Sarge would take it up a notch to see just how much "College Boy" could take.

At beer call at the local dive, though, Sarge and his counterparts would laugh their leathernecks silly at the day's latest installment of the ongoing Conrad commentary, secretly agreeing with most of the candidate's observations at some of the military's legendary wastes of time and energy.

Tacitly admiring the fact that "this little sumbitch ain't gonna break."

The man piloting that Learjet could still feel the swell of emotion of the day forty-three years before when ol' Sarge pinned his wings on him, and saluted him for the very first time. Pete Conrad was a naval officer.

Correction. A naval aviator.

# SEVENTEEN

**N**avy fliers are not crazy about the term *pilot*. Oh, they won't rise up to fight when you call them that; they may even use the word themselves. But in their minds, the term *aviator* is the appropriate one. The critical distinction is as plain as the nose on your face—to them, anyway. Only naval aviators are required to set a bird down on an aircraft carrier. And that makes all the difference in the world.

It is a surreal, pulse-pounding experience observing a full-tilt carrier op. Even with ear protection, it is mind-bendingly loud, as jet engines scream and roar; the blast out the back of one could easily blow you right off the boat. Color-coded squads move frenetically in a synchronized choreography, looking like space travelers in their helmets and goggles, signaling to themselves in a language only they understand, directing people, directing planes, *pushing* planes, smacking the deck, and getting the hell *down*. A giant steam catapult is cocked with fifty thousand pounds of pressure, a fighter jet weighing twenty tons is hooked onto a steel wire, and they fire it overboard like a slingshot with the engines going at full throttle.

Then, when the damn thing comes home, those same twenty tons of metal and jet fuel come hurtling down at 140 knots, hanging out a fist-sized hook, hoping to grab one of four steel cables. And the driver of the thing runs his throttle to the redline, just in case it doesn't.

When it's busy, this all happens every thirty seconds. If it's raining, or no-Moon dark, or the winds are way the hell up, or the waves are heaving the boat ten or fifteen feet this way or that . . .

Welcome to naval aviation.

# EIGHTEEN

It's not that pilots lie. They'll just never tell you the truth on this one. It's too ingrained in the *Right Stuff* mentality, and the world of military aviation is just too damn competitive. To show even a hint of a common human frailty is step one in your journey out of the cockpit.

But the truth is the truth. Outside of willfully picking up a healthy rattler or stepping off the ledge of a tall building, climbing into a jet aircraft and flying it 140 knots onto the deck of a moving aircraft carrier in a thousand feet of water, hoping to catch a wire that first time, is one of the most fearful moments a human being can inflict upon himself.

It's just not natural, trying to rein in gravity like it's one of Winn DuBose's cattle, flying a screaming machine onto a moving surface that looks the size of a postage stamp as you make that final turn into your approach. Regardless of your training, that first time your brain is whispering to you, "Man, this just can't be done."

They hooked sensors and electrodes onto some of the Navy jocks in the 1970s, just to measure their alpha brain waves and see if there was a way to quantify fear in a human being. And guess what? Guys who'd done it fifty times couldn't lie to the machine. The little back-of-the-neck-hair meter registered the exact same fight/flight/*what the hell are you doing to me?* response as a sleep-ending nightmare, or the flash of the subject's worst phobia.

The aircraft carrier *Roosevelt* looked about as big as *half* a postage stamp to Pete as he executed that final turn in his F9-F8 Cougar jet. He'd practiced enough pinpoint landings, even set her down right smack on the money on the painted outline on the field at Pensacola the exact size and dimensions of the landing site off to his left, steaming away at ten knots.

But the practice area hadn't been steaming away. Surrounding the painted outline were concrete and sawgrass and the Gulf Highway with people and Buicks passing by happily on good old terra firma, not rolling ocean. He knew screwing up a landing there full of jet fuel was just as sure a death sentence as screwing one up out here . . . there was just something different about the water.

He'd swiped a pillow to sit on so he could see better over the nose and reach the pedals. Fighter aircraft are not designed for the beanpoles, but five-six is still short.

Pete wouldn't remember fear on that first carrier landing (see above reference to fear and the naval aviator); he just remembered a quick set of calculations. He'd been in the landing pattern for nearly an hour now. The ship was a hundred miles out. He didn't have the fuel to wave this one off and head back to shore. Not that he would, but all factors must be considered in a full calculation.

A guy out of Meridian, Mississippi, had bought it two days earlier, coming in too low without enough power to pull out. Disturbing as that fireball tumbling down the deck was, especially for the guys who hadn't made that first trap yet, it held a weird reassurance in the end. Superstition runs high on a naval vessel. The accident for this cruise was out of the way now. Odds against two were way low.

Pete could see the lights and the Flagman. *Focus. Assemble data.* He'd practiced this run fifty times by now, sat in the backseat while an instructor did it. He knew the procedure; weather was no factor. The Cougar's approach speed is a little hot for a trap. It's tempting to try to eyeball it, think you're going too fast, and back her down so far you lose the ability to control her, like the guy two days ago. And you were a rookie. *Calculate.*

Chance of success: 60 percent.
Chance of failure: 40 percent.
Alternative: Ditch.
Chance of survival: 50 percent.
Chance of continued naval aviation career: 0 percent.

The *Roosevelt* was coming up fast, the LSO signaling him go, all the lights green. It was an out-of-body experience in the end—complete silence in the sealed, pressurized canopy as the voices from the ship gave way to instinct and training. His movements weren't coming from his mind; all tasks were so practiced they were automatic. He watched his fingers feathering the stick like he was watching another person do it: extending the flaps, powering the engine back to idle, dropping fast for the wires.

Pete was thinking about Father suddenly. And Morris. Lulu. Mr. Heyniger. And Margaret Lowell, God bless her. Smiling the smile of a human being doing what he was born to do. Not thinking about it, not calculating or going down a checklist. Just doing it.

He didn't even feel the Cougar's tailhook catch the number three wire, wasn't aware of his hand running the throttle back up to full power in case it *hadn't*. Bull's-eye, going from 145 to zero in a half second. They scored him a three . . .

*Perfect.*

He had to call somebody, anybody, just to tell them. Jane wasn't home; she was probably pushing weeks-old baby Peter down to the library in the stroller. So who else does a boy call in his moment of glory?

"Mother? Mother, it's Peter!"

"Peter. Yes. Where are you?"

"I'm in Florida. You know, the Navy?"

"Good, good. How are Jane and the baby?"

"Super. Listen, Mother, I'm calling to tell you—I landed on an aircraft carrier!"

"I'm sorry . . . ?"

"My airplane. I flew onto a ship today."

"Oh, Peter, that's nice. But what will you do with your airplane now?"

"Ma'am?"

"Now that it is on the ship, what will you do with it?"

"I, uh . . ." There was no reason to continue this. "I just wanted to call and let you know I was having a good day. I gotta get back to work now."

# NINETEEN

Perhaps in comparison to the turbulent 1960s, the 1950s are embedded in our national memory as a time of innocence. Simplicity. Hell, even boredom, if you ask some. It was a time of bobby socks, Bill Haley and the Comets, the Platters, cars with fins. Interstate highways connected us coast to coast for the first time; suburbs sprawled with pretty green lawns, mowed by the guys who saved the world in the Big One, then came home to have their 2.4 kids and fill their fifteen-hundred-square-foot American dream with every appliance GE could think of producing, paying for all of them slowly on easy credit. Ike was President. Times were good. It's a nice picture, and like any stereotype, there is a degree of truth in it.

What the picture doesn't show readily is the uneasiness creeping across the frame like the coming night. A fear. And the color of that fear was red.

Russia has traditionally been a fog-shrouded mystery to anyone from the outside. Carving out their own massive chunk of the globe a thousand years ago—from the Pacific to the Urals, from practically the North Pole all the way south to the Black Sea—Russia remained invisible to the West, able to go its own "savage" way virtually unknown to the rest of the world. Out of sight, out of mind. With the exception of Peter the Great, then Catherine, and a few great composers and writers with last names ending in -*sky*, Russia was simply not relevant to life in the young and growing United States.

The twentieth century changed that. Like a simmering pot left unattended on the proverbial back burner, Russia blew its lid right in the middle of the First World War. Bolsheviks, Mensheviks, Whites and Reds, and then they went and shot their own Tsar and all his family! What the hell was going on over there?

The Western papers called it the Russian Revolution, but few in the United States really understood it. When the dust finally settled, and a very unfriendly-looking man was shaking his fist at the Western world, calling us the enemy and extolling the virtues and sanctity of "the worker," he was setting the stage for the entire twentieth century.

Unbeknownst to Vladimir Ilyich Lenin, he was also firing the starting gun on a race—the race to the Moon.

Communism showed up in the mainstream American vocabulary by the 1920s. It was the buzzword of the intellectual set, largely railing against the drunken party going on down on Wall Street—the same party that would come to a crashing end for Charles Conrad and the rest of the country. During the Great Depression, the same intellectuals trumpeted communism as the highest human good, and a sure antidote to a morally and now financially bankrupt American economy built on that paragon of human greed and selfishness, capitalism.

Communism gained a powerful foothold in this country in the fear and anger of the 1930s. As did fascism. Even with a popular and charismatic Franklin Delano Roosevelt in the White House, there was a growing sentiment out there that our system just wasn't working.

Still, by the end of the decade we were digging ourselves out of the financial disaster we'd been in since the stock market crash of 1929. And of course, the whole communist and fascist flirtation went away on December 7, 1941. The good guys had been attacked. It was time to rally and go save the world again. And by the time World War II ended, America's capitalist-based economy was firing on all eight cylinders, and the good guys had marched right into Berlin together with those commie Russians who maybe weren't so bad after all.

As Pete Conrad was building hours in that Piper back in postwar Philadelphia, making the Darrow honor roll and dreaming of flying Navy, America was all alone on top, basking smugly in the glow of victory, calling the twentieth century the *American* century.

And then those damn Russkies went and ruined it for everybody when they set off an atomic bomb in 1948.

Patton had figured it out before the rest of us. In that great march on Berlin in the spring of '45, he'd been ordered by Ike—who'd been ordered by the President himself—to wait—*wait?*—for the Soviets to catch up and marshal their forces for the final push to decapitate the Nazi war machine alongside their American allies. Patton stewed with his idling tanks outside the city walls and waited for an ally he frankly regarded as an enemy.

The Soviets didn't fool Churchill either. He knew the final terms of the Yalta Accords were a raw deal for America and Western Europe, but with a fading FDR, the Lion was left alone in the ring with Stalin. And Stalin got his way.

And maybe we all agreed with MacArthur over there in Korea when he called it like he saw it, but we sure as hell weren't going with his recommendation: engaging the Chinese *and* the Russians in World War III now, while we had the muscle.

Instead, President Truman fired the Old Soldier. And we watched helplessly as the direst of warnings from Patton, Churchill, and MacArthur became reality with a vengeance. The Soviets dropped their iron curtain, rolled mercilessly into Budapest and Prague, made a mockery of the United Nations, and enlisted China as the newest kid on the Communist bloc—half a billion strong.

Even the temporary relief of the United States exploding a thousand-Hiroshimas hydrogen bomb was short-lived. Three months later, the newsreels showed the Soviets exploding their own.

\*   \*   \*

**T**he whole Korea thing had been a debacle, start to finish. It was a war by proxy. The United States and the Soviet Union weren't even directly fighting each other. Then, Senator Joseph McCarthy from Wisconsin joined a committee on un-American activities, and charged the State Department with harboring communists. And the Rosenbergs were executed for selling H-bomb secrets to Moscow.

This was the "time of innocence"? Maybe. It was also the era of backyard bomb shelters, "duck and cover" drills in elementary schools, and the blacklisting of Hollywood writers and directors who wouldn't take a loyalty oath. America had a new enemy out there, an enemy that wasn't shy about identifying itself, or its goal of taking over the entire planet with its glorious "workers."

Were we paranoid, or was someone really out to get us? Was the party really over this fast?

Sadly, it was. This was the first round of the chess match known as the Cold War. East versus West. Democracy versus communism. The good guys against the bad guys. And watching that mushroom cloud spread high and wide in our local theater, everyone in America knew the stakes couldn't be higher.

It became fashionable later to dismiss McCarthy's "Red menace" as little more than a grand play for his own political gain. He was demonized, his political career came to an ignominious end with his censure by a U.S. Senate that had grown weary of his extremist views and bullying tactics.

But damn if the bully from Wisconsin didn't have a point. When the KGB archives were opened up after the fall of the Soviet Union in 1990, the files confirmed what McCarthy was screaming about: There really were communist spies throughout the federal government.

The enemy was indeed among us in the 1950s.

# TWENTY

The Department of the Navy designates its aviation squadrons VF and VA. This nomenclature is a holdover from the dirigible days, when blimps and airships were designated L for "lighter than air" and airplanes received a V for "heavier than air" flying craft. F stands for fighter planes, A for attack.

Naval Air Station Jacksonville was home to fighter squadron VF-43 in 1955. The Korean conflict had decimated it: Some of its pilots had been killed; the rest quit when their tour was up. The planes that did manage to get back were wrecks, if they were airworthy at all. It fell to Al Taddeo, executive officer of the squadron, to rebuild the damn thing from the ground up. After two days on the job, he wasn't sure he was up to it.

"I'm there at my desk, staring at my quotas in one hand, and my lack of inventory and personnel in the other, popping my fifth Bufferin, when there's a knock on the door. And in walks this little guy, squeaky-clean, pressed tight in his brand-new whites, looking like he's maybe eighteen, clutching his orders like they're a ticket to Disneyland, smiling this gap-toothed grin."

"Ensign Conrad, reporting for duty."

"My first arrival." Taddeo shook his head, and reached for another Bufferin. "They didn't get any greener than this kid, and I'm supposed to rebuild a squadron with a bunch of rookies right out of school?"

God almighty, did Al Taddeo have a job in front of him. He didn't have time to nurture, to bring a pilot and an officer along. He needed fliers, experienced fliers. And he needed them now.

"Let's have a look at your orders, Conrad," he said. The kid looked fine—hell, they all looked fine—on paper. But getting this squadron into fighting shape came down to one thing, and one thing only: "How do you fly, son?"

"How do I . . . fly?" Pete wasn't 100 percent sure if he was being asked about a certain technique, or if he was being asked a trick question. "Uh, I can hold my own. Sir."

"Well, let's go find out."

The instructor's control stick in a trainer aircraft is a direct line to the student's mind. A seasoned pilot can literally feel the confidence or lack of same through the hydraulics connecting the two sticks.

They had barely leveled off when Al's initial suspicions were turned on their head. He called out a few basic maneuvers, just to warm the kid up, wring the aircraft out a little. But he didn't even need to watch how the move was executed, or the jet trainer performed. His ungloved fingers on the rear stick, barely touching, told him everything he needed to know.

Ensign College Boy up there, gap-toothed grin and all, was born to fly a jet. They did tactical runs, strafing runs, even spin-recovery tests Al would have hesitated to give a veteran; Pete couldn't get enough.

"Hell," Taddeo would remember, "we refueled three times till I just had to get back to my desk. It was like telling a kid at the fair that it was time to go home."

Rebuilding this squadron might not be such an uphill battle after all, he thought.

# TWENTY-ONE

With apologies to the good folks of El Centro, California, it is a godforsaken place. Blessings on them all, but there is a reason the Department of the Navy chose El Centro as their shooting range. Hot as a furnace in a burning building, it squats ignobly on the California–Arizona border, fifty miles inland from the garden spot of Yuma—nothing but rock and sand and scrub and lizards and snakes as far as the eye can see. It was and is the place the Navy and Marines bomb the hell out of decommissioned tanks, drones and outhouses with all the newest guns and missiles and bombs that aren't nukes. And of course, it was the place to do a little aerial one-on-one after hours, the kind that never seemed to make it into the logbooks.

It's also the place where, once a year, the Navy holds an invitational shoot-out to see who's got the best "air trigger" in the fleet. *Competitive* doesn't even begin to tell the tale.

**P**ete was duking it out for the number one spot in VF-43 with a guy named Hal Wellman. Al Taddeo had built the whole squadron around these two, actually—perfect yin and yang. Wellman the strong and silent couldn't have been more opposite from merry prankster Pete. But they had one thing in common: These boys could fly like bats out of hell.

Like attracts like, and good fliers just started showing up there in Jacksonville. As for the guys who weren't quite that hot yet? They *got* hot, or they moved on. It was textbook leadership for Taddeo—let the cream rise. And the one-two punch of Conrad and Wellman made them the squadron to beat in the '56 shoot-out.

**P**ete transitioned out of the jet trainer and into the F9-F8 Cougar as seamlessly as he'd moved from the Piper to the Navion. Unlike his peers, and a fair number of his superiors, he understood how these planes and their systems worked, and could explain things like fluid dynamics and structural airflow systems to nonengineers, which most of the twenty-five-year-old fliers were.

Gunnery was more an art form than a technology in 1956. There was no heads-up display, no laser-guided anything. There were a couple of new air-to-air missiles that packed a lot more wallop than the 20mm rounds they were replacing, but it was still largely just ready, aim, fire. Of course, it was now ready, aim, fire near the speed of sound, twisting and turning like a jet fighter will.

Conrad had two things going for him as a gunner: twenty-ten vision, and a brain that naturally practiced trigonometry. It probably came from learning to fly so young, but the three dimensions of flight, and the ever-changing values of X, Y, and Z coordinates relative to speed and altitude, were instinctual. It also helped that Pete had learned to think in systems. The logical, orderly steps in every operation overcame the reading thing for him, and nobody had a clue about his dyslexia, which suited him just fine.

When you got right down to it, Pete could shoot the eyes out of a jackrabbit on a dead sprint. Onboard cannon, new rockets—even with a prototype radar system that didn't work as advertised—it didn't matter what the gun was. Just like down at the ranch with Winn, shooting was shooting.

Pete loved El Centro. Besides the flying and the gunnery, this was where the best of the best were, shooting it out like a bunch of cowboys, then repairing to the squalid bachelor officer quarters, where they'd grill steaks and drink beer and drink some more beer, and shoot gophers and rats and snakes off the shimmering desert floor with their flight suit–issued .38s. Then they'd drink some more beer.

VF-43 was well represented. Pete and Hal took the whole damn thing, finishing number one and number two, respectively, in their division, the youngest ever to take the top slots. They were the only two in the top ten who hadn't seen combat.

Finishing just below was a fighter jock by the name of Alan Shepard.

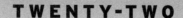

# TWENTY-TWO

**T**here are two schools of thought when it comes to the top of the flying heap. One school holds that combat pilots are the rightful occupiers of the number one seat, having flown and fought against people shooting at them—from other airplanes or on the ground.

The other school maintains that test pilots hold the high ground, pushing aircraft to their very limits, including some aircraft that never should have left the drawing board in the first place. Their enemies are more formidable and less beatable: wind, gravity, and the twisting, airframe-bending tactics of military flying.

This argument is almost as old as flying itself, and probably won't be settled in the foreseeable future.

That said, the words *Pax River* summon the same thoughts in the naval aviator as the words *Top Gun* summon in the general public. The best. Top of the heap. And whether you got there blowing Zeros, Messerschmitts or MiGs out of the sky, or you got there between wars because you showed them you belonged there, the point is, *you got there.*

Pete Conrad showed up in Patuxent River, Maryland, in 1958, wife and now two sons in tow. Pete was carrier-qualified, rated number one in his squadron, and had been in the top five of the El Centro shoot-out three years running now.

He'd shown up at Pensacola still a boy, and at Jacksonville somewhere in that gray area just south of fully realized adult.

He reported for duty in Pax River a man.

**W**hatever swagger he might have had in his dress whites, coming so far so fast, was gone by the end of week one. Yes, he'd arrived at the place to be if you flew Navy, surrounded by drivers of equal status: Jim Lovell, Dick Gordon, Wally Schirra, Al Shepard, and a lot more. But by the weekend he and Jane were dressing in silence for their second funeral. Some other guy, not even thirty, had a modified F-104 fall apart under him, clipping along at a thousand miles an hour. Yes, fall apart. Every weld just up and decided to quit, right then and there. The poor bastard never had a chance.

It slowly began to dawn on Jane Conrad, now pregnant with their third child, that her husband's nonchalance aside, this test pilot thing was dangerous business. *Very* dangerous business.

Although it's obvious now, it was not so then. Certainly not in the community of men who were paid to take the aircraft to their breaking points, even before anybody knew what those breaking points were. In those days, pilots didn't talk about work at home, not in Pax River. Not anywhere, really. It wasn't in the blood. Even when Pete made it home in time for dinner, there wasn't a lot of talk past, "How was your day, dearie?"

"Super. Super."

"Did you fly?"

"Yup. Lotta fun."

Then they talked about the boys some, whom they were having dinner with that weekend, and Pete was off to study his manuals or performance specs till late at night. He'd climb into bed after she was asleep, and climb back out most mornings before she awoke.

Like any other test pilot's wife, Jane comforted herself with the knowledge that her husband wasn't flying into harm's way. Nobody was shooting at him. He was rarely even landing on a carrier these days.

But what he was doing was flying right to the point of crashing—a word never used—and reeling it back in, then going back to the office to write a report on it.

And Jane wondered when it would be her turn to take the neatly folded flag and gaze tearfully at the sky as the Missing Man Formation screamed overhead, and wonder how in hell she was going to raise these kids by herself.

John Tierney was a flight instructor at Pax when Pete's class arrived. He too was a Princeton grad, and had done two tours as a combat pilot in Korea. Tierney was tasked to head up a first-of-its-kind class in spin-and-recovery techniques for all test pilots. The brass was getting concerned about the mortality rate around there, and the dirty little secret was that the fatalities weren't all the failings of the aircraft. More and more they were the failings of the *operator* of that aircraft.

Pete was Tierney's first student. Tierney had already been briefed that Pete was a natural stick and rudder man, the perfect prototype for this program.

"So we're up in a T2V trainer, a perfect airplane for this sort of thing, because it's got wild spin characteristics. I mean, e-ticket ride. Conrad's a great pilot; he can handle most anything I throw at him. . . ."

Tierney took the T2 into a straight vertical climb over the marshes of Patuxent River. The idea was to go to the top and kick the nose and rudder over when they got to zero climb. The plane would whip around like the blade of a pinwheel, then head straight downward in what is known as a Hammerhead entry. Pete would then recover from a light spin, and they would move on to the next evaluation.

The unplanned component was the engine flaming out, which it did as the T2 hit zero vertical speed, halting all hydraulics flow, and therefore steerage. There'd be no kicking anything over. The plane just started to fall back to Earth, tail-first, real fast.

The obvious thing to do would be to relight the engine, but that took air flowing through it front to back, and right now it was doing the exact reverse. Then, in the blink of an eye, the plane eased over and Pete and John Tierney found themselves in an inverted, twisting, rolling spin, like a race car that leaves the ground and flips its way down the track, over and over.

Except they were at twenty thousand feet, heading for the marsh like an incoming meteor, hydraulics out, no engine, in what was no doubt a death ride. . . .

"We're doing negative Gs, then positive Gs, restraints are popping out, we're getting the hell beat out of us," Tierney remembered.

Did he scream?

"I remember a few shouts, yes."

Tierney knew he was the instructor, and it was up to him to pull them out of this thing. But he'd never been on any ride like this one. Up until the shouts, student Conrad assumed this was just the mother of all spin-and-recovery exercises.

It turned out to be just that. The altimeter was spinning like a top: 20,000 feet, 10,000, then 5,000. . . . Now they were in a Hammerhead, all right, like an arrow whose feathers were missing—heading down real fast, but not even remotely straight. Pete had caught on by now, by the sincerity of Tierney's "shouts," that this was not a test. He could only imagine what this looked like to any idiot who'd decided to trespass on the government land below and fish these putrid waters.

They wrestled with the stick and the pedals, trying every trick in the book to get the engine relit, with their stomachs in their mouths and their vision going wacky.

Finally, at less than a thousand feet, the engine popped to life, and they roared out so close to the water they left the biggest wake in that swamp's million-year history, ruining the fishing for the rest of the day.

And Pete's grade for spin and recovery?

Tierney passed him.

# TWENTY-THREE

The pace of change for nations is mostly slow, gradual, even glacial. But the catalyst for change? Just as with individual people, nearly instantaneous.

The Red scare that had opened the 1950s settled from disillusionment and anger to resignation across the fruited plain. As Americans watched the Eastern European nations fall like dominoes, read about the carnage in Budapest, and saw Khrushchev ranting on TV at the UN, we knew the truth instinctively. The USSR was building H-bombs, and long-range bombers to deliver those H-bombs around the clock over there in the Siberian war plants. The USA was building them, too. And one day the thing might actually happen. Someone would press The Button, and we'd duck and cover and run for the bomb shelter we'd dug out back, and pray our bombs were bigger, better, and faster.

Or, more likely, despite the hysteria, and despite the disturbing images on those black-and-white Philco television sets, we'd just ignore it. The threat never seemed all that imminent, or even real. Americans have always felt the insulation of the two great oceans guarding our east and west coasts, and despite all the dark and scary news from Europe in this time, we just shrugged our shoulders and went on with our days.

It wasn't really denial; there was just no visible reason to feel vulnerable. If you didn't count Korea, which was a draw anyway (or a game called, due to lack of interest), the U.S. was 2-0 this century, and undefeated for our career. Go right down the list—we'd never lost since we kicked the Brits out in 1781. Our boys had always risen to the occasion, always won.

A cause for panic? An enemy cross those oceans and beat our boys? Forget it. Never happen. The worst-case scenario would be over in a nanosecond, so why even worry about it?

Then came October 4, 1957. A two-hundred-pound ball called *Sputnik I* orbited the Earth—orbited right over the Golden Gate Bridge, for God's sake!—*beep-beep-beep*ing its telemetry back home to Star City, announcing to the world that the game had just changed.

The Soviets were in outer space now. Outer space! And in case the rest of the world thought they just got lucky with that first one, they did it again with *Sputnik II* a month later. This time it weighed more than a *thousand* pounds. And it carried a dog!

The implication was lost on no one. Suddenly that slow-talking Texas senator Johnson didn't sound so funny when he warned about ". . . those Russkies planning to put platforms into outer space, and lob 'nucular' bombs right on top of our little children's heads!" Suddenly it wasn't so paranoid and hysterical to fear and loathe going to bed by the light of a Communist Moon.

This was real.


Pete Conrad got the same top-secret letter about a hundred military pilots got late in '58. They were looking for twelve guys—it didn't matter which branch of service—to report to the Lovelace Clinic in New Mexico for a series of tests and evaluations to determine their suitability for long-duration flight. You didn't have to be a mind reader to figure this one out. They were looking for pilots to go head-to-head with the Russians, and make damn sure the first *man* in space was an American.

And who was this mysterious *they?* President Eisenhower had bypassed the Joint Chiefs of Staff, who naturally just assumed it would be the Air Force, or so the secretary of the Air Force assumed, anyway. The USAF had been going full-bore with their DynaSoar Project since 1957. A couple of test pilots had even dropped out of a balloon at 110,000 feet, breaking the world free-fall record. That was as close to space as anybody had been. Those guys out at Edwards raced rocket sleds in the desert and trained for zero G, and the X-15 rocket plane was just getting off the drawing boards, but it could be sped up.

The Navy was still smarting over Ike's New Look national defense policy. He'd placed the Air Force in the lead of all the services for the possibility of a "massive retaliation" if the Soviets decided the nuclear game was on. They were the only ones with the long-range capability to deliver a counter or pre-emptive strike.

Still, the Air Force had been in existence as a separate branch of the Armed Forces only eleven years. The Navy had been instrumental in air combat and reconnaissance since the airplane was deployed. They set the gold standard for astronomy in guiding their ships around the globe, and were going like gangbusters with their long-range Polaris missile program. Surely they were the ones to handle this one!

Ike wasn't President for nothing. He wasn't named supreme commander of the Allied Forces in World War II because he'd made good grades at West Point. He was a clearheaded, unlobbyable, ruthless decision maker. His firsthand experience and assessment of the cooperation of the branches of service was spot-on. He knew the Army, Navy, Air Force, and Marines couldn't and *wouldn't* cooperate with one another. They would fulfill the role of any massive bureaucratic beast: guard their territories jealously, and fight to preserve and increase their respective budgets. No goal superseded these.

It would have to be a civilian agency, lean and mean, with one singular, if unofficial objective: beating the Russians in getting a man into outer space.

\*   \*   \*

**P**ete read the letter again in his office at Pax. There was no indication of how long he'd be off the flight line, or even what kind of bird they were thinking of taking up there. There were rumors that it was just a can at the end of a ballistic missile.

What would this mean to his family? Would they have to move? Where to? How long would this hitch run, anyway?

It wasn't a light decision; no call for volunteers ever is. And it wasn't an *open* call—he was chosen. Sure, the letter stated that "not volunteering will not be held against you in any way, shape, or form" but he knew it would get noted. Somewhere.

Pete liked this job. He'd barely been at Pax for a year. But this funeral-a-week stuff was wearing on him. It was surely wearing on Jane. With three boys now, the chances were that he wouldn't be in the Navy forever.

The more Pete thought about it, the more he realized that it would probably be a great ride. Every equipment upgrade for him had always been that—from the Indian to the Piper to the Navion to the Cougar, and every wicked-ass piece of flying machinery parked outside or flying overhead right now here at Pax. Lord knew what kind of ride awaited him at the National Aeronautics and Space Administration, or NASA.

What the hell. It sounded fun. He checked the box, signed his name, and threw the letter in the outgoing mail bin on his way out to the flight line.

# TWENTY-FOUR

**"T**he process has begun to select the U.S. citizen who will become our twentieth-century Mercury, orbiting the Earth in space. . . ."

So began the January 1959 statement to all prospective volunteers from T. Keith Glennan, administrator of NASA. The absence of anything even remotely smacking of military was conspicuous—and intentional. This was a civilian agency, headed up in our nation's capital, not at some military base in the middle of nowhere behind miles of barbed-wire fence. Even so, the credentials they were looking for were clear enough:

- College degree in engineering or physical sciences
- Graduate of a military test-pilot school
- Minimum of fifteen hundred hours in his flight logbook

- Younger than forty
- Not taller than five-eleven
- In superb physical condition—"physically and psychologically suited for spaceflight" (whatever that meant)

Only one professional class even came close to these qualifications—an active-duty military test pilot.

NASA had narrowed it down to 110 men; they'd whittle the group down until they were left with twelve. They were summoned to a hotel in D.C. in groups of thirty or so to hear the top-secret pitch.

Instructed to register as Max Perk, Pete had just finished the check-in procedure at the front desk when he recognized another Max Perk having a cold beverage at the hotel bar. Turned out there were thirty-six Max Perks registered that weekend. This Max happened to be Pete's Pax River buddy Jim Lovell, and it was all they could do not to giggle like kids at their ridiculous undercover name.

When they entered the hotel ballroom, it looked like any other business function at any hotel, except for the plainclothes government security guys guarding the doors and lobby, scanning the field with eyes constantly going left and right. The giggles didn't last long—it was obvious this was damn serious business. Glennan's pitch was short and sweet, as was the Q and A that followed. These guys knew why they were there, and they wanted some details. But few were forthcoming.

Other than the initial qualifications, there was one thing shared by every guy in this room and the other seventy-four who would follow—a hypercompetitiveness. *How high can I go? How fast? How do I make sure I'm the guy?* The words were carefully chosen: *pilot-astronaut, rigorous training, first manned orbital flight.* None of this "duty, honor, country" crap. The between-the-lines message was irresistible to this class of human: *Are you really the best?*

That was the button, all right, and the only one they could push to make sure the twelve best pilots in all the land would give up the world's greatest day job and jump on board an enterprise so loosely defined.

NASA wanted to signal—to *this* community in particular—that it was going to do this thing, and do it right. The initial government response to *Sput-*

*nik* had sent precisely the opposite signal. Overnight things had become a circus—literally. Trapeze artists were considered. Human cannonballs. Daredevils. Even demolition-derby drivers! More than any other factor, the chaotic fervor to just get *something* up there was why most of the cream of the crop out at Edwards Air Force Base decided to sit this one out in '58. They could smell a disaster a mile off, could smell an organization that didn't have the first clue as to what they were doing. All anybody could talk about was the risk, how only a "special breed" could ignore the specter of probable death in the service of his country, defeating the dreaded Communists in getting a man out of this atmosphere first.

Wrong approach. Besides, the guys at Edwards had the best deal going in military aviation. Why would they give away their slot to jump in some crazy, half-baked rocket race with the Russians?

Glennan laid it out pure and simple. NASA was looking for the twelve best in the world, and they'd go from there.

All 110 in that hotel ballroom bought the pitch.

**T**he leap in technology and equipment that would be required was daunting, to say the least. Not to mention the knowledge that didn't exist yet, anywhere. This had never been done before on the American side, not even with a two-hundred-pound beeping ball. Orbiting the Earth from space was the stuff of Jules Verne, astronomy professors, or rocket scientists who'd had too much to drink. Every man in that ballroom drinking lousy coffee knew that the vehicle to pull this thing off also didn't exist yet—not for human orbit, anyway.

Of course, it would have to be a rocket—a missile, more precisely. Missiles were still in their infancy, little more than tubes packed with highly volatile propellant and explosives, designed to go up, come down, and explode. And the only ones who seemed to even get that right were the Germans, many of whom drew up and built the first viable Soviet rockets after the war—which beat the hell out of chopping rocks in a gulag, anyway.

This was the two-A.M. discussion going on in Pete's room with Al Shepard and Wally Schirra. Did these guys even know what they're doing? Navy test pilots at the mercy of politicians and administrators? *Civilians?* Say what you would about the military, but they got the damn job done, offered Pete, re-filling Shepard another shooter.

Rocket testing for this enterprise had already begun, and it wasn't going well. Four stories of liquid hydrogen exploded spectacularly on the pad; birds spun out of control a thousand feet into it, some toppling over and crumbling like a child's block tower. Dangerous was one thing. Suicide was another—a nationally televised one at that!

But that wasn't the thing troubling these shit-hot Navy jet jocks. The real issue was the career.

Pete was a lieutenant; lieutenants wanted to make commander; commanders wanted to make captain, and if the stars were with them, admiral. They didn't care so much about the pay grade and the title; what it came down to was the *flying*. The cause didn't matter, or the urgency of that cause; you had to keep flying if you wanted to keep moving up that ladder—to the newest and hottest planes, the squadrons right on the pointy tip of the spear.

What would this hitch mean to Pete's career? How long was the commitment? Programs in test flight came and went. It was a gamble, like betting on the right horse—except Pete would be betting with his career, not dollars. Look at all the Air Force guys who'd bet it all on the DynaSoar Project. They were scrambling now, trying to make up for lost time.

Suddenly it was about a lot more than the ride.

Pete went back to his room alone. Wide-awake with worry, he poured another shot and dragged a chair over to the window to stare out at the lights of D.C. and perform the standard Conrad calculation: amass the data, assess the cost, execute a decision.

As his chin dropped to his chest in sleep, the decision was made. He wasn't going to do it.

Pete woke at first light with a start, that heart-racing, breathless, where-the-hell-am-I jolt, like waking up in the middle of a boring lecture or a strange bed.

Maybe it was the familiar sight of all the icons of the American dream bathed in that first light of a cold gray winter day. The Washington Monument. The Jefferson Memorial. The Lincoln Memorial. Maybe it was the flag rising slowly over the Capitol Dome. Or the thought of a threat to all this, real or imagined.

Maybe it was just the wild hair.

What Pete Conrad did know was that he loved his country for all the right reasons, and didn't give a rat's behind how cornball it sounded. And he was at his best when he was part of something, especially something bigger than himself.

Would he chuck it all, then? The greatest ride anybody could imagine in 1958 was his five-day-a-week job at Pax River. Would he just let that go? On the possibility that these guys might actually figure this out, and find a way for a man to sit down on top of a rocket and go for a ride around the Earth at a hell of a lot more Machs than anything he was flying right now could go . . . *in outer space?* Would he lay it all on the line for a shot at that?

Yeah. He would.

# TWENTY-FIVE

The first red flag was flying high before Pete had even checked into his spectacularly bland motel room in Albuquerque. His welcome packet included two warm-water enema bags and a stool-sample kit. He'd get the day's agenda the next morning when he reported at the Lovelace Clinic.

NASA had already narrowed down the field to that elite 110 based on medical criteria. The head of NASA's Aeromedical Committee was able to narrow it down even further to thirty-six by the time Pete reported for "a series of intensive physical and psychological tests, which include studies of the candidate's ability to cope with the stresses of spaceflight, and other biomedical and environmental aspects of flight, under confined conditions, for a long period."

Sure sounded solid. This would, in fact, be the most thorough physical examination in medical history, and whittle that thirty-six down to the chosen twelve.

Day one for Pete Conrad, fondly referred to as examinee number eight, started with an eight-A.M. report to the lab, stool sample in hand. At nine Miss Thomas would deliver any "special instructions," and he would proceed to X-ray for a series of no less than twenty (*twenty?*) high-powered radiological images of his heart and lungs. At one, the test pilot began the first in his twenty-four-hour urine-collection safari.

Day two, number eight brought in another stool sample, and the twenty-four hours of collected liquid waste. EKG for four mind-numbing hours, report again to Miss Thomas for "further instructions" (none given today), sent back to the motel room until tomorrow. Nothing to eat, drink, or smoke after ten P.M.

Day three. Blood work. Briefing at Dr. Secrest's office for the upcoming proctoscopy examination that afternoon. Noon, back to the motel to "prepare" for the proctoscopy examination. One forty-five, proctoscopy examination, which was the mother of all cavity searches, aggressively administered by a limping and clearly angry, bitter man. Three P.M., X-rays of the spine. Four P.M., briefing by Dr. Plank on the correct semen-specimen collection procedure. Five P.M., dinner, suggest light snack late, as he would be fasting until afternoon the next day. And, yes, another stool sample.

Day four. Turn in semen sample along with stool sample, provide urine sample as soon as possible. Report to Radiation Therapy Building for body-water test. Proceed directly to Lasseter Lab for BSP liver-function test. Lunch at two, then exercise test, followed immediately by opthalmology and more "special instructions" from Miss Thomas. Today's briefing was on preparations for tomorrow's colon test and X-ray. Return to motel to wash hair (*wash hair?*), no oil to be applied. Seven to midnight, stock-still electroencephalograph. No food, drink, or water till afternoon the following day.

Day five. No breakfast, report to Colon Lab to drink twenty ounces of liquid chalk for gastric analysis. Report for colon X-ray. Rest quietly for one hour after.

Normal lunch. (*Yee-fuckin'-haw.*)

One P.M., report to Miss Bernalise for audiogram, then dental and esophageal X-rays. Lots. Then report to fourth floor for otolaryngology. Miss Thomas to provide instructions for tomorrow's stomach X-ray ("It's a bit uncomfortable"). Report to Dr. France at five P.M. for thorough dental exam and cleaning. No food, drink, or smoke after midnight. Please provide another stool sample upon arrival.

**"P**ete, what the hell are you doing?"

"I'm having a goddamn drink, Al. What are you doing?" Pete entered Shepard's room carrying glass and bottle, and flopped onto the other bed, scowling.

"You know we're supposed to fast after midnight."

"Well, it's eleven fifty. You oughtta see the one I'm gonna build at eleven fifty-five."

"Okay. Give me a belt, would you?"

"Attaboy." Pete handed the bottle over. "It'll loosen you up for your stool sample."

The men sat in silence a moment, watching the TV sign off with the national anthem.

"How are Wally and Jim holding up?" Pete asked.

"About like us, I guess. Have you noticed they're staggering our schedule so we don't get to talk to one another?"

"Jesus, Al. We've got another week of this. Are we gonna get to the flying, or is it just about what's up our ass?"

"I don't know."

"I don't know, either. But I want some answers."

"Pete, be careful. They're watching everything we do. And taking notes."

"What the hell does this have to do with *flying,* Al? Give me a damn physical, and let me out of this place!" Pete slammed the remainder of his drink and poured another. The clock read 11:57.

Al finished his own. "I got the dope on the psych test. It's that ink-blot thing. They're looking for virility."

"Virility?"

"Yeah, so no matter what it looks like, make sure you see something sexual."

"Oh, for chrissakes."

*     *     *

**"O**h, a vagina. That's definitely a vagina." Pete handed the Rorschach card back to the psychiatrist, who wordlessly noted his response and handed him another. "Hmmm. This is interesting." Pete studied the blot. "This is a man and woman doing it."

"Go on, number eight."

"Well, it's . . . what it is. They're doing it."

"Tell me a story about what you see."

Pete shifted uncomfortably in his chair. His backside was sore as hell after another cavity search this morning. He suspected this whole charade was all about pain, the way the proctology guy shoved his finger up there. And if that six-foot-five male nurse hadn't been holding him down, he'd have laid that angry, limping, sadistic SOB out right then and there.

*And now this twit wants me to tell him a story.*

He gritted his hypersensitive and overfluoridated teeth, and smiled. "Well, it's a pretty scene. Pastoral, medieval. She is, I believe, a nobleman's daughter. And he must be a knight. Yes. Those are definitely chain-mail pants around his ankles. It is a time of strife in the land. Civil war and famine. And he is, shall we say, *blessed* by his Creator. She's enjoying it." He flipped the card back across the desk, ready to lay *this* sadistic SOB out too.

The psychiatrist scribbled more notes, muttering to himself. Then he turned his trump card over with a wan smile, holding it in front of him like he'd just hit blackjack. "Tell me a story about *this* one, number eight."

The card was blank. Pete squinted at it, deep in concentration. "I'm sorry, Doc. I can't."

"Oh?" The guy leaned forward, excited suddenly. "And why can't you?"

"Because you've got it upside down."

**A**nother semen sample, followed by another stomach X-ray. Then cardiology. Bioacoustics. And a flight to Los Alamos for neurological examination. More "special instructions" from Miss Thomas, followed by another stool-and-urine-sample kit.

When they finally administered the stress and fatigue tests—like this whole damn thing wasn't that to begin with—Pete was convinced they were making this thing up on the fly. Stationary bike for three hours (*why?*), blowing water through a tube, sticking the men in a hot box for an hour, then putting their feet in a goddamn bucket of ice water—just to see how long they could keep them there?

*What the hell does this have to do with flying, Al?*

On day eight, number eight was directed to the "special functions" wing, and told to sit down so the behemoth male nurse could strap his arm to a stainless-steel table and alcohol-prep his hand. If that wasn't a clear enough early warning, the doctor rolled toward him on a metal stool, holding a two-inch needle connected by wire to a power source.

"What are you going to do with that?" Pete gasped.

"It just stings a little; it'll be over before you know it."

"You're going to stick that needle in my hand?"

"We will introduce it to the thumb joint, yes."

"And run *electricity* through it?" The guy didn't answer, just stared blankly at the examinee. "What exactly are you looking for?"

"It is a necessary part of the evaluation, Lieutenant."

"What could possibly be necessary about it?"

"It's a lot to explain quickly."

"Try."

"Number eight, this will take less than five minutes, and there are men waiting. Other candidates." He nodded at the nurse. Pete shot the behemoth down with the look of death. Then he ripped the strap right off his arm.

"You're not sticking any fuckin' needle in my thumb till you can tell me why."

Stress and fatigue, all right. So this was the benchmark for the chosen twelve. The divine disciples of pain they'd throw inside a vehicle they hadn't even built yet, to launch their asses into a zero-G proctology exam?

If this didn't suck bad enough, what was really killing Pete was the hours he could already be logging in that brand-new, faster-than-hell F-4D Phantom that arrived the very day he shipped out of Pax to subject himself to this insanity. Somebody else was getting his hours! And here he was in a backless gown, holding an enema bag in the middle of freakin' New Mexico, where they wanted to introduce needles and electric current to his thumb joint for reasons clear to no one? And by the looks and scribbles going on, it was more than obvious he'd already been tagged as an "attitude problem."

What the hell was the point?

On day eleven, Pete breezed right past Miss Thomas with his sixth full enema bag, and walked right into the office of the commander of the facility.

"General—something to remember me by." Pete tossed the bag on the startled man's desk. "Have a nice day." Examinee number eight turned on his heel and walked the hell out of the Lovelace Clinic.

Pete's letter was waiting in his mailbox when he got back to Pax River. *Thank you for volunteering, for the service to your country, etc.* However, mitigating factors would preclude his further participation in the Mercury Program. And they wished him well in all his future endeavors.

For Lieutenant Conrad, the stated reason dripped with between-the-lines pleasure: *Not suited for long-duration flight.*

This letter was also dropped into the Pax River out box, the cylindrical one by the door. And with that Pete walked down to the flight line to strap on that new F-4 Phantom and take her for a ride.

# BOOK THREE

# ASTRONAUT

# TWENTY-SIX

February 12, 1996
Learjet N10BD
On the ground, Sal, Cape Verde
2101 Zulu

"Learjet 10BD, turn left onto taxiway four, and proceed to your fueling area."

"Ten-BD."

Pete goosed the throttle toward a flashing spotlight at a temporary setup a mile away from the Sal terminal. Two fuel trucks were standing by, waiting to move into position. A small army of personnel stood at semiattention in front of a good-sized crowd of a hundred or so who'd turned up to see the record-attempting Lear as it stopped by. The engines hadn't even finished spinning when each truck was in position, hoses out and waiting, and the power cart feeding her current to run the fuel pumps and crank her back over, saving the batteries. A guy was already washing the windshield like they'd pulled up to a full-service gas station.

"This is a little more like it, boys," said a smiling Pete.

A tall, elegant-looking black woman was in command of this operation. It was surprising—not that a woman couldn't do the job as well as a man, but that the men were so clearly deferential to her. This wasn't a part of the world where that was commonplace. But one look at her barking out commands at the trucks and personnel who snapped to when she did made it clear that this lady was in charge here.

The trucks filled the fuselage, wing, and auxiliary tanks quickly; 10BD's crew had the rest of the drill down on this second stop. But Calkins got so busy with the pleasantries and the poster exchange and customs and clearance stuff that he forgot to initiate the transfer to the 110-gallon tank. They lost five minutes before Dan figured it out.

"Mark, what about the tank? You start it?"

"Oh, man—"

"What? What were you thinking?"

"What *was* I thinking?"

"Shit, man, you're costing us time!"

It wasn't a small mistake, and Mark knew it. They were already thirty minutes behind schedule, with six stops to go. If they lost another hour along the way, their shot at breaking the record was lost too. But this was a direct challenge to Mark as captain. It would either set a precedent or break one. It was up to him.

The woman ground chief noticed the exchange. Pete pretended not to watch as he handed the nozzle back through the emergency hatch, curious how Mark would handle this.

"I screwed up, Dan," he said through gritted teeth. "Now get back to *your* job."

Perfect. Pete smiled, nodding approvingly as he wiped down and sealed the rear hatch. Dan was young; he'd learn. You didn't yell at the boss. You didn't embarrass the chief.

"Okay, boys, we're full. Let's do this thing!" Pete called. He was back up front, strapping in for departure. "We got a clearance, Mark?"

"Yeah, Pete. We're good to go."

"Close the door; let's get the hell out of here."

The trucks were clear, the power cart turning the left engine. Pete glanced out the side window; the crowd cheered him, and he waved with a quick pang of regret. *Dammit*. He should have stepped out to shake a few hands. He glanced at his watch. No time. The ground chief stood in front of her crew, hands on hips. She was a serious, competent individual, good at her job, and obviously proud of their quick turn: thirty-six minutes touchdown to rotate.

The astronaut gave her a salute as he rolled clear. She nodded, satisfied.

**Learjet N10BD**
**Heading 025**
**Nineteen thousand feet, climbing**
**2150 Zulu**

"You know about our tail numbers, right? Mark grinned at Pete.

"No."

"Ten-BD. Think about it."

"BD . . . Bill Daniels, I guess?"

"Nope. Bo Derek."

"Bo Derek?"

"Perfect ten. Just like this jet."

Cleared all the way to Olbia, Italy. Pete smiled, nosing "Bo" over to their assigned altitude of 37,000 feet. Ahead lay the western Sahara, Morocco, Mauritania, and Sicily, taking them right into the Italian boot. He glanced out at the tiny cluster of lights to his left—Tenerife, the Canary Islands. Tenerife airport was where a KLM 747 and a Pan Am 747 collided as one tried to take off over the other in March 1977, killing 583 people, the worst accident in aviation history.

"How ya doing, Pete?" Mark asked, reading his mind. Their flight was eighteen hours old now. It would be a frequent question each asked the other, as fatigue would lead to mistakes, and mistakes could lead to accidents.

"I'm fine, Mark. I've got her to Italy; then we'll rotate. You haven't slept a wink, and you need to."

"Roger that." Mark joined the other two in some shut-eye.

Pete settled back, scanning the gauges. Black sky tonight, just a sliver of his old pal the Moon coming up. In the clear, cold air up here, up out of the ground clutter, Pete could see the lights of a satellite whizzing by. Way up there in space.

Yeah. Space.

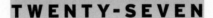

# TWENTY-SEVEN

The election of 1960 was a squeaker, with more than a few disputed ballots out there, not to mention some deceased voters heading to the polls two or three times in some precincts—for both sides. But it didn't matter. Richard Nixon, Ike's Vice President, would have his day later in the decade. He bowed out gracefully, and made way for John F. Kennedy and the New Frontier.

It was a new decade, with a new man in the White House. He was young, movie-star handsome, graceful, and charismatic—with a drop-dead gorgeous wife to boot! JFK's swearing-in sent a clear and unmistakable signal to the whole wide world.

There was a new sheriff in town.

It was time. The fifties, like most decades, ended with a whimper, actually more like a weary sigh. Ike had mustered enough strength after his heart attack to go all out in a bridge-building effort to Khrushchev and the Kremlin. It wasn't going too badly, either, till the USSR blew Gary Powers out of the sky over Vladivostok in a U-2 spy plane we denied we even had. Khrushchev made not a sound until the highly charged Paris Summit, where he made President Eisenhower look like a fool and a liar.

Would Ike have done the same had we shot down one of theirs? Despite their indignant denials, everybody from the Pentagon to Pax River to Portland knew they were flying their birds over us, snapping away.

But embarrass the President? With the whole world watching? No. That was crossing the line.

If the roles were reversed, Ike would certainly have flayed Khrushchev. He just would have done it through proper diplomatic channels, and used it to gain some advantage in this superpower chess match. Khrushchev took the opposite tack, and chose to embarrass the President.

Americans have always been funny about things like this. You can yell and scream and insult and complain all you want about the guy in the Oval Office. That's the American Way if you call this place home. But if you don't . . .

Then don't embarrass the Chief.

Kennedy was a smart guy. He knew bluster and saber rattling could be dangerous, especially with the kind of sabers both sides could rattle—or launch.

The new President chose a more neutral battlefield—the high ground of space. And it would be a race, not a battle. NASA had figured out how to stop the rockets from blowing up by the spring of 1961. The space vehicle was built, and it was spring-loaded, ready to go down at Cape Canaveral. The twelve guys who survived the Lovelace Clinic were further whittled down to seven. And after a lot of trial-and-error training, one of the seven was set to ride a Redstone rocket into space, and splash down in the Atlantic Ocean.

And in May 1961, Alan Shepard did just that, putting an exclamation point on the New Frontier. America was in this game now. And we were in it to win.

No matter that the Soviet Union had already gotten a man up there. No matter that Yuri Gagarin even got a full orbit in before landing on the ground out by Lake Baikal. Kennedy looked across the table at Khrushchev and changed the game on him, from chess to poker.

He called the USSR's Gagarin play and raised the ante, putting all of America's chips on the table. The U.S. would land a man on the Moon, and bring him home safely before the sixties were over.

It was an electrifying moment. Overnight the flag-waving hero worship of the Mercury Program became a national mission statement. It was bigger than Kennedy, bigger than Shepard, bigger than any one person since Jesus himself. The Moon in under a decade? Even the NASA optimists gulped in dismay when JFK laid down that gauntlet. The greatest challenge in history was America's destiny now.

And as Pete Conrad watched that helicopter pull his old Navy buddy Shepard out of the Atlantic on the TV in the pilots' breakroom, his mind drifted back to an enema bag on a desk in the Lovelace Clinic.

And he knew he'd blown it.

# TWENTY-EIGHT

Christopher Conrad was born at Pax River in 1961. Chris was number four for Jane and Pete, joining Peter, Thomas and Andrew on the latest line on Thones Kunders's descendant chart. They were a beautiful family: rapidly advancing Navy test pilot, four fair-haired kids, and the perfect officer's wife.

The wives on base had their own seniority and ranking system, even if it was unofficial. Jane's stature rose right along with Pete's as one of the first ladies on base. Always gracious, Jane was the first to volunteer for a worthy cause, play hostess to important visitors, and even shoulder the most dreaded of duties with warmth and compassion: comforting a brand-new Pax River widow.

Pete was now instructing the new pilot classes in the F-4, the meanest, fastest fighter jet on the planet. Fat and heavy, with two monster turbo-fan jet engines slapped under her belly, this baby could flat-out go at speeds that had been unimaginable for an airplane when he'd joined the Navy. The damn thing was a flying muscle car. Not much in the twisting, turning department, but in a straight line the F-4 could outrun a bullet and give a pilot the best ride he could have with his pants on. Pete loved that plane. It reminded him of his old Indian bike, the way she smoked and roared and pinned her ears back in a full sprint.

He'd been assigned to armaments after graduating test-pilot school, but his engineering and airframe experience pretty much made Pete the de facto naval aviation expert on the flight characteristics of the F-4. He went to VF-96 as an instructor, even wrote a few chapters in the Pax "book" on the jet—along with Jim Lovell and Jim Stockdale.

Yes, Pete had a beautiful family, and a career on the fast track. Hell, he might be one of the lucky few who got to take the F-4 into action over in that thing heating up in Southeast Asia. These were good times to be a test pilot, right?

Well, yeah. But old Thones's DNA was stirring. Could it be that going Mach 2 with his hair on fire suddenly wasn't fast and furious enough?

Pete couldn't help but see it everywhere. He'd have to be living in a cave not to feel the United States putting the pedal to the metal in this space-race thing. One naval aviator already got his ride on the rocket; another was waiting in line. Sure, it was all about the ride. And rides don't get much better than the F-4 in flight test.

But Wally and Al were riding *rockets*. Into outer space. What kind of a ride would that be?

It was a complex heart beating inside that G-suit, pushing the aircraft past its structural and performance limits. Pete loved his job, loved his life right now. But knowing he could have been right in the middle of the *space race*? With all the smiles, and jokes, and wisecracks, and high-G turns, every now and again Pete would get a familiar feeling. It was just like the day his family had left the Roadside Cottage back on the Main Line for the little carriage house in Saint David's. Or getting canned by Haverford.

The greatest something the world had ever seen was going on full tilt out there. And Pete had been left behind.

*   *   *

"Pete Conrad? Holy shit, Al, is that old *Squarewave* over there?"

Pete turned from the bar, hearing a familiar voice calling him by his Navy call sign. There, strutting into the O-club for beer call on a Thursday afternoon, were the Navy's two rocket jocks themselves, Wally Schirra and Alan Shepard. "Hell, yes, it *is* Squarewave, Wally. Crying in his beer, like always."

"Just crying for you two. Riding in a tin can with a monkey when you could be down here flying the F-4 with me."

They were all at the same table in a flash, laughing, talking with their hands as all pilots do, making more noise than anybody else in an already noisy bar. The conversation could get to only one place, and eventually it did, as Shepard waved for another round.

Al: "You still lightin' it up down here, are you, Pete?"

Pete: "Aw, same o' same o'! You guys are doing pretty good yourselves."

There were the usual barbs about Pete's dramatic exit from Lovelace. They all reminisced about those glorious two weeks down there.

Wally: "It's all changed now. We've got our shit together."

Al: "We're going to the Moon, by God."

Clink of the beer bottles. Pregnant pause, then laser-beam eye contact from Shepard to Pete.

"Mercury's all done but the flying. We're tooling up for a new class."

"Oh, yeah?" Pete was nonchalant.

"Yeah. We've been talking you up. They all know the Conrad legend now."

"Super." Pete rolled his eyes at his well-known reputation as the body waste delivery man.

"They also know you're a shit-hot pilot." Pause. "You want to give it another shot?"

"Yeah."

# TWENTY-NINE

**N**ASA's Mercury Program was a success by anybody's definition. After Shepard's brief suborbital flight atop the Redstone rocket, the dream had gone from drawing board to reality. Mercury was just a baby step. Like a child learning to walk, NASA was getting stronger with each stride, gaining momentum and confidence. And looking way past the low-level Earth-orbit phase.

The original name for the Gemini Program was Mercury Mark II—a continuation, and gradual expansion. But words are important, names and titles more so. Mercury had been about getting a man into space. Now, after JFK had challenged NASA to put an American on the Moon, there was a new mission, a new way of thinking, and a new program. And it needed a new name.

Gemini is a constellation, a medium-sized cluster of stars surrounding two giants—Castor and Pollux, as dubbed by the ancients, or the Twins. The next step for NASA would be a two-man crew, working as a team to accelerate the learning curve needed to get a crew 241,000 miles to the Moon. Unlike the zodiac sign named for the Gemini (pronounced Gem-in-eye), the NASA guys preferred pronouncing it "Jiminy" (as in Cricket). In early 1962, the program was so named.

Gemini had three primary objectives: achieve rendezvous with two spacecraft, perfect reentry, and make certain humans can survive two weeks outside the Earth's atmosphere, which would be the length of time required for a round-trip to the Moon and back.

There'd be a lot of baby steps in achieving these objectives. A bigger and better rocket; a bigger and better spacecraft; better fuel and more efficient energy consumption; an exponential leap in communications and tracking, computer capacity, and programming; and a vastly improved and cheaper reentry and landing system—on land, as well as the water. It wouldn't be easy or cheap. NASA budgeted the Gemini Program at $250 million, an (ahem) astronomical sum in 1961.

Pete knew one thing for sure when he was selected in August 1962 with eight others: This was a different NASA from the one he'd been introduced to four years earlier. It no longer felt like a hastily slapped-together government agency hurrying the hell up to get into space.

The men running the agency weren't sure exactly how they'd have a man standing on the surface of the Moon before 1970, but they had no doubt that they would. It was a charged atmosphere at the Manned Space Center in Houston. People were showing up every day, rolling up their sleeves, throwing on those ubiquitous pocket protectors, and getting to work. They'd bother with their badges and paperwork and clearances later—right now there was a job to do, a big, huge job that was mobilizing an entire nation.

What it felt like was a team.

And Lord almighty, what a team it was. It's easy to envision those early days at NASA as a high-tech skunkworks and factory and launch and recovery and Mission Control and suit manufacturer and rocket-fuel mixer-upper, all under one roof at some Willy Wonka kind of magic science castle in Texas and Florida.

To some extent, that was true. NASA's reputation as the best and brightest in the land when it came to the mechanics of putting machines and people into outer space was and is accurate, and well deserved.

What Pete didn't know until he got there was how deep this dream team really was. It wasn't under one roof; it was a whole lot of roofs, all across the country.

McDonnell was the prime contractor. Then there was Thiokol rockets. Motorola. Martin Aviation. IBM, GE, Westinghouse, Honeywell, Northrop—even Studebaker for a while!—Lockheed, Philco, Bell Aerospace, Rocketdyne, North American . . . and these were just the big guys. For every one of these heavy hitters, there were twenty little guys—small machine shops in towns you never heard of, start-ups, people tinkering with motors and wires and fuels and fabrics and metals, just like young Pete and Morris out in the garage. But they were doing a lot more than tinkering. They were building Project Gemini.

Pete was part of something, all right. It looked like half the working population of the country was in on this dream, all playing for the same team.

On September 17, 1962, Manned Space Center director Robert Gilruth named the nine members of the new Astronaut class. From the Air Force, Frank Borman, Jim McDivitt, Edward White, and Tom Stafford. From the Navy, John Young, Jim Lovell, and Pete Conrad. There were two civilians Pete had never heard of: Elliot See, and some guy from NASA's predecessor agency, the National Advisory Committee for Aeronautics (NACA): Neil Armstrong.

The physical exam was done in one day. No ink blots this time, no buckets of ice, no needle with current going into his thumb, and no special instructions from Miss Thomas. Pete didn't even mind the backside finger wave this time around, comforted by the fact that the bitter, limping guy was gone, and there was no professional wrestler-class orderly standing dourly by. He turned his enema bag in to the proper personnel in the proper way, with a smile on his face.

Wally was right: NASA had indeed gotten its stool sample together. So had the test pilot. He wasn't gassing her up and flying solo anymore. He was part of a team.

The team was very busy in 1962. The Mercury flights weren't even half done, the Gemini Program was cranking up, and the engineers and planners were furiously scribbling away at the Apollo drawing boards.

They'd need a bigger rocket than the Redstone to get them to the target altitude of 160 miles. They'd also need a bigger capsule for a crew of two. Complex Fourteen at the Atlantic Missile Range in Cape Canaveral worked fine for Mercury, but a whole new launchpad, blockhouse and launch control center would have to be built.

For the new class of astronauts, it was back to school. Pete found himself immersed in astronomy, upper-atmosphere physics, meteorology, navigation, computers, and medical science. He even had to take desert and jungle survival classes in case they had to abort a launch over Africa and were able to defy the considerable odds against surviving a separation and hard landing from 200,000 feet. These guys walked in here test pilots—they'd walk out astronauts.

They weren't the celebrities the Mercury Seven were—not yet, anyway. They were way too busy and, as trainees, out of the public eye. The job description was changing. Chuck Yeager's "Spam in a can" quip was a distant memory now that Gemini was under way. *Astronaut* and *Pilot* were the same thing now. These guys wouldn't just be payload; they'd be *operating* this machine.

The Mercury boys may have been Buck Rogers to their adoring public, but the engineers largely saw them as little more than that payload—at least at the beginning. Test pilots being test pilots, they didn't sit still for that very long. And Gemini and Apollo vindicated them. Going up and down, maybe an orbit or two . . . yeah, the engineers could automate that. Even let a chimp or a dog or even a human cannonball go along for the ride. As long as he didn't touch anything.

But rendezvousing and docking, interpreting data and unforeseen circumstances, making mission-saving judgments, and eventually taking one of these things all the way to the Moon and climbing out and grabbing some rocks? Maybe one day the guys with the pocket protectors would be able to make a machine that could do all that, but in 1962, it would take a human being.

And the best human beings fitting that job description were pilots. So the pilots flew—and flew some more, which suited Pete just fine. They flew jets high and fast, and then flew in the simulator every day once the interior design and console of the capsule were approved. They even rode the famed Vomit Comet, a KC-135 flying a high parabola, giving them about thirty-six seconds of weightlessness to tumble about and get a dry run at a possible spacewalk—the official term was EVA, or extravehicular activity.

The real training, though, was in the mind-set. There was a reason the Mercury boys and the engineers locked horns—test pilots by their very nature are lone rangers. Their job is to start the bird on her takeoff roll, light the burners and go, push her as far as she can go, and bring her back in for a landing—*alone*.

Spaceflight is a completely different animal. The first thing to be engineered out was that lone-ranger mentality. The astronauts would be sitting on top of a ballistic missile, climbing straight up, leaving the atmosphere, circling the globe, performing their mission, then slowing down from seventeen thousand miles per hour to reenter at just the right angle so that they wouldn't fry alive. Then they'd have to drop right on target in the middle of the ocean so they could be picked up before they sank.

Without a vast network of computers, without an army of guys gulping coffee and smoking three packs a day as they furiously calculated and barked into their headsets, without those forty big-guy contractors and the little guys and half the American workforce working for *them*—without the Army, Navy, Air Force, and Marines working on this flight . . .

You're screwed, man.

There'd be no lone-ranger test-pilot swagger around here. This was a team, and never was the phrase "only as strong as the weakest link" truer than on the NASA team. Pete and all the pilots figured this out quickly, and it defined the rest of their lives.

That was the man who turned his jet onto final toward the Navy's Centrifuge Complex just outside Philadelphia, and had a good look at the roof of the old Conrad place in Saint David's, off the Main Line. He'd left there a brand-new pilot, barely certified in the Piper. Now he was bringing in a brand new T-38 to strap into that centrifuge, preparing him to fly a Gemini ship into outer space . . . not ten miles from where this ride began at Pennsylvania Hospital thirty-three years before.


**S**omething was wrong, very wrong. Pete didn't know the guys helping him out of the T-38, but he could tell something awful had happened. He trotted inside the complex quickly. No one was up front. Everyone was gathered in the breakroom around the television. Ashen. In shock.

"What happened?"

Before anyone could answer, Walter Cronkite took a bulletin handed to him. "The flash from Dallas, apparently official—President Kennedy died at one P.M., some thirty minutes ago. . . ."

# THIRTY

It rained cats and dogs at the newly named Cape Kennedy on August 19, 1965. The rain caused another set of problems with the fuel loading into the *Titan II* rocket. Astronauts L. Gordon "Gordo" Cooper and Charles "Pete" Conrad never even left the blockhouse. Chris Kraft scrubbed the launch at noon.

The only real glitches in the run-up to the manned Gemini flights had been in the *Titan II*, an Army missile designed to carry nuclear warheads, not humans. The *Titan* had its share of stability problems, specifically an annoying tendency to pogo in the initial stages of flight—which was exactly what it sounded like. Overthrusts and thrust interruptions gave it the exact same characteristics as a hundred-foot-tall pogo stick as it went from sea level to orbit. It was not a pleasant ride.

The Army didn't give a damn. The thousand pounds of enriched plutonium had never complained, and fixing this problem was going to cost a lot of dollars—*budget* dollars the generals did not want to spend. But the NASA guys did the math, and came up with a conservative estimate of seven or eight Gs these boys might be pulling as they rode the *Titan* out of the atmosphere. No big deal for a nuke, but they weren't about to launch two corpses into space to save a few million. The Army engineers bit the bullet and fixed it. Sort of.

Gemini was tremendously overbudget at the end of its first year. Two hundred fifty million barely paid for their capsules; it would be well over a billion 1965 dollars before they were through. The Air Force, and therefore the Department of Defense owned the entire launch complex at Cape Kennedy, and it was no secret that the Pentagon thought they should have been running this show all along. With NASA's 500 percent budget overrun, rumors began to fly that Defense Secretary Robert McNamara was going to make a play in Washington to take over the entire program for the DOD.

Pete and the other astronauts suddenly found themselves in the peculiar position of touring the contractor facilities, lobbying to keep NASA on track as *the* space agency. It was peculiar, because nearly all of them were still considered active-duty military personnel—DOD employees—simply on loan to the civilian agency.

Pete loved the tours, and was a favorite of the workers. It was obvious his visits weren't scripted. As an engineer he knew the questions to ask, and actually understood their answers.

But more than that, he was one of them. He wasn't tall; he wasn't movie-star handsome. He may have been able to fly the wildest machines imaginable better than anybody, but he never acted like it. He didn't cop any astronaut attitude. He was just one of the guys, walking the floors of the labs and facilities and wind tunnels, going out after hours for shooters, telling story after story with VPs and mechanics, drinking beer side by side with them. No script, no sell job.

"There's no way in hell I'd climb on top of that thing," he told a Thiokol manager who'd made it clear that he'd rather be in business with the Air Force, "if I didn't think the best in the world weren't backing me up."

Talk about a testimonial. Pete didn't have contract dollars on the line; this was his *ass*. It worked. The engineers and machinists and electricians and craftsmen understood better than the politicians and the bean counters that the best did not come cheap. Whatever NASA was doing down in Texas and Florida, they were doing it right—if *this* guy was in the middle of it. The message sent back to Washington was strong and clear: NASA *ain't broke, so don't fix it.*

McNamara backed off.

**T**he weather cleared two days later on August 21, and this time Gordo and Pete left the blockhouse and headed the four miles to the launchpad. The technicians sealed them up in the Gemini capsule, saluted them, and left them alone atop the hundred feet of rocket.

Gordo smiled at Pete. "You ready, rookie?" He noticed Pete was white as a sheet suddenly.

"I'm not sure, Gordo. . . ."

There was a long, difficult pause in the silent capsule. Conrad milked it for all it was worth till he couldn't hold back his laugh another second.

"Gotcha. Light this son of a bitch, and let's go for a ride."

**"F**ive, four, three, two, one . . ." *Boom.* It was like a bomb going off under him, then a shake, rattle, and roll like a '55 Buick blasting down a bumpy gravel road—louder than hell. *Gemini 5,* sitting on top of that *Titan* rocket, was on its way.

And, oh, man what a ride. They'd engineered most of the pogo stick thing out—*most* of it. But zero to a thousand in a few seconds going straight up is still some serious gravity slamming you back into the couch. It was the same G-pulling feeling as a really tight turn in the F-4 going Mach-plus and then some, which was right up there with sex for Pete Conrad. They'd pull seven Gs before they were out of the atmosphere.

"Go, you mother, *go!*"

Pete let it fly, didn't give a damn whether he was transmitting or not (he was), didn't care whether it was cool or not. He flicked all his switches at the proper intervals, giggling like a schoolboy in that metal helmet. He even got the usually ice-cool Cooper going. Yeah, he was one of the best-trained operators in the world. Yeah, he'd done this in the sim a thousand times. But this was no simulation.

This was the real McCoy. Pete was riding the rocket. And as the first stage dropped away, and the second lit off, pogoing him and Gordo right on out of this atmosphere, something told him he was on the ride of his life. No matter what he flew after this one, there'd never be a ride quite like this one.

And he was right.

*Gemini* 5 was the third manned flight in the Gemini Program, and it was about getting down to the serious business of shooting for the Moon. They were going for 121 orbits—eight days in space, the longest-duration flight ever.

A nonstop, action-packed, pulse-pounding space adventure, right?

Pete remembered it more like this:

> *The romance ended fairly quickly. We were really confined in an extremely small space. My knees began to bother me. It felt as though my knee sockets had gone dry. I hurt and I didn't want to stay in there. If they had told me I had to stay up longer than the eight days, I believe I would have gone bananas. My body ached, and my mind was not active enough. I was the rookie and Gordo was the pro. We had trained together for a year and there weren't any stories left to exchange. We had some systems failures, and this precluded us from doing some of the tasks we were supposed to do, so all we could do is sit. You can't go to sleep; you just don't get tired. Your body is uncomfortable, you don't do any work, and zero Gs makes you lethargic. We didn't have continuous communications with earth and there was an eight-hour sleep time when the ground wouldn't talk to us. We had thruster failures on the third day and we spent a lot of time in drifting flight. It didn't take long to realize that eight days was going to be an extremely long period of time. Houston had ordered us to shut down due to the thruster failure. Gemini would vent hydrogen and oxygen occasionally. Whenever it vented, it would give the capsule a little motion*

*and it would rotate. And that's when I learned about "the fickle finger of fate." It was very frustrating. Whenever we were over land, which was the one thing that was always fun to look at, the craft would be pointing up at the black sky. I was the loneliest I have ever been on this flight.*

The problems began less than an hour into the flight. The heating coil failed, which crippled the brand-new fuel cells, which threatened the oxygen pressure, which threatened the entire mission. Houston was ready to call it a day on the sixth orbit, but flight director Chris Kraft wanted to give the coil time to repressurize itself. It eventually did, but not even close to its operating capacity. It was just enough to keep going, and make the call day by day.

*Gemini* 5 carried a suitcase-sized box of electronics, a pod that would act as their rendezvous vehicle. Containing a radar transponder, batteries, and a flashing beacon, the "Little Rascal" rendezvous craft was twenty years ahead of the technology curve. The true highlight of the mission would be kicking her out, circling the Earth a full revolution, then finding her and locking on as they came back around. This was what the networks were talking about; this was what the engineers had spent three years on. Forty support guys were standing by in Mission Control for the most critical component in the eventual flight to the Moon: rendezvous.

It never happened. Shortly after ejecting the pod, the oxygen pressure problem required an extreme power down of the spacecraft, thus interrupting the planned rendezvous sequence. By the time they were back online, the pod had reentered the atmosphere, disappearing over California.

And it got worse. There were fuel problems in the thrusters Cooper would need to maneuver. Gordo and Pete had to dump fuel twice, and the fuel cells suddenly couldn't heat or even power the ship. They had to revert to the batteries NASA had hoped to abandon and replace with the cells on future flights. They'd be lucky to get thirty percent of their workload done.

For the last three days of their mission, they had to power the bird down so as not to use any electrical power or thrusters at all, saving them for the critical reentry phase ahead. So Gordo and Pete drifted like a tin can in a river, with not much else to do but look out the window and listen to the Al Hirt records the controllers piped up there to them. They had reverted to what the test pilots–turned-astronauts affectionately referred to as "chimp mode."

**"E**ight days floating in a garbage can" was one way Pete would remember the flight. Another thing he would remember was the silence. Pete and Gordo were workmates, and they were friends, but other than the workload at hand, which dropped off the table by day five, there just wasn't much to talk about. What made the silence even more noticeable was that the machinery and console brains and cooling fans of the Gemini capsule had all been placed in a separate firewalled compartment. It made for a very quiet ride.

Gordo got a little surly, too. As commander and the veteran aboard, he wasn't thrilled that the two primary objectives of the mission had become merely "learning-curve opportunities," as the public affairs officer called them. If you listen to the tape of the communication between the *Gemini* 5 astronauts and Mission Control, you can hear the frustration in Gordo's voice with CAPCOM Wally Schirra, advising mission planners that their nifty onboard telescope—which had to be taken apart twice to work— should go straight to the Cape Kennedy Dumpster when they returned. And when the fuel cells wouldn't work and the ship was flying at 10 percent and the mission planners kept their full work schedule on the guys anyway, he snapped, "You guys oughtta take a second look at that."

NASA tried to salvage the rendezvous operation by firing an electromagnetic pulse for the capsule's radar to lock on to, but it was chasing an imaginary target that both veteran and rookie astronaut shrugged off as little more than giving ground controllers something to do.

The food was M&M-sized pellets with meat inside. They couldn't stretch their legs out in the cramped compartment; their knees got sore as hell. Garbage floated everywhere, and the whole human-waste-neutralization procedure with plastic bags and antibacteria tablets was something to be avoided at all costs.

One bright spot was the "space vision test." NASA had set up huge rectangles of gypsum on the ground in Texas, which only Gordo seemed to be able to see. Pete nearly leaped from his couch when he spotted a missile launch from Vandenberg. "I see it, *I see it!*" he shouted. Then it got quiet again.

A failure then? Hell, no. The most important objective of *Gemini 5* was achieved. They made their eight days. Well, seven days, twenty-two hours, and fifty-five minutes, but that was a gimme in anybody's book. Even the Russians begrudgingly acknowledged the record, while chiding the United States for needlessly risking our astronauts in a headlong pursuit of dominance.

Right.

There was concern, even outright fear in the medical community at subjecting the human body to eight days in zero G. It added to the drama of the talking heads on TV, desperately trying to fill the airtime now that most of the experiments were falling by the wayside. What would eight days in space do to a body? Nobody really knew. Jim McDivitt and Ed White came back from *Gemini 4* visibly tired and drawn, and that one was just four days.

The fears were justified. Respiration is definitely affected, as are blood flow and neuromuscular response. Bone deterioration had been proven when they X-rayed the previous crew. It was certainly logical to predict these problems getting worse over time. The guys might lose the ability to swallow. Air and pressure problems could lead to "space madness," posed one scientist who feared crew psychosis from oxygen-starved brains.

Hell, Pete and Gordo could come back after eight days stark, raving mad. Or worse, in the height of their high-altitude dementia, they could take over manual control and try to fly the Gemini capsule all the way to the Moon, or even Venus. Kamikaze the thing in the first televised flaming Hammerhead reentry in broadcast history!

What horseshit. Doctors have always been a pilot's worst enemy, and now they were *putting them on TV!* Pete and the others laughed themselves silly at this nonsense. It didn't matter what happened to the rats they left in the running centrifuge for *eight days* (*my God, can you just* imagine?), or what the computer models showed, or the talking heads blathering away to Cronkite. The boys knew it wasn't a factor. And it wasn't.

They got their eight days. More important to the national psyche not even two years after JFK was shot, Pete and Gordo crushed—*crushed*—the Russian mark of five days the year before. If astronauts could live for eight days in a trash can, they could make it fourteen. And if they could make it fourteen, they could make it to the Moon and back.

Jane Conrad shuffled groggily into the kitchen at four A.M. to make a cup of coffee. Then she walked outside and sat down right in the middle of their subdivision street, looking up at the sky over Taylor Lake, Texas. There were no reporters now, and the boys were sound asleep, as was the rest of the world, it seemed. It was just her. Her and the stars.

It had been, without question, the most insane week of her life. Pete Conrad had become an international celebrity overnight, and his young family was suddenly as fascinating to the world as he was. Television cameras, *Life* magazine, newspapers from everywhere, all wanting to know what it was like being married to the man streaking through the heavens right now, as though she'd even had a minute to stop and think about it.

Well. This week four-year-old Christopher rode a bike for the first time without training wheels—right into the station wagon parked in the driveway, skinning his elbows and knees. The maid called Tuesday, and couldn't work because she'd gotten stabbed in a fight. The kitten kept having accidents on the floor; six-year-old Andrew sprayed an entire atomizer of Jane's best perfume on one of the offerings. Nine-year-old Tommy and eleven-year-old Peter decided it would be a fitting tribute to their father's upcoming splashdown to leap off the roof into the pool . . . again and again and again, yelling at the top of their lungs. Then they went out barefoot to help the local cop direct the tourist traffic in their street. The neighbors were kind, but the novelty of it all was wearing off. Jane gave four or five interviews a day, sticking to the NASA-approved "astronaut wife script" Trudy Cooper had memorized on Gordo's first Mercury flight. Oh, and the air conditioner broke. Again.

Other than the TV cameras, it was pretty much business as usual in the Conrad home.

Mission Control had given Jane a "squawk box" to listen to the spacecraft chatter twenty-four hours a day in her bedroom. Some nights she'd lie there in the dark, just listening to the charmer from Philly who used to take her up on single-engine airplane rides around Bryn Mawr, now talking in a language of three-letter acronyms and numbers that might just as well be Swahili. It was Pete, all right, but it felt as though she were listening to someone else.

Ah, the trials and tribulations of the test pilot's wife. She smiled to herself. Now the astronaut's wife. Same old story. Gone all the time. Even when he was here, he wasn't. Not really.

Pete had his work. Jane had the kids. Conversation had become an endless checklist and status report from home base. She wondered lately if they knew each other at all, or if they were just too busy to.

But here he came again.

Her heart raced, watching that tiny light blink across the predawn Texas sky, heading east. That was her Pete up there, pushing buttons and laughing and cracking jokes at seventeen thousand miles an hour. Like it was the most natural thing in the world.

The best part of reentry and recovery? Being done. Gordo used the last little bit of fuel they had to fire the thrusters and get her in right on the money. Suddenly they were sitting stock-still, looking straight up, ass-down, which is as unnatural a flight attitude as a pilot can ever find himself holding.

The stillness was a complete illusion. They were actually in a free fall, heading downward at a frighteningly high speed. There just isn't enough air at 400,000 feet to give you that sensation. There would be soon enough.

The capsule heated up quickly as gravity took over. She started rocking and rolling again, glowing red as stowed gear and garbage started flying. Mission Control faded into a hiss of white noise as they headed into the ionosphere, watching the black above them turn to blue. Not much to discuss, just hang on, and hope all the boys you backslapped, bought drinks for, and told dirty jokes to did their jobs right. Especially the parachute guys.

The drogue chute popped out at sixty thousand feet, right on program. It slowed them down just enough, pitching them over thirty degrees. Then the main chute. Pete was able to lean up just enough to look out the porthole, and see the wake of the aircraft carrier *Lake Champlain*, which was steaming toward them eighty miles away.

It looked nice and gentle to us, like a beach ball floating down for a featherlight touchdown on the water. But if you're in the damn thing, it gets your attention when the four tons of Gemini capsule hit the surface of the Atlantic, going about thirty.

And did they shake hands and congratulate each other on the new world's record? No, there was a decision to be made, as the air bags were inflating around the capsule. The chopper could come pull the whole thing, Cooper and Conrad inside, and deposit them right on the deck of the carrier or any of the destroyers coming their way. Or they could blow the hatch, climb out, and let the frogmen help them into the harness to be pulled up like a gaffed tuna. Looks fun. Isn't.

"What do you think, Pete?" Cooper's face was bright red, sweat beading up over his lip.

"It's gotta be a hundred thirty in here, Gordo. I'm sweating my ass off."

"Yeah."

The frogman was already there, banging on the hatch, wanting instructions.

"I can't do another minute in here. Open the son of a bitch."


**T**wenty minutes later, the chopper was setting down on the deck of the *Lake Champlain*. Two smiling, Cool-Ray Polaroid–wearing star voyagers who desperately needed a shower and shave bounded out to the roars of the assembled crew, happy they'd set the record, happy to be home. Mostly, though, they were happy to be out of that orbital garbage can that was still bobbing in the water two miles off the starboard bow.

Pete Conrad couldn't have smiled any broader. He was a Navy man, coming home to a Navy ship and a traditional Navy victory welcome—a coffee cup full of Scotch.

One of the Navy's own. Pete "Squarewave" Conrad. Naval Aviator. NASA astronaut.

Francis Conrad holding the newest member of the Conrad family, baby Charles Jr.—
known as Peter—on her lap, next to his big sisters, Bobby and Patty, 1930

Charles Sr. standing next to
balloon apparatus during WWI
in Fort Sill, Oklahoma

Peter, age one, with Lulu, his nanny,
1931  CONRAD COLLECTION

Peter, age seven, poses
with his father's pipe.
CONRAD COLLECTION

Peter takes his first aircraft for a test flight, age four.  CONRAD COLLECTION

Peter with football, 1938, age seven CONRAD COLLECTION

Peter, age eight, at the Devon Horse Show with Charles Sr., 1938 CONRAD COLLECTION

Front row, left to right: Bobby, Francis Conrad, Patty. Back row, left to right: George Kaufman (Bobby's husband), teenage Peter Conrad, Sam Hooper (Patty's husband).

CONRAD COLLECTION

Peter Conrad, pilot, Paoli Airfield, about
1946

Applying the methods he learned as a pilot to his
studies at the Darrow School, Peter was able to
overcome his dyslexia and make the Honor Roll.

Peter in cockpit of plane

Peter the Princeton thespian, costumed in pith helmet, monocle and pipe      CONRAD COLLECTION

Showing off his three-point stance for the Darrow football team      CONRAD COLLECTION

Pete's father-in-law Winn DuBose, with Christopher Conrad, age four, in his lap, is backed up (top to bottom) by Thomas (age eight), Andrew (age six) and Peter Conrad (age ten).      NASA

The aviator Conrad Collection

Pete at Naval Air Station, Miramar

Conrad Collection

Pete poses with a T-38, a high-altitude supersonic jet trainer. NASA

Pete relaxes on the deck of an aircraft carrier while at Miramar.    CONRAD COLLECTION

The Official Conrad Family Photo, from November 13, 1969. From left to right: Christopher (age eight), Andrew (age ten), Pete, Jane, Peter (age fourteen), and Thomas (age twelve).    NASA

The Gemini astronauts, Class of 1962. Front row, left to right: Elliot See Jr., John Young, Jim McDivitt, Pete Conrad and Neil Armstrong. On steps, from top left: Jim Lovell, Ed White, Frank Borman and Tom Stafford.                    NASA

The *Gemini 11* crew: Dick Gordon and Pete—not your typical NASA astronauts...                    NASA

Clockwise from top left: Dickie-Dickie, Pete, and equally goofy *Gemini 11* backups Neil Armstrong and Dave Scott, showing they are up to the task
                    NASA

The astronaut life wasn't all fun and games. Pete, head in hands, at a NASA lecture.

NASA

Pete couldn't help but have a good time at NASA. Even Irving, the stuffed gorilla adopted by the *Apollo 12* crew as their mascot, seems to be slyly grinning at Pete's humor during the prelaunch breakfast.

NASA

Pete and Al Bean get to examine some of the rocks and soil samples they brought back from the Moon.

NASA

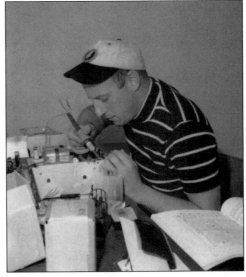

Pete was a world-class engineer and hands-on tinkerer. Even with the engineering might of NASA behind him, nobody could stop him from picking up the soldering iron.

NASA

Pete's first ride into space aboard *Gemini 5* turned into "eight days in a floating garbage can" with Gordo Cooper, setting a new duration record.                          NASA

Pete and Dick Gordon on USS *Guam* after the *Gemini 11* splashdown          NASA

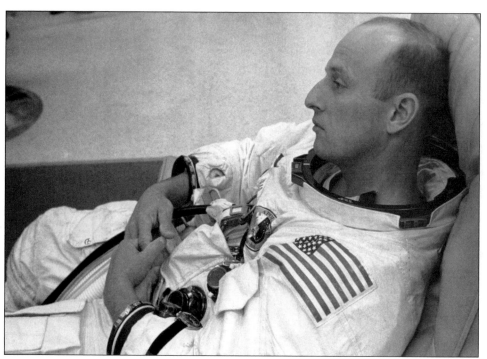

A pensive preflight Pete, *Apollo 12*                          NASA

The rocketmen of *Apollo 12*—Pete, Dick Gordon and Al Bean—and their matching Corvettes    NASA

Three good friends— Pete, Dickie-Dickie and Bean-o—also known as the *Apollo 12* crew, pose in front of the simulator. NASA

*Apollo 12* lifts-off from Pad A, Launch Complex 39, at 11:22 a.m. on November 14, 1969, heading for the Moon.    NASA

A view of a lightning bolt during the launch of the *Apollo 12*. A similar bolt struck the *Saturn 5* rocket about 36.5 seconds after liftoff, when the rocket was at about 6,000 feet altitude.    NASA

Pete's official *Apollo 12* portrait    NASA

*Apollo 12* flight patch    NASA

Pete checks out Surveyor on the lunar surface, the LM in the background.    NASA

Left to right: The first *Skylab* crew—Dr. Joe Kerwin, Pete Conrad and Paul Weitz—pose with a model of the orbiting space station.                                                        NASA

Pete demonstrates the comparatively luxurious sleeping accommodations on *Skylab*.                                       NASA

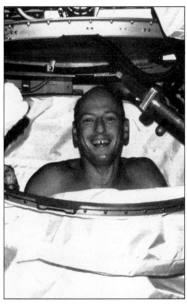

Pete enjoys his outerspace shower on *Skylab*.                                       NASA

Paul Weitz, Pete and Joe Kerwin (in dress whites) received congratulations from President Nixon and Soviet Premier Leonid Brezhnev, who was thrilled to meet the American astronauts after their return from a month in space. NASA

Pete was a natural filming a commercial for McDonnell Douglas to counter the bad publicity of the DC-10 that lost an engine and went down outside of Chicago. CONRAD COLLECTION

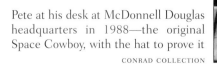

Pete at his desk at McDonnell Douglas headquarters in 1988—the original Space Cowboy, with the hat to prove it
CONRAD COLLECTION

A time-lapse photo of the successful DC-X test flight demonstrating vertical take-off and landing

ROGER RESSMEYER/ CONRAD COLLECTION

Pete shows off a model of the DC-X model like a proud papa.

CONRAD COLLECTION

The flight team of 10BD that set the still-standing round-the-world speed record for a business class jet: Pete, Mark Calkins, Paul Thayer and Dan Miller

DANIELS FUND

Bill Daniels, the Father of Cable Television. Friends with Bill for thirty-five years, Pete jumped at Bill's idea to make a go at the round-the-world record in the Lear 35.    BILL DANIELS ESTATE; PHOTO BY NICHOLAS DESCIOSE

Pete and Nancy at Angel Falls, Venezuela, in 1991, exporting fun to South America

CONRAD COLLECTION

Pete Conrad, self-portrait, White Sands, New Mexico, 1998

CONRAD COLLECTION

Nancy and Pete, 1998    CONRAD COLLECTION

# THIRTY-ONE

If you were casting the role of an astronaut in a movie, Dick Gordon would be your guy. He was as handsome as a silver-screen idol, possessing a quick wit and a million-dollar smile. Seattle born and raised, a University of Washington alum, he also was one of the Navy's hottest F-4 jocks, showing up at Pax River just a little before Pete had arrived.

Dick and Pete were friends instantly. Flying together, waterskiing, drinking beer and doing shots, the two shit-hot jet jocks, laughing louder than anybody in the bar, were known for closing the place down their share of times, and then showing up on the flight line six hours later, clear as bells.

Dick missed the cut in the second astronaut selection for Gemini. He was as competitive as any of the other guys, and none too pleased. "Pretty pissed off," in his words, he'd started sending out query letters to aviation companies, preparing to retire from the Navy. In a déjà vu scene of Wally Schirra and Al Shepard paying a happy-hour visit to Pete, Dick looked up from the bar after work one night to see a certain gap-toothed grin heading right toward him.

"Still crying in your beer, Dickie-Dickie?"

"Just crying for you, Pete, ya poor dumb sumbitch. Stuck in a garbage can in space with some Air Force puke while I'm out smoking the field in my Phantom." He nodded at the bartender for another round. "Let me buy you a beer, pal. Tell ol' Dick all about it."

Did someone mention the word *competitive?*

"So, Dick. They're gonna fill out this Gemini Program now that Apollo's approved. At least ten more slots. I think you oughtta apply again."

"And why would I do that?"

"Because you miss me."

The beers arrived and were hoisted. And before the night was over, Pete convinced him to give it another go. And in October 1963, Dick Gordon didn't have to miss Pete anymore. He joined the third group in the Gemini/Apollo pipeline.

Flight Crew Operations director Deke Slayton's philosophy in crew assignments was twofold: Keep crews together, and fly the rookies with veterans. Guys who knew each other just performed better. NASA was looking at the long haul now, developing a group of teams for future Moon flights. Putting Pete and Dick together for *Gemini 11* was a no-brainer for Deke. Dick was a hell of a pilot, the two had known each other since their early days at Pax, and Pete was completely comfortable with him.

The flights after *Gemini 5* solved most of the serious problems. The engineers worked out the bugs in the fuel cells, and in the radar tracking and rendezvous. *Gemini 11* would be about rendezvousing and docking with an Agena rocket, launched about an hour before, and doing it in the first orbit. It was a tall order, but the two Navy jocks sailed through the simulations, and couldn't wait to get up there and do it for real in September of '66. The mission also called for an EVA. Dick would step outside the spacecraft and run a series of power-tool tests on the capsule, while docked with the Agena.

Pete was breezing down the hall one day in Houston when Deke sum-

moned him into his office. Flight Director Gene Kranz closed the door behind him, and it was obvious something damn serious was up.

"Pete, we need to discuss an operational procedure with you," Deke began. "About the EVA."

"Okay."

"As you know, it's kind of a ticklish procedure. We've got a ways to go on
this thing."

"Aw, Dick's kicking it in the pool. He'll do terrific."

"We've got no doubts about that, Pete," Deke continued. "It's if he doesn't,
that's what we need to talk about." It was a weighty enough statement. Deke
waited for Pete to put two and two together. He didn't.

"If Dick can't get back in the ship, you have to leave him." The pause was
predictable.

"Say again?"

"If there's a problem—" Deke continued, trailing off.

"You close the door and come home alone," finished Kranz, never a word
waster.

"Okay . . ." Pete was puzzled here. "But if he gets in trouble, I can certainly help him out. He's on a tether, for God's sake."

"The hatch is too small for the two of you," Kranz reasoned. "You won't
have room to maneuver. Under no circumstances—zero—are the two of you
to be outside the vehicle at the same time. We are clear on this, right, Pete?"

What the hell. They had to do it. He was a commander now; he had to be
briefed on that procedure. He shrugged it off as the burden of that command, heading out to the parking lot. But as he got into his red-on-red
Corvette, it hit him. He'd never thought about it before—well, not since being here at NASA—the big D. Death.

Spaceflight was dangerous business, no doubt about it. The process had
begun to appear routine, but it wasn't. There were a hundred potential ca-
tastrophes in the launch alone. Honestly, Pete felt the risk element was
higher in test flight, but that was just the price of the ride. You might die.

But it was you. It wasn't somebody else. It was closing the door on your
best friend, waving good-bye through the window as he faded out into noth-
ingness forever.

What would you even say over the comm? *See ya? Sure sorry about it all. Have a nice reentry.*

It wasn't going well. Dick's heart rate was at 150; he was out of breath, sweat dripping into his eyes and fogging his faceplate. And he was dangling on a string outside *Gemini 11,* 161 miles over the Earth.

"How ya doin', Dickie-Dickie?"

"I'll be okay."

The capsule was spinning slowly, trying to wrap the tether around itself where they were docked with the Agena. They'd chased the Agena down on the first orbit, docking successfully with her on the first try. Gordon had to constantly fuss with it. And in the design phase, it was never considered how hard it was to grab onto a smooth, spinning metal surface with thick space gloves and boots, while trying to run a cordless ratchet wrench.

He was having a hell of a time of it, actually. And for the first time since he'd been an astronaut, Pete Conrad got scared. "What do you say we call it a day, huh?"

"No, I can get it." Gordon grunted, cussing under and over his breath as he gutted through the checklist. He wrapped the slack in the tether around the Agena's docking bar and across the adaptor segment. It was helping, but he was clearly struggling out there.

Pete winced at the wrapping of the tether. If they started spinning any faster, that thing would tangle, sure as hell. Dick might be able to extricate himself, might be able to make his way back to the hatch with no tether and try to cram himself inside.

Then again, he might not. He was completely out of breath now, heart rate right at the max. Even the ground guys were getting concerned.

*Gemini 11* commander Conrad was nervous as hell, and even if it was his best friend, he'd rather pull rank now than make the command decision Deke and Kranz had talked about. Besides, this struggle wasn't Dick's fault. He'd remember this first EVA as "like trying to tie your shoe with one hand while holding on to the drawer with the other."

Yeah. Except he was also wearing thick gloves and a stiff heavy suit, and hanging in space on a thread, and his dresser was going seventeen thousand miles per hour with no drawer handles to hold on to.

"Okay, Gordon. Item D-thirteen has ascertained that we definitely need handles and footholds on the Gemini. I'm calling this one a wrap. Get back in here, and let's go find a beer somewhere."

Dick got back inside, but it wasn't easy. The man was exhausted.

They undocked from the Agena after doing some infrared star photography. Command Pilot Pete lined them up for a pinpoint reentry, and nailed their landing in the West Atlantic after a three-day flight.

The whole thing went in the logbook about as perfect as it gets. Fuel cells, check. Chase down and dock on the first orbit, check. Pete drove the *Gemini 11* right into the Agena's docking port like it was a runabout out on Clear Lake. EVA? Difficult, but it taught them what they needed to know. Dick saved the other spacewalkers a heck of a lot of struggle and needless danger.

So what would Pete have done if Dick couldn't get back inside the *Gemini* on his own? Would he have done something stupid, and jeopardized the craft just to save one man? Or would he have followed procedure and closed the hatch, cut Dick loose, and saved the ship, leaving his best friend to die up there all alone? Would he have followed that direct order?

Nope. Not a chance in hell. And nobody, certainly not Slayton or Kranz, really expected him to.

# THIRTY-TWO

The pessimist gets nervous when things go too well, expecting a disaster to rear up. The better things are going, the worse the disaster will be. The optimist, on the other hand, sees nothing but positive—a good thing, but leaving one terribly vulnerable when something eventually does happen, destroying that illusion.

The realist, of course, lives in the middle and understands that Murphy's Law is one of the immutable truths of this life. If something can go wrong, eventually it will. And the more moving parts it's got, the wronger it will go.

Test pilots, by necessity, are realists.

On January 27, 1967, Murphy landed on Pad 34 at Cape Kennedy like a ton of bricks. After six glorious, batting-a-thousand years, something went terribly, terribly wrong. And it went wrong on *Apollo 1*.

Gus Grissom, Ed White, and Roger Chaffee were inside the *Apollo* capsule, performing a "plugs-out" pressurized cabin simulation, when an errant connector threw a spark, igniting the pure oxygen atmosphere in the cabin, incinerating the entire capsule, including the men, before the support team could get the hatch kicked in from the outside.

*Kicked in from the outside.* That was what did them in. The only way to open the sealed door was *inward.* And with the cabin fully pressurized, a draft horse in his prime couldn't pull that hatch free from the inside, much less a panicked crewman with less than fifteen seconds from recognition to expiration. Pure oxygen environment, pressurized seal, no explosive bolts, miles and miles of wire with connecting posts. Murphy had been waiting in the wings with this deadly combination. And in the blink of an eye, he woke everybody back up to the reality of this business. People could die doing this.

Three just had.

The dream ride of *Apollo 1* came to a screeching, heart-wrenching halt.


Pete was driving home from a T-38 hop at Ellington Field in Houston when he heard the bulletin on the radio that there was some sort of accident down at the Cape. The broadcasters were initially ho-hum about it—it was probably a small building fire somewhere on the vast Atlantic Missile Range complex, newsworthy only because NASA was there.

Pete knew instinctively that it was worse than that. The only way news like that made a wire was if an outside emergency agency was scrambled to the site. And the only way that happened on an installation with more than adequate facilities and personnel to handle every disaster up to and including a rocket explosion was that someone panicked and dialed the fire department or an ambulance. And the only way that happened was that something really bad had just transpired.

Pete exited the freeway, whipped his brand-new Corvette around, and floored it back toward Manned Space Center.


Equipment fails. Accidents happen. People die. Test pilots know this from firsthand experience. But they show up for work, fix the problem, bury their dead, and get back up there.

The general public is not wired like this. Especially after the roll NASA had been on since Al Shepard left the pad in *Friendship* 7 back in 1961. The press was in on this dream, and they are an awesome mover of the public mood when a cause becomes theirs. The most routine of the Mercury flights became super-galactic affairs in the newspaper and on TV, each surpassing the other. Gemini was the next step in what was surely just securing our birthright to this solar system in the name of freedom and democracy. These guys could do no wrong.

And why not? Who could argue with success, and who could help but love our boys? And who wasn't moved deeply and mightily, as one of our rockets roared to life, reigniting JFK's bold challenge: "We choose to go to the Moon in this decade. . . ."

Apollo and the Moon were as manifest destiny for twentieth-century America as the western frontier had been for nineteenth-century America.

And then three men died.

The horror and shock gave way to a brief unity and comforting period, as it always does. "We will go on," was the drumbeat in the press, and to one another—NASA and civilian. As in any tragedy or attack, Americans were drawn together to join hands, circle the wagons, mourn, and remind ourselves of the dream.

Then the questions got asked. The search for the cause, so that "this will never happen again." Someone must have known. Rumors were whispered in corridors, suppressed memos suddenly surfaced, "off-the-record" chats occurred with reporters in dark Houston and inside-the-Beltway bars. Accusing fingers were pointed.

Suddenly the whole space program came under scrutiny. Why were we doing this, anyway? Why spend $20 billion to get someone on the surface of the Moon when we had more than enough problems that needed to be addressed here on Earth? What were we gaining, really, other than beating the Russians in this all-consuming race? And now three men were *dead* because they couldn't get the damn door open?

It was strange to be putting on a suit for a pilot's funeral, instead of a uniform. Other than that, the ritual was exactly the same as it had been for Pete and Jane back at Pax. Only today they were in a D.C. hotel room—just the two of them. The boys were down at the Ranch with Granddaddy.

"Pete?"

"Yup?"

"How long did it take for them to . . . ?" Jane didn't finish the question, but she didn't have to. He knew what she was asking.

"It was over like that." He snapped his fingers.

"Couldn't they have done something?"

"Nope." He slipped on his jacket, checking the mirror quickly. "They didn't have a chance."

In all the test-pilot years, she'd never gotten used to it. Proud as she was of Pete, she'd always thought the whole high-risk business of flight test and combat was a needless waste of human life. But NASA had made it seem as if they'd engineered all the risk out of it. There were hundreds of thousands of people working at some level on the Apollo Program. Could not *someone* have foreseen this set of circumstances?

"What's gonna happen now?"

"We'll figure it out, we'll fix it, and get back to work."

Pete was deeply affected, no doubt about it. Grissom, White, and Chaffee were his friends; he worked with them every single day. Their kids played together.

But the pilot in him knew that nobody had forced the three *Apollo 1* astronauts to do this job. The risk was more than worth it—all three had made their own assessment of that. There was a list a mile long of guys who'd change places with them in a heartbeat, just for a chance at that ride. At least Gus and Ed had gotten theirs.

The pilot in Pete refused this line of thinking. He was ending this discussion before it even began. He grabbed the room key.

"Let's go, Jane. We're gonna be late."


The next weeks were the first since he'd joined the program—since he'd joined the Navy, really—that Pete wasn't working seventy-hour weeks, completely consumed by the job. He was like one of those legendary Japanese soldiers they rescued off a remote Pacific atoll years after the war had ended, having no idea the fighting had ever stopped.

For the first time since he could remember, Pete read the paper. He actually sat in a chair and thought about what he'd just seen on Huntley and Brinkley's nightly broadcast—my God, how the world had turned. This was a different America now. *Really* different.

The sixties are remembered fondly in this country as a time of liberation: a modern great awakening, an era of freedom and social justice, not to mention some great music. To some extent, this is true.

But like all memories, time has sweetened this perception, and edited out a fair amount of reality. The truth is, it was actually a dark time: a time of anger, strife, and violence that ripped the fabric of this country apart again and again. As the Cold War got colder and colder, we found a new enemy out there—*ourselves*.

The irony is, it all started with such noble intentions. When JFK followed Eisenhower in committing forces to Vietnam, it was to stop the flood of communism, not to gobble up land eight thousand miles away. Oh, how that would spin out of control.

When LBJ pushed Kennedy's Civil Rights Act through an ambivalent Congress, it was about righting historical wrongs and uniting us as a people. As a Southerner, he knew there would be resistance, but he never dreamed police would be fire-hosing people in the streets. But the real ticking bomb out there was among America's youth. And just like a countdown at the Cape, they were about to go off.

November 22, 1963, might be the closest mark on the timeline for when it all began. Our President, symbolizing youth and beauty, this breath of fresh air, was cut down. Murdered. And it further stirred this pot of paranoia and fear that had become a fact of life in the postnuclear world. The young weren't as interested in the space race as they'd been with Shepard and Glenn and the Mercury Program. Besides, all the flights were starting to look the same.

They changed the channel and saw a half million marching on Washington, demanding change for people of color. They went to their room and turned the radio up, listening as rock and roll changed from the joyful exuberance of the early Beatles to the anger and mistrust of the Doors. They sneaked out and smoked marijuana, got sick of being virgins, and laughed as everybody over thirty wrung their hands, wagged their fingers, and lectured them endlessly. This was the generation gap, and it was about to turn ugly.

Young Americans turned their TVs back on, and saw Dan Rather standing in a grass field in Vietnam. Behind him were bags about six feet long, being loaded into a helicopter. And what was in the bag was *them*, our country's young, dying by the hundreds every week in a war they didn't start for a cause they didn't believe in, in a place they'd never heard of till now. And Johnson was ramping this thing up? Calling for another million of us to register for the draft?

*Hell, no. We won't go.*

Now the angst of youth had a cause. "Us and them" wasn't about the United States and the USSR anymore; it was about "us" and anyone over thirty. Rock concerts became protests. Protests became marches, and sit-ins, and teach-ins. Which was all well and good, and the American way going all the way back to the Boston Tea Party . . . until it got violent.

And it did get violent. "The cause" wasn't just about the Vietnam War, and though it sounded great, it wasn't about peace and love, either. The cause was about overthrowing the *establishment,* at least in the minds of the truly militant and most vocal. Suddenly buildings got bombed. Race riots broke out in Watts, Detroit, and Newark. The 1968 Democratic Convention in Chicago, the symbol of democracy itself, would be made into an utter shambles in front of the entire world. Some punks even set fire to Old Glory.

And in the year to come, a couple nutcases would kill Bobby Kennedy and Martin Luther King.

Pete snapped off the TV in dismay and stepped out into the warm Houston night. When had all this happened? All this time behind the gates at NASA, in the silence of space, he'd been living in a bubble. His world hadn't been the one on the evening news. Until now—now that the rockets were cold, and the Dream was grounded.

Suddenly he and the guys weren't heroes. They were crew-cutted, uniformed "squares." Even in a painstakingly civilian space agency, everybody knew they were *military* pilots. The military in 1967 might just as well have been the Gestapo to this new movement.

Cronkite did his best to raise everyone above the hate and noise, and pause us just long enough to reflect on the fact that Grissom, White, and

Chaffee were men willing to give their lives in the service of this country, in the service of humankind, making the ultimate sacrifice to fulfill the vision set down by their fallen commander, who was rapidly moving into American sainthood. For a few days America did pause and grieve.

But it didn't last. Now the ire turned on the once-bulletproof, sacrosanct NASA. The criticisms grew more shrill and personal. Some irresponsible hack even cashed in on his crackpot theory by writing a book charging that NASA had cooked up a conspiracy to kill Grissom before they'd let him be the first to walk on the Moon in retaliation for losing his Mercury Liberty Bell capsule in the ocean after a malfunction at splashdown.

*And people believed it!*

Expressing all of the astronauts' exasperation, Frank Borman cut right through the bull droppings in yet another Senate hearing when he declared, "The question isn't whether we trust our own agency; the question is whether *you* trust *us.*"

Suddenly people didn't.

NASA's engineers would sort it out, fix the problems, and move on. You didn't see a single astronaut joining this fray, because they *did* trust their agency, their team, and their country. And they all knew, to a man, that an accident with machines this complex and with such physics-defying audacity was all but inevitable. Pete was quietly surprised a fatal accident hadn't happened before *Apollo 1.*

But the writing was on the wall. Even when NASA did redesign the hardware and procedures, the clock was winding down. Apollo was gutted before the program began. They'd never get to *Apollo 20,* as they'd originally planned. The base on the Moon was long gone—too expensive: in dollars, political careers, and now lives. Pete kept a good face on it all down at work, understanding that his most important job right now wasn't flying and engineering; it was keeping his smile. Keeping everyone around him laughing and looking up, as much as they could in this excruciatingly long, soul-searching internal investigation time. They saw the writing on the wall, too. The ride was coming to an end.

When Vladimir Komarov augered in a month later out on the Siberian plain, stopping the Russian space program right in *its* tracks, nobody was smiling. It didn't matter what flag the guy was wearing, or what race they were in; he was still one of them. His ride was just as over as Ed's, Roger's, and Gus's. And it might just be over for everybody.

Pete watched the Moon rising above Clear Lake, and felt a tiny hand slip into his own.

"Daddy?"

"Yes, Christopher?"

"Are you really gonna fly to the Moon?"

"I hope so."

The boy nodded, thinking on this, then wondered, "Can I go, too?"

Ah, youth. Who else could break your heart, or launch your spirit to the heavens, in the blink of an eye? Pete picked little Christopher up and held him tight. "I hope so, my boy. I hope so."

# THIRTY-THREE

True to form, the media made more of the rivalry for the number one spot—who would be the first to land, and walk on the Moon—than actually existed. Deke Slayton's job as crew chief was as complex as the computer engineers', managing the skills, schedules, health, and personality dynamics of the astronaut corps. Part football coach, part production manager, part psychologist . . . Deke had a task as challenging as herding cats. The flight assignments had been set long ago, but the loss of Gus's crew had thrown the whole thing into a scheduling nightmare. Crews had to be switched, guys had to learn new jobs, and resentments flared when teams were broken up.

But there wasn't any grumbling about Neil Armstrong. He'd earned it. He had been with NASA as a test pilot when they were NACA, had flown the X-15, became an astronaut in 1962, and piloted *Gemini 8*. Neil was quiet, reserved, seeming to compete only with himself—the perfect choice to be the first, if for no other reason than how he seemed to shrug the whole thing off as just another day on the job.

The world stood still, watching TV together on Sunday night, July 20, 1969, as Neil stepped off the ladder and set the first human foot onto the surface of the Moon. Even the criminals took a break for a few hours, as police world-wide reported a 90 percent drop in nefarious activity for those hours Neil Armstrong and Buzz Aldrin walked on the Moon, collected a bag of rocks, and snapped some pictures while Michael Collins whizzed by overhead in the command module.

NASA had fixed its problem. The engineers found some more problems in the downtime, fixed those too, and launched Neil and Buzz and Mike out of Earth orbit and into the Moon's. Now there were Neil and Buzz up on the big screen in Mission Control, taking humanity's baby steps on another world.

And amid the yells and cheers, the fat cigars and popping champagne bot-tles down in Houston and in living rooms, breakrooms, barrooms, shop floors, and even hippie communes across America this Sunday night, a quiet awe set in over the country.

By God, we'd done it.

America had ignored the distractions, the finger-pointing, the generation gap, an unwinnable war, all of it, and kept working. And damned if Neil Armstrong didn't check off the last line on the biggest to-do list in history, completing John F. Kennedy's vision.

The United States had put a man on the Moon before the decade was out. And with a nod and a respectful salute to our adversaries in this race—whom all the people in this business quietly suspected we'd be working *with* someday—Pete signed off with the rest of the astronauts and engineers and administrators on the last line of the plaque left at the base of the lunar mod-ule *Eagle* as Neil and Buzz blasted out of the Sea of Tranquility for home:

"We came in peace."

# THIRTY-FOUR

It was an all-Navy crew settling into the command module on top of their *Saturn 5* rocket four months later. And don't think everybody at NASA didn't know it, as Pete Conrad, Dick Gordon, and Alan Bean made damn sure they didn't forget.

*Apollo 12* was going to the same place, in the same kind of vehicle launched by the same monster rocket with the same basic mission parameters as *Apollo 11*—yet the mission couldn't be more different. All along in this program, especially after the fire, the unspoken objective had been: *Let's see if we can actually do this and not die.* Neil Armstrong, Buzz Aldrin, and Mike Collins, all on hand for today's launch, proved that yes, we can.

Missions are like companies, or football teams, or families. They take on the same characteristics as their leader. Neil was focused, serious, not given to a lot of chat. With him as commander, their flight reflected that. Perhaps that was how it should be. The first crack at anything as large as a Moon landing would have a rather serious and focused approach.

And then there was the commander of the second flight, *Apollo 12*, a guy named Pete, who was as focused and serious about the job as Neil, and not exactly an average jet driver himself. But there the similarities ended.

There was plenty of chat, a lot of laughing, attaboys, way-to-gos, and thank-yous. Astronauts are not generally given to this kind of kinetic energy or personality. It's not that they aren't excited about the job, or grateful to the hundreds of thousands of people working behind them, or unable to tell a decent joke. It's just that the profile guy sitting on top of that *Saturn 5* rocket wasn't Pete. He was more like Neil: focused, serious, and reserved. Taller, too.

There was even a joke going around that Pete had *talked* his way into this program, and talked so fast nobody noticed till it was too late to fire him. But damned if they didn't find themselves tossing 'em back after work with him, listening to his stories, laughing louder than profile at his jokes. And you'd better believe, to a man, they'd kill to fly with him. Nobody laughed at that joke harder than Pete.

Loading these three and their equipment into the command module more resembled three fraternity brothers climbing into a surf wagon with their boards and Frisbees for a beach day. The only thing missing was the beer. But when they strapped them in, plugged them in, and closed the door, the grins gave way to the profile-astronaut focus and seriousness, the ones that had gotten mission commander Pete Conrad to the top of this rocket in the first place.

**A**l Bean was the perfect third to join the dynamic duo of Conrad and Gordon. A Texas boy, and a naval aviator himself, Al joined the third group of astronauts in the middle of Gemini as Apollo was just getting under way. He loved flying, loved being an astronaut, and was as comfortable as Pete talking about it (another nonprofile trait). Al actually had the ultimate one-word answer when people asked him the inevitable, and ridiculously abstract question:

Public: "What's it like being an astronaut?"

Al: *"Great."*

As lunar module pilot, Al would separate from the command module with Pete, and land and walk on the Moon. Their two scheduled EVAs had them spending about eight hours outside, gathering samples, taking pictures, and, if all went spectacularly well and spot-on target, checking out the *Surveyor* craft still parked on the surface there, no longer streaming its data to NASA home.

It was a tall order, that last one. A pinpoint touchdown from a quarter million miles away with about 10,000 variables on the second landing in history was optimistic, to say the least. When Neil was bringing the *Eagle* down, he could see that their intended landing strip was a huge boulder field that would spell the end of him and Buzz. He had to steer the thing miles away from the original target.

Talking about Pete's landing, after all the calculations and orbit projections and burn rates and double and triple checks of the math, one of the mission planners candidly admitted that if they hit their target, it would be more "lady luck" than anything else.

Chuckle, chuckle. Pete shrugged that opinion off when pressed on it by the media. "We'll give it a shot. See what happens." Between the lines was a message to his well-meaning, but misinformed nonflying teammate on the ground:

*The hell you say, pal. Give me a clear landing site; I'll hit it.*


The word *awesome* is overused in our lexicon, tossed around about a pretty day, a good café latte, or a very attractive man or woman. But the *Saturn 5* surpasses the strongest definition of the word. *Awesome* doesn't even touch that bird.

At 363 feet tall, the Saturn is a lot of rocket. Pour several thousand tons of liquid propellant inside, strap on five huge engines, weighing her in at more than six million pounds, firing a volcano of thrust out the back when she's rockin' and rollin' . . . this bird is one hell of a candle. Which is exactly how the ground guys referred to the truly awesome beauty they rolled out to Pad 39-A a month prior.

Even standing still on the pad, the *Saturn 5* looked for all the world to be a living, breathing thing. With liquid oxygen and hydrogen gassing off her, the metal skin popping and groaning as it expanded and contracted with the supercooled blood coursing through her veins, casting a sunrise shadow of nearly a half mile, the *Saturn* was an otherworldly beast you were drawn to and scared shitless of at the same time.

Pete sat in the saddle of his Harley in the marsh grass alongside her on the Sunday before launch. All was quiet as he watched a blue heron circle the *Saturn* lazily, not a care in the world. If Pete thought anything at all, it was only how tiny he felt, looking up at the little cone where he'd be sitting in a few days, going for the ride of rides.

There were a thousand people working into the night down here at the Cape, preparing—on a Sunday. A thousand more over in Houston. Nobody ever seemed to pay attention to the shift whistle on this job. Nobody ever wanted to leave.

People don't get any happier than that—giving everything they had and then some to a singular goal; forgoing sleep and comfort and a normal life to make damn sure nothing goes wrong on their end, expecting the same of everybody around them, and never doubting them for a second. All those people, all those hours and days and years and sweat, all their hopes and fears . . . just to put him inside that cone, and let him take the ride for them, then come back and tell them about it.

Yeah, he felt tiny. And damn lucky.

# THIRTY-FIVE

It was sixty-eight degrees, overcast, and raining at Cape Kennedy on November 14, 1969—ceiling 2,100 feet, winds light. There was discussion while the men were in suit-up of scrubbing the launch, but that would mean ramping this whole thing down, draining every drop of fuel out of the monster rocket, and sitting on their hands for a twenty-eight-day hold.

Going to the Moon is not like driving your car from point A to point B whenever you feel like it, just hitting the gas and steering. The Earth and Moon need to be perfectly aligned, rotations accounted for, gravity fields exited and entered at precise placements in the space-time continuum, or you'll need a hell of a lot more rocket than the *Saturn* 5 to pull it off. You couldn't. You'd have to wait.

Was there pressure to launch on schedule, even in a storm? Why, hell yes. And nobody applied more pressure than the pilots to just *go*.

Think of it. The countdown clock for *Apollo 12* started when Armstrong, Aldrin, and Collins hit the water in *Apollo 11*. For days, weeks, and months the entire machinery of NASA had been moving toward that big zero, intensity and anticipation growing as the day drew near, test-pilot adrenaline pumping under those skins, under those white pressure suits and clear helmets, ready to climb in and light 'em up . . .

To have the game called on account of rain? It would be like stopping the Super Bowl as the kicker sprinted toward the opening kickoff.

Twenty-one hundred feet was enough. Besides, it looked like it was breaking up. They'd be up and over it right damn quick driving *this* bird. The three naval aviators were ready to rock. Houston and the Cape finally agreed.

All systems were *Go* for launch.


**"T**en, nine, eight, ignition sequence begin, engine start. Four, three, two, one . . ." *Whooo, boy.*

If the *Titan II* was an e-ticket ride, the *Saturn 5* was all of Disneyland slammed into a few seconds. The ignition boom could be heard from five miles off, and the crew sure as hell heard it just a football field above the engines, even in a sealed, pressurized capsule. It was a smoother ride than the *Titan,* but not by much. Four times their own body weight pressed down on the astronauts, and this bird liked to pogo a little herself as she picked up speed. And did she pick up speed.

It was all going right on program for the first half minute of the launch. The second half minute? Commander Conrad remembered it well:

> *The funniest thing of all was in the first thirty-six seconds of the flight—it's funny now; it wasn't very funny then.*
>
> *The entire time we're training, running up to this mission, there's never a doubt in anybody's mind—Dick Gordon is the driver. I mean, I may be commander, but the pilot—the guy driving the rig—that's Gordon. And he makes damn sure every day that nobody forgets it. Touch a*

*switch without asking, he'd slap your wrist like a pissed-off piano teacher.*

*We're in the simulator one day, and I just instinctively put my hands on the stick—I mean, for God's sakes, I am a pilot—I thought he was gonna have a baby right there and then.*

*So I'm in the left seat, the commander's seat, and the countdown hits zero, we're shaking and rattling, blowin' and goin', I mean, this is it. We are on our way, blasting right through this thunderstorm, heading for the Moon, when . . .*

*Whammo! Sounded like a baseball bat smacking an aluminum pole— and we're the pole! All eleven system warning lights fire at the same time. Now, in the most catastrophic simulations, we've seen maybe three or four go off—but right now in the real deal, the whole board looks like a Christmas tree.*

*Of course, we'd just been hit by lightning. A thirty-six-story hydrogen bomb with three guys hanging on for dear life as we accelerate to nine miles a second, and we're nailed by a full strike. And then it happens again! Every alarm buzzer and light we have is going off now, data just stops coming in. . . .*

*And Dick Gordon, our fearless pilot, driver of this rig, throws his hands straight up, and says, "Okay, Pete. She's all yours!"*

They'd grown their own lightning, was what they'd done. A thunderstorm is a supercharged cauldron of static electricity, and lightning comes flying out of it when clouds and particles rub together, just like walking on a carpet in your socks. Introduce a flaming metal rocket going like a scalded dog into this mix . . . well, in retrospect, nobody should have been surprised they'd just created the world's most truly awesome flying lightning rod.

But they were. Pete's hand moved instinctively to the abort handle as all screens went blank. The voices from Houston and the Cape weren't panicked, but they were mighty *urgent*. And there were lots of them. The commander had a fast decision to make—*real* fast.

While it was better to gain more altitude to give the chutes more time to open, the longer they went, the farther from the Cape they'd be when they came floating back down. If the capsule did manage to get separated from the roaring, flaming *Saturn*—and there was no guarantee of that—there was no telling exactly where it would end up. They'd trained for a hard landing in the desert or the jungle in Africa or thereabouts, but hell, nobody'd actually *done* it. They would probably hit water, but *where?* There was a whole lot of ocean underneath them, and capsules won't float forever.

Could they ride it out? What if they weren't able to restart the system? What if the thousand miles of wire they'd need to keep going had been fried by the lightning?

What if this bird was dead?

Pete's fingers closed around the handle. He looked at Bean and Gordon for a split second; they were as out of ideas as he was. Assemble data, assess the options, execute decision—

"Flight, have them turn the SCE switch to AUX." The voice belonged to a young flight controller in Mission Control, John Aaron. He was talking to Flight Director Gerry Griffin, who was furiously processing the information coming at him from the other engineers and controllers.

"What?" Griffin responded, not even sure who was talking.

"SCE to AUX, Flight," Aaron repeated.

Griffin to CAPCOM Jerry Carr: "CAPCOM, SCE to AUX."

Carr responded, "What?"

Griffin repeated, *"SCE to AUX."*

Finally Carr told Pete, "SCE to AUX."

"Say again, Houston," Pete fired back.

Lead Flight Director Gerry Griffin looked up and over at all the consoles in Mission Control Houston and saw young John Aaron staring right back, nodding, utterly sure of himself.

Griffin looked at Carr. "Tell him again."

"SCE to AUX, Pete," Carr barked. "Switch SCE to AUX."

"What the hell is SCE? And *where* the hell is it?" Pete scanned a hundred switches as quickly as possible. In all his training, he'd never heard of, much less thrown, switch SCE. And by the deafening silence on the other end, apparently none of them knew where it was either.

"I know what it is!" Al Bean hollered, and quick as a flash, he reached across the sea of dials and switches on the *Apollo 12* console, found SCE, and moved it to "AUX."

Immediately the screens in Mission Control blinked with streams of data. Once data was restored, it was recognized by Aaron that the fuel cell power sources had tripped offline, causing the severe power brownout in the spacecraft. The crew was told to place the fuel cells back online by activating the fuel cell reset switches. The whole thing had taken less than thirty seconds.

Pete released the abort handle, and shook Al Bean's hand. Then he grinned at Gordon. "Okay, Dickie-Dickie. Fly us to the Moon."

Two guys saved *Apollo 12* less than a minute into it: a kid barely out of college, and Al Bean. Out of all the engineers and flight controllers and designers near the radio, he and John Aaron were the only guys who had a clue which of the hundreds of switches *might* restore all the control settings. But only Al knew where that switch *was*.

The only one not surprised by that was Pete, who knew that the Creator had left the gift of detail out of his own makeup and dumped it all into Al, the detail guy's detail guy. Even if Al hadn't been a damn good pilot—and he was—he'd saved this entire mission, and earned his seat right there.

It takes about three days to cross the miles between Earth and the Moon. You're traveling awfully fast with that slingshot out of Earth's gravity and no air or wind or anything to slow the capsule down, but it doesn't feel like it. The stars are still way the hell away; the only sensation you're making any headway is the Moon getting larger and the Earth smaller. But you're making headway, and you better pray they did the math right, or you'd be making it forever.

"Kinda boring," Pete remembered the journey out in the command service Module, *Yankee Clipper*. "Everything was automated until we got to the Moon, so there wasn't a lot to do other than shave and brush your teeth." The CSM was a lot bigger than the *Gemini* capsule, but other than the three-across couch and the crawl space leading to the docked lunar module, there wasn't a great deal of elbow room. Nor privacy. Good thing these guys liked each other.

Music had become a staple of spaceflights. The astronauts seemed to perform better with the stereo on, and time seemed to pass quicker. They had cassettes given them by record label owner Mickey Kapp, and a player mounted in the bulkhead just like it was a car. Mission Control piped a few requests in during down times. Pete and Al preferred country; Dick wiggled and danced to "Sugar, Sugar" by the Archies so many times that Al was ready to scream. Just like boys on any long road trip—arguing over the radio.

The Moon looked just like it did in the photos, only a lot more real—and closer. Beat to death by meteors and micrometeors, it looked to Pete like the door of the old pickup rusting out at the edge of Winn's ranch. Every cowboy and hunter passing by for the last thirty years just had to put a bullet or a shell in its door.

At orbital altitude, the Moon was nothing but craters and pockmarks. *Surveyor* was down there somewhere. Pete wondered looking at that very unfriendly landing zone down there, how the thing had even set down without crashing. He wondered how he would, too.

All the power-up and preflight were done aboard *Intrepid,* the spiderylooking lunar module. Looking at it stuck on the nose of the command module, you wouldn't think the gangly, wingless, foil-wrapped LM would even hold together, much less fly. But it actually could. Although it was a brick with legs, it did have rocket motors to slow them down and launch them out, and thrusters to give the pilot just enough power and maneuverability to steer away from the side of a crater or a boulder field.

NASA had eliminated seats in the LM, so the two-man crew stood side by side. As an engineer, Pete was instrumental in this design change, as it improved human performance, especially in a straight descent.

Gravity is gravity, even if the Moon exerts only a sixth of the Earth's. The LM was essentially designed to drop to the surface as gently as possible, sit for thirty-one hours, and provide life support for Pete and Al Bean until they blasted right back up to Gordon and the command module. Then they'd set her free to crash-land right back down where they came from, and study the seismic echo.

There was a thought they trained themselves not to think, but they knew it. Especially here and now: *There's only one way for this to go right . . . and a thousand ways it can go wrong.* And almost all of them would mean Dick was driving home alone. And Pete and Al would stay behind, shining down on their friends and family, affecting the tides, and the moods and cycles of all the women on this blue planet—for the rest of time.

They didn't think about it, but they knew it.

**A**l was in the LM and situated, already flipping switches. Pete crawled through the hatch for the last time, and looked up at his old buddy Gordon, grinning down at him like a possum.

"Let's go over it again, Pete. The gas is on the right; the brake is on the left."

Pete only smiled. He was speechless for once.

There was a split second when Pete's eyes met Gordon's in one of those looks that can only be given and received by one who slogged through that same swamp *with* you, the same government-agency political bullshit, the daily near-death, Mach-2 experiences right alongside you, to get right here. This place.

Pete knew there'd been the same quiet moment back on the ground when Deke Slayton and Gene Kranz—probably Chris Kraft too—had pulled Gordon aside, just like they'd done with him on *Gemini 11,* and reminded him in so many words that if something were to go wrong down there on the surface, something that would keep that little spidery ship from making it back to lunar orbit to meet up with him, there was nothing he could do. He'd have to point his nose toward home, fire that engine, and leave his friends behind. The look they shared over the surface of the Moon—all one second of it— was the same as when Gordon stepped out of the *Gemini* for his spacewalk three years earlier.

Then Dick Gordon, friend for life, thrust out his hand. "Go get me some rocks, partner."

"See ya tomorrow, Dickie-Dickie." With that, Gordon closed and sealed the hatch.

# THIRTY-SIX

*Intrepid* was eighteen thousand feet above the lunar surface, dropping twenty feet per second. Separation was nominal, every move right on program. Although the computer was humming right alongside him, it was Pete Conrad bringing this ship down. Commander. Pilot.

Neil had been just about here, calmly minding his business and letting the computer handle most of the descent, when he'd had to take over, coming into an unlandable field of boulders. Heart racing at nearly 160 beats a minute, Captain Cool found a spot, and set her down like a pilot with six seconds of fuel left.

There'd be none of that computer-glitch monkey business today. Pete was on stick the whole way down, aiming right for what appeared to be the planned landing site, which indeed looked unlandable from here. He was hoping *Surveyor* was there, but he sure couldn't see it yet.

Armstrong was a hell of a pilot and hell of a good guy. He saved the LM and his and Aldrin's asses by setting her down like he did. The first human to set foot on another world, he was every bit the hero the world made him out to be, and deserved every Corvette or free lunch or free house the taxpaying public would buy him for life. Pete had no desire to try to better Neil, or do something that he hadn't done on his own flight.

But all pilots want to nail their landing, whether it's from Paoli Field to West Chester, or Cape Canaveral to the Ocean of Storms. Starting from Pad 39-A, a quarter million miles away at the Cape, Pete wanted nothing more than to bring her in and drill the target like an F-4 Phantom hitting the number three wire.

The reference point was the "Snowman Crater, Ocean of Storms, Moon." They needed to hit him right on the shoulder; the *Surveyor* was there.

Only it wasn't. From this point, Pete was sure they'd missed. By a frickin' mile.

Al was calling out altitude, rate of descent, and fuel, glancing at Pete goosing the thrusters, tipping *Intrepid* over five degrees to have a look out the window. Getting frustrated.

"Five hundred, doing fine . . . need to slow her down, Pete . . ."

Then out of nowhere: "Son of a gun! There it is, Al! Right down the middle of the road!"

"You nailed it. Watch for dust."

And they both held their breath as the dust of the Moon, kicked up by the rocket motor, obliterated their view in the last fifty feet.

Touchdown. Main engine stop. Pete Conrad was on the Moon, one of only four people in all of human history who could say that in November 1969. But that didn't matter yet.

What did matter was that the pilot had nailed his landing. He pegged that Snowman son of a bitch right on the shoulder—five hundred feet from the *Surveyor*, right here in the Ocean of Storms.

Bull's-eye, baby.

\* \* \*

**P**ete and Al laughed out loud at CAPCOM Gerald Carr, passing along the flight surgeon's suggestion that they rest up a bit before venturing outside.

*Rest up?*

After all this. All the training, preparation, the dreams and visions of humankind for thousands of years, and here they were, the third and fourth in the history of the species to set foot on this thing . . . *and you expect us to sit down for a smoke break?*

*Right.*

They did the power-down and suit-up like a couple kids cleaning their rooms as fast as they could so they could get outside and play in the snow.

Everybody wondered what Pete would say when he put his boot down on the sand. Hell, what *could* he say after Neil? Contrary to common (and cynical) assumption, the astronauts weren't scripted. Pity the twit who would try to script a bunch of test pilots and fighter jocks, egos fully intact, riding a rocket to the Moon.

No, they were on their own on this one. And knowing Neil, Pete figured he probably didn't think about it till he was at the bottom of the ladder. And then he uttered the phrase that will live forever: "That's one small step for man, one giant leap for mankind."

Follow *that*.

At one of the hundreds of dinners for Buzz and Mike and Neil after *Apollo 11*'s return, a journalist asked Pete about his upcoming walk, and what his first words on the Moon would be.

"What are they gonna have *you* say?" she asked, barely hiding a contempt for the Big Brother spin some of NASA's lesser fans were crafting in the nonmainstream press.

Pete laughed. He was enjoying this line of questioning more than she wanted him to. And he was turning on the charm—Pete may not have been Paul Newman, but his energy was irresistible. And he knew it.

"It's up to me, darlin'." He was laying it on thick with his Texas-Pennsylvania drawl. And she didn't believe a word of it.

"I tell you what. Let's you and me decide right here and now what I'm gonna say when I set foot on the Moon. It's on TV real time; I can't lie to you. If I say it, you owe me five hundred dollars. If I don't, I owe you. Deal?"

Deal.

\* \* \*

**P**ete stopped on the last step, looking down at the gray-white sand. That last one was a doozy, almost three feet. And like pausing before leaving a diving board, he took a breath, then backed off the ladder in a half jump.

And Pete Conrad, stuffed into a hundred pounds of space suit, floated gently down, and stood on the Moon, the third human being in history to do so.

What were the thoughts of the man at this moment? What were the words the history books would immortalize?

*"Whoopee!* It might have been a small one for Neil, but it was a *big* one for me!"

They were prepared remarks all right—prepared right there at a banquet table with that pretty-yet-cynical journalist, a self-deprecating joke about the five-six-and-a-half astronaut's height. There was no more significance in the words than that. They boomed over the speakers in Mission Control and were met with the usual response of those in Conrad's presence—big belly laughs. Yep. That was their Pete up there. The one and only.

Pete laughed too, secretly knowing he'd just won his bet with the journalist. Only he never saw her again. And he never saw his five hundred bucks, either.


**A**l stepped off five minutes later, and they got to work immediately. Instruments to set up, experiments to prep for, Pete started digging for soil samples right off the bat—just in case of an early departure. It was easier to move than in the bright-white lunar-surface training room back at Houston. In the Moon's gravity, a hundred pounds was less than twenty. Bulky yes, and restrictive; but the movement was a lot easier here than there. EVA 1's checklist was done in half the allotted time.

"Dum-dee-dum," the astronaut from the Main Line sang while he worked. People who didn't know Conrad listening to the transmissions were sure space madness had set in. Or maybe Pete had smuggled hooch aboard the LM, and it was beer-thirty on the Moon.

Nope. Just a guy well trained, and familiar with every procedure ahead of him. And having a hell of a great time. He and Al giggled at how close he'd actually come to the edge of the Snowman crater, setting *Intrepid* down. Fifty more feet and there wouldn't have been much to giggle at. Pete tromped to the edge of the crater where old *Surveyor* was waiting. At the end of EVA 2, they'd head down and inspect her up close.


**P**ete lay in the LM's hammock bunk for the "good night's sleep" block in the mission profile. Right. *I'm the third man to set foot on a world outside his own, I haven't even been here twelve hours, and I damn sure won't get back anytime soon—and they expect me to just go to sleep?*

Besides, Pete and Al were so afraid they'd break a zipper or rip a seam in the puffy suits—canceling the second EVA if they did—they just took off their helmets and boots and gloves and racked out in the things. It was as comfortable as sleeping in football pads. It didn't seem to bother Al. He was snoring away in his hammock.

Pete looked out the window at the black sky, blacker than any black he'd ever seen. The stars weren't brilliant; he could hardly make them out at all in the harsh white light bouncing off the sand. It was all so cold, really, and as silent as silent got.

Here was Pete Conrad, at the top—the very pinnacle of the NASA dream ride, with half the Earth's population a quarter million miles away probably looking up at the night sky right now, wondering what he and Al were doing, wishing they were right there right now.

It should have provided comfort. Company. But it didn't. Pete suddenly found himself lonely. Unsettled. No one to talk to, nothing to do till the boys down in Houston gave them their wake-up call in six hours.

Sitting still never sat well with Pete. It certainly didn't up here. Wide-eyed, he found himself thinking about Father. Charles had passed away four months before this dream ride. He'd seen his boy ride the rocket twice, but couldn't hang on long enough to see him walk on the Moon.

Pete grabbed the extra cassette-tape player NASA had allowed him to take on board the LM—after a lot of pleading and bargaining for the extra twenty-four precious ounces of weight—and hit play. Keeping the volume super soft, so he wouldn't wake Al, Pete hugged the player to his ear, closed his eyes, and let Patsy Cline sing him to sleep.


They were absolutely filthy. NASA would never release these photos—Pete Conrad and Al Bean covered head to toe with soot and Moon dirt on this second EVA, like two little boys who'd been in the dirt pile with their Tonka trucks all day.

"You know, Pete"—Bean laughed—"you look just like a big puffy Pigpen with a space helmet on."

"You oughtta see you, Bean-o. How'd you get so damn dirty? Was it the core samples or did you fall down and go boom?"

When everything was all said and done, walking on the Moon had just been a kick in the ass. Twenty-eight hours since the landing, and Pete and Al were at the end of the second four-hour EVA. They made their measurements, took their readings, and got their rocks. Checklist complete.

This one was different from *Apollo 11*, to be sure. Neil and Buzz barely got a quarter of this much time on the surface—even so, there were a lot of nerves and trepidation. Who really knew if the ground on the Moon was stable and solid when they had landed last July? They'd set down off target, and burned a hell of a lot of fuel finding a place to land. Would the hookup with Collins work? What if they missed? It was a very real possibility.

*Apollo 12* was pure Conrad—fun, and relatively glitch-free. Yeah, Bean-o had fried the TV camera, accidentally pointing it directly into the sun, which you absolutely cannot do with a video unit. Like he was supposed to know that? The man was a pilot, an astronaut; he wasn't a damn TV cameraman. Besides, NASA hadn't gotten the thing to them until three days before launch, gave Al and Pete a quick how-to, and that was that. Pete even tried to get it to work with his geo-hammer, kissing *Apollo 12*'s TV coverage good-bye for good.

People on the ground were hotter than hell over that, especially the networks and the advertisers. *Screw 'em. You experts want it fixed so bad, get your ass up here and do it yourself,* Pete thought. It was an accident. No way in hell would Pete let Al feel bad about that. He sure didn't.

The entire traverse over to *Surveyor*, Pete hopped like a bunny—seeing just how high he really could jump in one-sixth gravity, once again giggling like a kid on the playground.

"You know, Al, even if I am a runt, I believe I could dunk on Bill Russell right now."

And there was an incident that could have taken place only on a Conrad mission. Pete was halfway through the EVA checklist book NASA had Velcroed on the wrist of his suit, when he turned innocently to page seven. . . .

And there, smiling at him, was the prettiest face, the nicest hair, and the biggest, firmest, roundest hooters this astronaut had ever laid eyes or hands on—Miss October, 1968. *Seen any hills and valleys?* was the caption.

"Holy shit." Pete gasped, forcing down a laugh. "Hey, Al, you want to flip over to procedure seven? I might need your help on this."

And there they were—America's finest, standing in the Ocean of Storms on Earth's only Moon, checking out some bodacious ta-tas. They lost five minutes of EVA laughing, flipping madly through their checklists, searching for another picture, or at least the *Playboy* party jokes. Wondering which of the boys back home had slipped these pages by the mission director.

Throughout time, wolves and men have howled at the Moon. This day, the first in recorded history, the Moon howled back.


Pete hadn't stopped, really. Hadn't taken the opportunity to just look around. That hadn't been on the mission time line. Every activity, every move was scheduled, preplanned. There was just a set amount of time, and a set amount of oxygen. Then he had to go.

Pete watched Al disappear back inside *Intrepid*, and for the first time in eight hours of jumping, dancing, twisting, and shouting while they performed the sixty-eight preprogrammed tasks . . . he stopped and looked at the Earth over that tiny horizon.

The Moon wasn't the be-all and end-all of his life and career. He'd never looked longingly at it as a boy, nor boldly declared that *someday* he'd walk upon her surface. Pete Conrad was a pilot, and the Moon was the objective of this mission. Landing on target and getting his crew home safely were the most important things to him. But now he looked. He needed to.

The Moon had so little color. It was ice-cold, black and white and gray, with just a hint of blue and green in the sand, like pulverized glass. And so small. You really had the sensation of standing on a ball, seeing that tiny horizon dip away from you.

But there above him, the tiny Earth. Silent, blue, tranquil . . . fragile as crystal. All alone out there. Home.

As an engineer, Pete had never given a lot of thought to the possibility of life on other worlds. The mathematical odds were in its favor, but now, as he stood here . . . what even littler thought he'd given to a Creator, and the possibility that we really were *it* out there . . .

It seemed quite likely that Pete, Al, and Dick whistling by overhead were the only three complex life-forms in this universe *not* on that tiny blue ball.

She looked so quiet. So small. So vulnerable. There was no sensation of America tearing herself apart from the inside. Or of a poorly planned war in Asia that wasn't accomplishing a goddamn thing but killing people, including a lot of Pete's old squadron mates—those who hadn't landed in a prison camp in the middle of Hanoi. And here he was laughing and skipping on the Moon.

There was no sense of madmen gunning down the Kennedys and Martin Luther King, police trying and failing to beat a generation into submission. And certainly no sense of towering rockets on opposite edges of that little blue planet, pointing menacingly at one another, ready to fire.

None of that. Just a timid, lonely little world rising silently above him against an endless expanse of black.

Mother was down there, looking up at him in the early-morning sky. Jane, too, probably. The boys were still asleep. He felt a little like God, watching over them from above.

The crackle of a voice from that blue ball and the little whistle at the end of the transmission reminded Pete that time was his enemy. He had to go.

"Roger, Houston. Heading in now."

Then astronaut Pete Conrad saluted his dad, somewhere out there in those stars now, smiled that gap-toothed smile, and started up the ladder of the LM. One last look at the mountains, the side of the crater where *Surveyor* slept, the flag he'd planted to tell someone long in the future that they'd been there, and his and Al's bootprints in the dust . . .

"So long," he whispered as he crawled inside, pulling the hatch closed behind him on the Ocean of Storms.

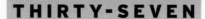

# THIRTY-SEVEN

They were finished, gear stowed—*Intrepid* was ready to go. Pete looked over at Al, who was taking his own last look at the Moon, lost in his thoughts.

"You want to do it?"

"Do what?"

"Take us out of here. You're the LM pilot."

"Yeah, but you're the commander."

"You want me to order you then?"

Pilots fly. Bean-o was a pilot. Of course he wanted to fly it. Pete didn't have to offer him that; it was his lunar mission. It was the commander's privilege to fly, but it was also the commander's discretion to turn over the controls. He'd had his fun; it was Al's turn.

The lunar countdown hit zero, and Captain Bean hit the EXE button,

launching them in silence toward Gordon and the orbiting *Yankee Clipper*.
The Moon was behind them now. They'd done it.

Al would never forget the simplest, most natural gesture Pete offered, the
only time it happened in the Apollo Program—the commander let the rookie
drive.


The reunion joy on the *Yankee Clipper* lasted for about two seconds. Dick
Gordon took one look at the two Pigpens on the other side of the docking
hatch—in a *cloud* of lunar dust, no less!—and slammed it back.

"Dick, what the hell?!"

"You're not coming in my ship like that, Pete."

He wasn't being an orbiting Felix Unger; he was right. NASA had sealed
and launched the *Yankee Clipper* from a near-sterile clean room for a reason.
Dirt particles clog filters and shut down the airflow process, which is a bad
thing a quarter million miles from landing.

"Strip down."

"Say what?"

"You heard me, Commander. Get out of those suits and you can come in."

And so they did. The crew of lunar module *Intrepid* weightlessly re-
boarded the command module naked as jaybirds, giggling like they were
skinny-dipping in the community pool at two A.M. Even the usually poker-
faced Gordon couldn't help but laugh at the ridiculous sight of two astronauts, great galactic explorers, heroes to all the world, floating into his
cockpit in their birthday suits in zero gravity.

"So picture this," said a laughing Pete. "Something really bad happens
right now, and we're done. And somebody finds us a thousand years from
now. Just like this. What do they conclude?"

"That I'm a sick and lonely man," answered Gordon, the only clothed one
at the moment, "and I went to a lot of trouble and expense for some privacy."


By the third orbit, everybody was dressed and ready for separation. Dick
counted it down . . . three, two, one . . . and *Intrepid* was undocked. Pete
watched Dick working the board, firing the *Clipper*'s thrusters to make sure

they were clear when the *Intrepid*'s engine fired, driving her right into the surface of the Moon like a piece of space garbage, so the boys could measure the impact with the seismometer Pete and Al had left behind.

Dick Gordon was the classiest guy Pete had ever known—ever would know. Traveled 240,900 miles, but didn't get to go that last hundred. Didn't get to set foot on the Moon. And he never said a word about it. He just did his job and did it very very well, happy to be on this team.

The tiny LM's engine fired, taking her straight into the Moon, disappearing from their sight. The impact reverberated for a full thirty minutes before going silent.

And in the quiet of performing the procedures leading up to their slingshot for home, all three men smiled as Pete hummed the chorus to a popular song, looking at one another and wondering the same thing. . . .

*Is that all there is?*

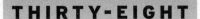

# THIRTY-EIGHT

**February 13, 1996**
**Learjet N10BD**
**On the ground in Olbia, Italy**
**4:02 a.m. Local Time**

It was a mob scene reminiscent of the days right after Pete had splashed down in the *Yankee Clipper* twenty-seven years before. The Italians have long identified with Americans, and taken the same exuberant pride in many of our accomplishments as they would their own. And as this crowd proved again that they are just so damn good at *being* exuberant.

"Peeeete, Peeete . . ." they chanted more and more fervently, until he finally tore himself away from the rear tanks once they were full and capped. The ground crew and spectators roared as if he were a rock star. Once upon a time he had been. All the astronauts were.

Mark watched as Pete obliged every outstretched hand, every picture or shirt to be autographed, laughing and even attempting to converse with them in broken Italian. They ate it up.

"I actually had some hair then," he quipped, signing an *Apollo 12* photo to their adoring delight. *This guy knows how to work a crowd,* Mark thought.

They cheered like mad as Pete waved and jumped back aboard, engines already screaming. Dan was at the controls, blown away by the scene, obviously too young to remember the whole *Apollo* thing. He wasn't even alive when Pete was on the Moon.

"Damn, man. You're like Elvis!"

"It's just my looks," Pete said dismissively as he belted himself in. "These chiseled features are the cross I bear." He sighed, about as serious as he was tall.

They were up and out of Italian airspace in a flash, the cockpit settling down to the quiet of four-plus hours to Riyadh, Saudi Arabia—which hadn't yet issued clearance to land. Ally or no ally, the Middle East was no less tense than it is now. The crew hadn't really worked out an alternative yet—just had to wait and see.

"That's gotta be a great feeling to be remembered like that after all this time," Mark observed.

"So did you, like, ride in parades and all that?" Dan wondered.

"Yup."

"So . . ." Dan searched for the right way to put it, but Pete already knew what was on the twenty-five-year-old's mind.

"Yes, Dan. There were groupies." And that was as far as a gentleman from the Main Line was going, to Miller's obvious disappointment.

"That must be top of the heap for an astronaut," Dan said. "Walking on the Moon. I mean, how much better does it get than that?"

Pete didn't respond, just looked out the window at the Italian boot giving way to the sea. Mark had vowed not to pepper Pete with astronaut questions—he must get so sick of answering the same ones over and over again, he thought.

But to heck with it. *How many times am I gonna get forty-eight uninterrupted hours with a guy who walked on the Moon?*

"Does it, Pete?" He broke his vow. "Does it get better?"

"It did for me, Mark. A lot better." He turned from the window and winked. "On *Skylab.*"

# THIRTY-NINE

**G**od, she was beautiful—118 feet long, thirty-two feet around, a wingspan of nearly a hundred feet, weighing in at a svelte two hundred thousand pounds.

The average person looking at *Skylab* without the dramatic Earth shots in the background might think a little less of her beauty. To be honest, it did bear a physical resemblance to a giant barrel with flatiron wings, looking like it couldn't fly even if something could actually manage to throw it.

But not to an engineer. *Skylab* was the state of the art of space vehicles in 1973, the largest, most sophisticated man-made body ever to orbit the Earth—before or since—and held the keys to the universe, in ways *Apollo* couldn't.

If the United States could just afford to keep her there.

On May 14, 1973, she roared off Pad 39-A on top of that other beauty, the only rocket with enough beans to get her out of our gravity, the *Saturn* 5. She was unmanned, so there was nobody aboard to complain about the pogoing they still hadn't quite engineered out of the monster. *Skylab* left the Earth's atmosphere as flawlessly as the other *Apollo* flights, then settled into a perfect orbit.

And within minutes, it was obvious. Something had gone very wrong up there.


Pete had turned his attention to the Skylab Program in 1968, when Richard Nixon, the newly elected President, promised the nation that his attention was fixed firmly on "the serious issues facing us here on the ground."

It was a loaded statement, and sent an unmistakable signal to NASA. At a billion dollars a flight, Apollo's blank-check days were numbered.

It was no surprise. Everything from the war in Vietnam to poverty to pollution to civil rights was at critical mass in this country. The economy was suffering record deficits from a recession that seemed to worsen every month. It would cost another $20 billion to take the program all the way to *Apollo 20,* then fund a sustainable lunar base, then colony, when nobody was sure what it was we were actually doing there other than winning the space race. Nixon would turn off the lights on Apollo at 17. And that was that.

Heartbreaking as it was, Pete agreed with the decision. After they landed on the Moon, the game was over. Yes, the technological, engineering, and managerial achievement was the greatest in all of human history, but in spite of all the fabulous advancements and futuristic possibilities, it was lost on no one: This thing started as a race to beat the damn Russians.

It wasn't a tie. We won. You didn't keep playing the game after it's over, especially when the other team sacked its bats and called it a day, which was essentially what the Soviets did, turning their eyes and resources to a manned space station. It was cheaper, easier to accomplish, and paid off with a lot more bang for the ruble.

Pete saw the logic in that. He also saw that an Earth-orbiting space station was the only way to keep the ride going at NASA, as the public agreed with their new President. We did need to address some pretty serious and expensive problems here on Earth, and after dealing with them, *then* we could push toward the stars.

*Skylab* was a way to do both. Pete got in on the ground floor—as an engineer. Nobody is better suited to design a machine than the one who would operate it. Especially if that operator understands the engineering that makes it work and, more important, what *won't* work.

Less than two months after *Apollo 12*'s splashdown, Pete was done with the state visits and parades and speeches, and the moonwalker was back working sixty-hour weeks on the long, fat, beautiful bird, shuttling back and forth between Houston and Huntsville, Alabama, in a NASA T-38. Everything from driving *Skylab* to taking a shower in it—all had to be designed and built from scratch or adapted from Apollo. And it had to be done for about a tenth of the cost of a flight from that program.

The limits were what made it a challenge. And it was, without question, the most fun Pete Conrad had ever had: drawing, building, welding, wiring, testing . . . then throwing it away and starting again. In its own way, it was just like sitting at the workbench alongside Morris the chauffeur back in the garage of the Roadside Cottage, building something. Except this was NASA. And he'd get to fly it when they were done.

The only time he could remember coming up for air for more than a day or two was when his old pal Lovell ran into some seriously bad luck on *Apollo 13*. Pete and all the guys working on *Skylab* came running when Mission Control called all hands on deck to help Jim fix the thing and get home alive. He and Jane were dispatched to Lovell's home to stay beside Jim's wife, Marilyn, comforting and strengthening her. Pete translated the blizzard of technical language streaming through her Squawk Box and gave her what she needed most right then: an understanding of what was really going on. Marilyn feared they weren't telling her how bad it really was.

It was bad, no two ways about it. Jane was prepared to resume her old Pax River duties of being first-on-scene with a brand-new widow. Pete never doubted the engineers nor his old flying buddy would work this thing out and get home in one piece.

And by the grace of God, and the world-class skill of NASA's Dream

Team, they did just that. Pete cried with Marilyn, celebrated Jim's splash-down, then got back to work on *Skylab*.


**W**hat had happened on *Skylab*'s launch is that the Big Bird wounded the Lit-tle Bird, causing a combination of problems. First off, the *Saturn V*'s shake, rattle, and roll launch ripped away a portion of the micrometeorite shield that surrounded the exterior of the *Skylab* workshop, which tore away one of only two solar panels, and a piece of the shield wrapped around the other, preventing its opening. With no solar panels, she had no way to power herself outside of her batteries. And with the shield gone, she began overheating im-mediately after going into orbit. When the data started rolling in, the cabin temperature was climbing past 150 degrees. If the bulkhead material started to melt, the pressure integrity of *Skylab* would be compromised. This would be life-threatening—to the crew, the ship, and the future of America's manned-spaceflight program. Fortunately, the ATM, the non-cash-dispensing Apollo Telescope Mount, which was the Big Science that got this bird funded to begin with, was working.

Pete would be commanding two rookies on the first *Skylab* mission: Paul Weitz, another Pennsylvania Navy flier who had joined the Astronaut Corps late in Apollo, and Chicago native Joe Kerwin, who would be the first physi-cian to take the Big Ride. They were originally set to follow *Skylab* into orbit one day after it left, rendezvous, and dock, and get right to work on a variety of experiments and observations. That itinerary was put on hold as Mission Control went into crisis management mode to try to figure out how to save this bird, whose orbit was already decaying.

*Skylab* wasn't just a malfunctioning unmanned space vehicle to Pete. It wasn't a prototype jet fighter at Pax that never should have been built to begin with, much less flown. This was his baby in trouble up there. There wasn't a nut or bolt or wire that he wasn't intimately acquainted with; he loved this bird like he did his old Indian bike. He'd given her over a year of his life, and he wasn't about to cut his losses, as the all-knowing media was instantly advising NASA to do, warning that a rescue was all but impossible under these circumstances.

"Like hell." When he got his Options and Assessments Report the first day in the Engineering War Room, the first thing he did was cross out Option #5, the Worst Case Scenario:

Let the ship die, start again.

In more than ten years at NASA, Pete had never lost his temper with anybody. Never even raised his voice in anger at a soul other than himself. But he did on day six of the war room deliberations. Speaking to no one in particular, he jolted the entire room out of a sleepwalking reexamination of a low-odds scenario that hadn't worked the twelve other times they'd tried it.

*"Just get me up there, goddamn it!"*

That wasn't the engineer talking. It was the commander—who'd decided they'd talked about it long enough. Even if the way-smarter-than-all-of-us engineering committee resented his nonscientific approach, they were quietly relieved that it was Pete who said what was clear to all of them: this endless-loop discussion was an exercise in futility. And nobody spoke with more authority than the pilot-engineer who was on *Skylab*'s design and construction teams, and knew how to fly it.

The engineers had been brilliant in saving Jim Lovell's crew on *Apollo 13*. They did the math, built a prototype, and developed a procedure. They talked Jim and the guys through every step of it, and it worked!

But there was a critical difference here: There was no Jim and crew aboard *Skylab* right now, just computers and wires and provisions and a nifty new telescope. The engineers could talk and upload data till they were blue in the face, but not one of *them* was gonna open the door, crawl out on a tether, and fix the damn thing. They couldn't rely on math, science, and technology. It would take a man. It wouldn't be pretty, but a man with a tool belt was the only shot they had.

Three days later, *Skylab 2*, the modified Apollo Command module, was on its way with Conrad, Kerwin, and Weitz. As they lifted off, Pete got his usual relieved laugh from flight controllers when he radioed, "And Houston, *Skylab Two* with you. We fix anything."

When Pete finally got a good look at *Skylab* after a flawless launch, he got the same feeling as you would when seeing a classic car you'd invested four years of your life in restoring now mangled in a heap in the town junkyard. The commander's indomitable spirit sank as he flew the CSM around the wounded bird, letting Weitz open the hatch to conduct a stand-up EVA to check it out up close. One solar panel was long gone, the other was stuck fast, and the heat shield on the port side stern was nowhere to be found. She was wounded all right, maybe beyond repair.

Docking was a bitch. Most of the transcript of this part of their flight would read EXPLETIVE DELETED, a term about to come into vogue from the Watergate hearings in '73. The ship's docking probe's capture latches didn't work. Pete gave Weitz the controls, depressurized the command module, and opened the tunnel hatch. He and Joe dove headfirst into the bank of circuits and gizmos, Pete cussing a blue streak as he sorted through the wires, cutting and splicing like a pissed-off Maytag repairman trying to get a dryer to work again. Kerwin had to turn away to hide a smile, despite the seriousness of the situation. The only thing missing from this cussing and grunting wire-snipping Mr. Fix-It was the low-creeping work pants revealing more derriere than anybody would want to see.

But damn if it didn't work. After another hour of rerouting and connecting, skinned knuckles, more and better EXPLETIVE DELETEDs, and a very difficult EVA into the docking tunnel, Pete got the two vehicles docked. Two hours after that, they opened the hatch and cautiously entered *Skylab*, breathing their own oxygen.

It was dark. And hot. The air was fine, with no poisonous gas present, but it was 130 degrees and climbing. They had to fix this problem, and they had to fix it fast.

The solution to problem one, the solar panel, was simple: a twenty-five-foot square parasol made of Inconel—the same foil they wrapped the Lunar Module in, giving it that Reynolds-wrapped appearance—would cover the gash in the heat shield and deflect the sun's rays back into space.

Sounds easy. It wasn't. First, the thing had to get made. During the first ten days of the flight, the backup crew, led by Rusty Schweickart, developed and practiced an EVA method for freeing up the solar panel. Pete and Joe rehearsed it on days eleven and twelve inside the *Skylab* workshop, preparing their equipment and making adjustments. On day thirteen, they went outside.

*   *   *

**T**he moonwalkers who've also walked in space tell us that one doesn't even compare to the other. There is something particularly ethereal, slightly divine about floating over the Earth and looking down like an angel on rain forests, cities, mountains, and oceans. Pete didn't have a lot of time for ethereal just now. He had a full tool kit and a big job to do, or *Skylab* was over.

Pete and Joe assembled a twenty-five-foot pole with a Southwestern Bell Telephone Company limb lopper on the end, and brought it as close as they could get to the stuck solar panel. Pete held Joe's legs while he attempted to place the jaws of the limb lopper on the aluminum strap that was holding the solar panel cover down about twenty feet away. The first try didn't work.

Neither did the second, or the third. More cussing and grunting, adjusting their "persuader." Joe reattached his tether and gave it one last try, Pete holding the tether rigid for stability. Joe pulled the jaws halfway closed on the panel's restraining strap, using the lopper's long rope.

Now came the time for space acrobatics. Pete went hand-over-hand down the twenty-five-foot pole and attached another line they called the BET to the cover of the solar panel. He and Joe closed the jaws of the limb lopper fully, freeing the panel's cover from the twisted and mangled aluminum strap. It opened a little more, just about to deploy . . . then stopped. The hinge was frozen solid.

More cussing. No more Mr. Nice Guys. If Pete had had a chainsaw, he would have fired it up.

Joe cinched down his end of the rope to a handy frame, and he and Pete both wriggled their bodies between the taut BET line and the side of the workshop. Now, like a couple of Olympic powerlifters, they both "stood up," pushing mightily against the BET, which pulled on the solar panel cover. . . .

It's a shame that sound waves don't travel in space, because Pete's cosmic samurai scream of "WHOOO-YAAA! WE GOT IT!" might still be traveling toward God Himself on the other side of the Big Bang. The frozen hinge unfroze, and the snarled arm let go, throwing the massive solar wing suddenly open, bonking him and Kerwin on the head as it went. The two astronauts tumbled ass over elbow back against the workshop. There they were, laughing and slapping five over Hawaii as the wing locked into place, pretty as a picture, just like they'd drawn it. The inside temperature started dropping within five minutes.

And of all the awards Astronaut Pete Conrad ever had hanging on a wall or sitting on a shelf, none meant more to him than the "Hands to Work" trophy given by his alma mater Darrow School, honoring him for this afternoon's job: a silver hammer.

He and Kerwin headed victoriously inside for a cold one. A dry-ice-cold bag of Tang, that is.

# FORTY

**P**ete had seen Stanley Kubrick's 1968 film *2001: A Space Odyssey* about the time the interior cabin of *Skylab* was being put together up in Huntsville. And he would always wonder who'd imitated whom. The 360-degree running track in the film was a dead ringer for the one they'd designed for the combination storage bins/physical-training area on board NASA's ship. Either Kubrick had a spy inside NASA, or the spacecraft designers were blatantly ripping off the movie.

But the onboard running track was an apt symbol for this first *Skylab* mission, once things settled down to its version of normal: a rumbling, tumbling romp for three guys shifting the hell out of the manned-spaceflight paradigm, and getting down to some serious work.

The weightless "physical training" Kerwin, Weitz, and Conrad performed on the track mostly consisted of chasing each other around, rolling and flip-ping like fourth graders at recess, determining who could turn the most som-ersaults or do the best back walkover. It was Pete, of course, who'd done gymnastics in high school and college. He badly dislocated a finger in one of the contests, but he'd be damned if he'd tell Houston about it, especially when they had a doctor right here, turning cartwheels himself, giggling like a kid. Dr. Joe yanked the finger back into place, taped him up, and they were right back at it.

They even invented a new human event in this orbiting Olympics, which could be possible only in zero G: Push off from one end of the station, and see who could fly to the other end the fastest. Kerwin had a considerable height advantage, and took the gold easily.

But the true business up here was science—science in the service of the Earth's environment and industry. It seems as unlikely a relationship as Democrats and Republicans, but think about it. Not only was *Skylab* look-ing down at the ground from a 270-mile vantage point, a view unavailable to anyone other than those in a satellite, but the crew had observation and measuring instruments that had never existed before. Pete and NASA were keenly aware that without some serious down-to-Earth applications, *Skylab* would soon enough be a distant memory, as Apollo was rapidly be-coming. The public wouldn't long pay for the Conrad Olympics or the Vel-cro darts the crew had been given, no matter how cool it looked on the evening news.

Pete and Joe and Paul were quickly doing eight-hour workdays with cam-eras, radar, infrared, and spectrometry; studying insect infestations in Texas, flooding in Africa, south Atlantic currents, typhoons gathering near Java, gypsum deposits in New Mexico, strip mining in Kentucky and West Vir-ginia; and logging the data in onboard and Earthbound computers.

*Skylab* helped Venezuela find the oil that exploded them into first-world status, and, as a key trading partner of the United States, the South Amer-ican nation would keep OPEC from literally bringing us to a grinding halt, which was suddenly a real possibility brought home by the Arab Oil Em-bargo of '73.

They'd even be uninvited witnesses to a supersecret atmospheric test of a Chinese atomic weapon, and supply the CIA with all the appropriate data. What could the Chinese do about it? Scramble MiGs 270 miles up to chase *Skylab* out of the demilitarized zone of space? *Just observing, Mr. Chairman.*

The $2.6 billion to gather in two weeks what corporations, universities, and governments would otherwise have spent ten times that amount on, in dollars and years, was the justification of the expense of a space program. And as Pete saw it, the guarantor of their future. This thing was a bargain.

Pete agreed that billions and billions to go to the Moon or Mars just to pick up rocks and take pictures was absurd, and a waste. But if spaceflight could be used to find and manage resources, make money for industries, help protect Earth's environment, deliver to America and the world all the medical, communications, and computer breakthroughs the program was already yielding, and perhaps even help to solve all these very real problems the critics of the program were citing, it was worth every penny.

It was a lot more than Velcro that NASA was offering the world. The cost-benefit analysis of *Skylab* should be as plain to everyone as the nose on President Nixon's face.

And, oh, man, had the ride changed since Pete's "eight days in a garbage can" aboard *Gemini 5* with Gordo Cooper. *Skylab* was the size of a decent house, and solved nearly every function and comfort issue the thirty-some-odd previous manned NASA flights had raised. For instance:

- Food: No more two-by-two-foot food lockers with flat bags of God only knew what, until you opened it and squirt-gunned not-very-hot fuel-cell water into it. This bird came with a ten-by-ten-foot kitchen! And none of that freeze-dried bilge, either. The veteran of three previous flights, Commander Pete would have retched at the sight and smell of one more cup of lukewarm reconstituted powdered minestrone; there'd be none of that. The crew had twenty containers of food on board, five of them frozen, like meats and vegetables and desserts—all microwaveable, and good.

- Shower: Sure, it was just a cylindrical curtain bag you zipped yourself into and hit a button for a quick jet of warm water and a vacuum drier . . . but, hey. It was a lot more than a no-rinse towelette, like the first three. It was a real shower!

- The "facilities": Real flushing toilets—which beat those miserable Mylar bags they'd had to tape to their backside and do their business while their copilot looked the other way (or in Dick Gordon's case, mocked Pete mercilessly). Even in the ultraadvanced Apollo days, Pete described the command module's head as "taking a dump in a can of Campbell's pork and beans . . . the *little* one."

- Data storage and retrieval: Three computer workstations, a mile and a half of printer paper, a substantial improvement over cuff checklists and upside-down writing pens. *Skylab* was actually the first full deployment of a computerized inventory-control system. Twenty thousand items were bar-coded, tracked, and counted. *Skylab* was the test of the system, which was a big deal then. Now, you'd be hard-pressed to find a midnight 7-Eleven clerk who couldn't run the same thing in his sleep.

- Clothes and shoes: These boys were looking sharp now. No more blue and white; NASA went gold on *Skylab*. The flight suits with zippers and Velcro turned into shorts and mock turtlenecks with a couple yanks. Ten pockets. Each guy had a color-coded Snoopy to ID his garment as his own; the commander got red. The shoes had canvas tops with aluminum soles, and removable cleats to fit into the mesh flooring, so the astronauts could walk on the walls and "ceiling" like flies. The crew even had 210 pieces of disposable underwear. If Pete had no other achievements to hang his spaceflight hat on, he'd be a legend for that one alone.

- Exercise: The Gemini and Apollo programs proved that long-duration spaceflight atrophies muscle and diminishes the body's capacity to do work. It's proven. Personal trainer Joe Kerwin used Pete as his favorite "lab rat" up there, having him run, lift weights, and ride a stationary bike daily, then charted every physiological change. It should be no surprise that Pete returned to Earth after twenty-eight days in orbit in the best shape of the three, even if he had lost about a third of his strength and endurance.

Pete was damn proud of being the first man in history to ride a bicycle around the world in ninety minutes as *Skylab* completed a full orbit.

Each astronaut could take five books along. Pete's favorite was *Jonathan Livingston Seagull*. Personal music was allowed, and Pete naturally took Patsy Cline, Hank Williams, and Willie Nelson cassettes. Space science and country music just went together for him, even if the other two were getting a little weary of steel guitars and twang.

There were some preliminary plans for including wine in the galley, but someone from the press got wind of it, and that was the end of that. Orbital Prohibition would be strictly enforced in flight. Curiously, Dr. Kerwin refused to answer an interviewer's question years later—whether Commander Conrad, known to enjoy an after-work shooter, might perhaps have gotten around the NASA quartermaster on that one. The good doctor only smiled.

Like all the great rides in Pete's life, it ended too soon. After twenty-eight days, it was time to clean up for Al Bean's crew, who were champing at the bit to get up here, power the girl down, undock the CSM, and head home. Kerwin and Weitz were already out, strapping into the CSM; Pete was the last to go. One more quick check. He floated over to the window—the biggest window yet on a NASA spacecraft—and watched the sunrise coming over Australia, drifting quietly by underneath.

This was it, and he knew it. The ride was over for astronaut Pete Conrad. He was forty-three; it was time to bring her in for a landing, and go find a new ride. Make some money, maybe. Get to know his children before it was too late. Get to know his wife again, after twenty years of going like a man on fire. At least he was going out a winner.

Walking on the Moon had been great; he wouldn't have traded it for anything. But *Skylab* . . . God, he loved this beautiful flying barrel of a bird. From graph paper to shop floor to floating here in her cargo bay as she whistled over the Outback at seventeen thousand miles an hour, clearly visible to anyone on the ground who cared to look up at the night sky . . . this girl was his. He'd put his hurting baby back together again, and just like a country song, it was time to go, never to return. Hank Williams warbling in his head: "I'm so lonesome, I could cry."

He patted her bulkhead one last time, a gentle touch like a father's, saying good night to his child. Then he turned off the lights and gently closed the hatch.

# FORTY-ONE

**D**r. Chuck Ross had just begun the huge battery of crew evaluations on board the *Ticonderoga*, eight hundred miles southwest of San Diego, when the phone rang from the bridge.

"Dr. Ross, it's the White House on the phone."

"The crew is in the shower, Captain."

"The President wants to talk to *you*."

Me? The doctor was wary as he lifted the receiver. He'd been at NASA long enough to know that practical jokes rule the day once the crew is home safe.

"This is Chuck Ross."

"Dr. Ross, this is President Nixon." There were some great Nixon impersonators out there, but Chuck knew the real thing when he heard it. He also heard his voice go up an octave.

"Yes, sir, Mr. President."

"I understand the crew is under quarantine. Just wanted to know how they were holding up."

"Terrific, sir. Fit as fiddles." It was a half-truth. Conrad was completely normal, as would be expected after spaceflight number four and his daily exercise regiment. Weitz was so-so, but Kerwin was pretty wobbly. *Why is he talking to me?* Chuck could only think.

"Fine. Super. I'd love to host the crew out here at the western White House for a little reception. How soon do you think you could release them?"

"Well, sir . . ." The standard procedure was several days "in the can," as they called quarantine—under heavy observation, decontamination, and careful reintroduction to Earth air and food. That concept being relative, of course, as Conrad was already smoking a fat smuggled-in Cuban cigar, having already thrown back a celebratory shot of whiskey.

"I only ask, Dr. Ross, because I have a guest here this weekend who would be awfully keen on meeting them."

Ross knew full well who it was: Leonid Brezhnev, the General Secretary of the Communist Party, who was there discussing such light and breezy topics as the Strategic Arms Limitation Treaty. The correct answer to the question should have been, "two or three weeks." The typically protective doctor stood his ground as official flight surgeon but Houston had already given permission for the crew to go, providing they wore surgical masks for their protection.

"As soon as you'd like, Mr. President."

Dr. Ross was on a Sea King helicopter with Pete and the guys the next morning, arriving at Marine Corps Air Station El Toro by nine, immediately tearing off the base in a bulletproof Secret Service car. Ten minutes later they roared off the freeway, turned onto a surface street, and were promptly pulled over by a San Clemente cop who thought it odd that four men were sitting in the back of a station wagon going almost eighty through a very sleepy beach town on a Sunday morning, three of them wearing surgical masks. He didn't even glance at the Secret Service guy's ID.

"Gentlemen, take your masks off."

"Officer, these men have just returned from space."

"Yeah, right. Drop 'em. *Now.*"

Weitz was nervous, Kerwin about to puke, Conrad trembling with laughter, but they complied.

"How about some ID?"

"Look, pal . . ." The Secret Service guy was getting pissed. "They're the NASA astronauts. You know, *Skylab?*"

"What the hell is a *Skylab?*" He stared at Pete, the face vaguely familiar all of a sudden. "Wait a minute. Him, I've seen."

They got it sorted out eventually. The guys even signed autographs for the embarrassed cop's kids, and he escorted the station wagon to the gates of the Western White House. Masks back up, they could see Nixon and Brezhnev approaching on a golf cart with actor Chuck Connors as the car pulled to a stop inside.

"You know," Pete thought aloud, "here are the two most powerful men on Earth, with the Rifleman himself. I'm making a command decision. I for one am taking this mask off, and I'll take responsibility."

All three of *Skylab's* crew removed the things for the last time, and got out to meet their President and the guy from the other side.

Brezhnev was a big bear of a guy who joked and laughed through his translator. He was clearly at home with Nixon, clearly in awe of Pete and Joe and Paul as they whipped through some impromptu ceremony the protocol aides had thrown together for the cameras. Gifts were exchanged, but the Secret Service got strange about it suddenly, along with the Soviet security detail, and tried to intercept the gifts. Nixon glared, and the Secret Service backed off. Brezhnev nodded at his own, and they followed suit.

*You don't embarrass the chief, boys.*

Brezhnev backslapped Pete a moment later. "Secretary Brezhnev would like to cordially invite you and crew to Moscow for dinner," was the translation. "Name the date, Commander."

Once again, both sides' security guys and protocol aides looked nervous and chattered quietly into their headsets. We were, after all, enemies with these people. The two chiefs were here at the beach dickering over how many ICBMs each really needed to destroy the whole damn planet a hundred times over. Pete looked to his President, who ignored the protocol officers and nodded.

"I'll fly anywhere for a free meal, sir. But let me talk to my wife. I don't schedule a thing till I've cleared it with her."

You can search the photo archives if you'd like, but you will never see a bigger grin on the faces of the two most powerful men on the planet in 1973 than the moment Brezhnev's translator gave the general secretary Pete's answer.

# BOOK FOUR

# HARD
# LANDING

# FORTY-TWO

**February 13, 1996**
**Learjet N1OBD**
**Over the Persian Gulf**
**0943 Zulu**

**"T**his isn't right," the astronaut whispered to himself, not wanting to wake anybody. The numbers on the GPS display didn't match up with the note-card in his hand, and flashed accordingly. Pete loved gizmos, was always the first guy in line buying the latest, greatest thing at Circuit City or CompUSA, but he also knew from the school of hard knocks that the more moving parts, even if they are just electrons, the more there is to go wrong. Murphy's Law had yet to be repealed in 1996.

The voice of the Algerian controller had just dripped with resentment when he'd given him these coordinates, and Pete wondered if maybe they were wrong. He also wondered if it was an accident.

The Lear wasn't exactly in friendly territory right now. From North Africa across the Arabian Peninsula and over the Persian Gulf, across Red China to the eastern end of Russia, friendly responses to American accents would be the exception, not the rule.

Military people who've been around the world know all about it. Jealousy, envy, and hate come with the territory of being an American abroad, especially around here. Whether it was politically correct or not—like he cared— the hair on the back of his neck told Pete that the voice on the other end of that VHF hated his guts, for no other reason than that he was an American, flying the very symbol of capitalist excess, a Learjet, over the man's war-ravaged airspace.

*What the hell ever.* There was really no point in a discussion on the geopolitical climate right now. Pete was at the controls; they were going six hundred miles an hour at 42,000 feet over Burma, with GPS numbers flashing at him, telling him what he already knew, the sickest feeling a pilot can ever know.

Pete was lost. And if that wasn't bad enough, he couldn't ignore the message on his chart: WARNING—Aircraft infringing on Chinese Territorial Airspace may be fired upon without warning.


**"M**ark, you gotta help me here."

Calkins was alert in an instant. "What is it?"

"I'm not sure about this radio frequency we're on."

Mark saw the flashing GPS, nodded seriously. "We're only seven minutes from the border. We need to raise Chinese air traffic control."

Mark shared Pete's alarm. They'd been warned by the State Department when they filed their flight plan that the welcome mat would not be out all over the world—singling out Iran along with Algeria, Libya, Iraq, and a couple others to avoid altogether. And if you couldn't avoid them, pray to God you could sail on by and not have to make an emergency landing. Stay on course and don't run out of fuel—which would happen soon enough if they had to circle outside of the Chinese border, as Pete feared.

Pete worked the VHF radios on the left side, while Mark tried different HF channels on the right.

"Yangon Control, Yangon Control, November One Zero Bravo Delta. Does anybody copy?"

Silence.

"Keep trying." Pete anxiously viewed the GPS display. Only three minutes to the border.

"Yangon Control, Yangon Control, November One Zero Bravo Delta. Does anybody copy?"

"Try Kunming Control on VHF frequency 133.6," a miraculous voice returned in perfect English from the HF radio. Pete wasted no time dialing in the frequency. One minute from the border. Where did that transmission come from? They would never know.

"Kunming Control, Kunming Control, November One Zero Bravo Delta," Pete relayed, raising a gruff voice on the other end.

"Learjet November 10BD, you are cleared to enter Chinese airspace via Route A599, flight level 12,500 meters."

"Well, my Chinese friend," Pete said with a relieved smile, "you may be on the watch list, but you are a pro." He stretched big. "You ready to drive? I'm whupped."

"Yeah, Pete. Let me at her." They did the seat-switch ballet, trying not to step on the feet of the other two guys.

"I was in this whiteout once," Mark remembered as he settled into the left seat. "Up around Nome. I hadn't slept in two days, the compass was screwy, I was low on fuel and running heavy. I couldn't see a thing—not ahead, behind, nothing. I had no idea where I was or what to do. It's the worst feeling in the world, isn't it. Being lost?"

Pete nodded silently. Mark suddenly felt a little pretentious, trading war stories with a guy who had flown to the Moon and back. "I don't guess an astronaut feels that very much."

"Oh. You'd be surprised."

# FORTY-THREE

**P**ete had been in his first civilian job since 1950 for precisely one week when he realized he'd made the mistake of his life. He'd sold the house in Houston, pulled the boys out of school, and moved the Conrads to Denver so he could go to work for his friend Bill Daniels at American Television and Communications Corporation. He negotiated a screaming good salary, and he was building a house on the up-and-coming southeast side of town, and getting in on the ground floor of what would become one of the most profitable industries in America and the world—cable television.

He settled into a new cockpit, one with six drawers, a credenza, and a vice president placard. And a few days into it, the most trusted gauge the pilot had, the gut meter, was pegged in the red. This was the wrong course, in the wrong craft.

And Pete knew it.

\* \* \*

**C**ongress had gutted NASA's budget for fiscally sound reasons after Apollo. The race to the Moon had been won, and there was no reason to continue the bottomless funding. Even *Skylab*, ambitious and successful as it was, became a much-reduced and streamlined operation compared to its original mission.

The Space Transport System, also known as the Space Shuttle, was actually on the drawing boards during Apollo, envisioned as the vehicle to get back and forth from *Skylab* as it ramped up into a permanent space station, a launching point for a lunar colony and a Mars mission. Pete was actually tapped to head up the shuttle program, but declined, knowing that with the post-Apollo dollars Uncle Sam was offering NASA to build it, it was ten years off at least.

And when it did manage to get up and flying, he wasn't crazy about the design. Even on the volatile *Saturn 5*, which could leave a Hiroshima-sized hole in the ground with a major malfunction, he had an abort handle. He could eject off the rocket if he had to, and he almost did once. But for the first two minutes of the shuttle's flight, at least at the beginning of the program, the astronauts didn't have that option. If there was a problem inside those two minutes, the crew was strapped onto that solid rocket booster. And if something went wrong with *it* . . .

And it would in January of 1986. Something went very wrong.

It was obvious that there would be no permanent space station, no colony on the Moon, and certainly no manned mission to Mars. And after a semi-mutiny by a surly crew aboard *Skylab IV,* even that was mothballed.

Pete could see the writing on the wall: The flying at NASA was done—and he'd come there to fly. He retired at the end of 1973.

He called Al Shepard, now back in the Navy. "Al, I'm thinking of coming back in."

"Don't do it, Pete."

"Why do you say that?"

"I know why you want to: You want to fly. But they won't let you. Your rank's too high."

"Come on."

"I'm serious, Pete. After the Moon, they'll promote you all the way up to admiral. It's a hell of a way for a test pilot to die. You want my advice? Go out and make some money."

Bill Daniels had been a Navy fighter pilot in the Second World War, and a decorated hero. After a Japanese kamikaze pilot slammed his Zero into the deck of the USS *Intrepid* in November 1944, Bill was the first guy below, freeing survivors from the twisted, white-hot metal of the flight deck till they pulled him out just before it blew. He was credited with saving the lives of more than fifty sailors that day, and very deservedly received the Bronze Star.

These were the qualities he brought to his business: loyalty, persistence, and a willingness to do whatever it took to prevail. By the launch of *Gemini* 5 in 1965, which he attended, Bill was already a very successful and wealthy man. After laughing out loud at a TV interview with rookie astronaut Pete Conrad, Bill cashed in a couple favors owed him to meet this wisecracking rocket jock. They were lifelong friends before their first dinner together was finished.

They had a lot in common: mostly the ride. Bill would drop whatever he was doing when Pete would call, flying something nearby with an empty seat. When Bill was ready to buy his first airplane, Pete was right there with him, advising, warning, and finally helping select the brand-new Learjet.

And then there were the cars.

Pete loved cars, and no other car captured his heart and soul like the Chevy Corvette—the automotive equivalent of the F-4. The original ones didn't have quite the sleek, aerodynamic lines of the later models; the car just pulsated with what every boy loves in his four wheels: *power and speed*. By the time he was named commander of *Apollo 12*, Pete owned two of them. And was quite proficient in their high-speed operation.

It's no breaking story that the rocket guys liked to race with each other, nor should it be any big surprise. It's difficult to imagine test pilots who would routinely top out past the speed of sound, pushing an aircraft to its limits and beyond, driving a sensible six-cylinder family sedan. And military pilots being more competitive than the vast majority of human beings, it's even more difficult to imagine them not lining up for a little test of their high-speed skills now and again.

For Pete and Al Shepard, it was a weekly ritual. Same with Gordon. Be it down at Cocoa Beach, or over at Ellington Field, or right out of the gates of the Cape, only flying lit Conrad's candle like the roar of that 400-plus horse-power Vette. Naturally, GM president and production shepherd of Chevy's premier muscle car Ed Cole, having heard of the astronaut's love and lust for his baby, was beyond thrilled to give him one, as he had with most of the Mercury guys before. And while he was at it, why not give one to Pete's entire *Apollo 12* crew? And hell, why stop there? Florida Chevy dealer Jim Rathmann asked. Why not give one to all the Apollo astronauts? And so GM did, brand-spanking-new 1969 Corvette Stingrays, making sure Conrad's crew got the gold ones.

When Pete stomped the gas on a deserted highway one day, slamming him and Bill into their seats like they'd just lit off a *Saturn 5* engine behind them, Bill was hooked. It didn't take long before the two of them were racing each other, and going to driving clinics and, of course, going to the mecca of all speed fans with Rathmann and Cole: the Indianapolis 500. When Pete, Dick Gordon, and Bill were hosted one year at the mother of all car races by friend Bill Yeager, it was only a matter of time before Bill Daniels would own a Formula car himself, especially after seeing businessman and race car owner John Mecom's face while he described the year he'd won it all.

Indy was where the lifelong friendship between Bill and Pete was truly forged. And never more so than when they rode in the pace car together in 1976.

Both men loved a good steak, a good Scotch, and a good joke. And they vowed that when Pete was finished flying around in the stars, he'd come back down and make some serious dough on Earth with Bill.

Bill had gotten a simple idea in front of his snowy-pictured television one afternoon outside of Denver. It was actually borne out of extreme frustration as he was missing a championship boxing match. And that simple idea would end up changing television forever.

Denver television stations, like most, had a theoretical broadcasting range of a hundred miles or so, with a decent tower. But the actual range was about half that, with the Rocky Mountains getting in the way of the signal. Bill conceived of a statewide closed-circuit subscription cable system, delivering television to homes that couldn't get the signal from Denver over the air. The prototype worked so well, and the coming generation of communications satellites was a technology literally searching for a larger application. . . . The global implications were exciting, to say the least.

Bill conceived and funded American Television and Communications in 1968, and took the company public four years later. Cable television was born, and calling Bill Daniels its "father" was not really an exaggeration.

When Pete told him he'd be leaving NASA and looking for a real job, Bill had a brilliant idea.

"Hey, Conrad. You remember the promise we made each other?"

"You were gonna make me filthy stinkin' rich, right?"

"I want you to come to Denver. I'm gonna give you a ridiculous sum of money to be a cable television executive."

"Bill, I'm a pilot. I don't know jack-shit about cable television. I don't know jack-shit about *business*."

"You got the fastest mouth in the South, everybody from here to eternity wants to buy you a drink, and I've got a feeling you could sell water to a fish. Get your ass up here, Conrad."

So he did. The new chief operating officer and VP of operations reported to CEO Monty Rifkin in January of '74.


It was a *job*. Pete had never had a job, really. Not since cutting weeds and gassing planes out at Paoli Field had Pete Conrad traded his time simply for money. The Navy, test piloting, NASA . . . yeah, he got paid for all of them—about a tenth what Bill was paying him now—but money had never mattered since he'd begun flying professionally. The particulars of life were taken care of, so he could focus on what he did best, and give that to a team.

Suddenly he wasn't doing what he did best. He didn't feel part of any team; there was no "Something Bigger than Myself" in this suite of offices. Pete was surviving the corporate jungle, and neither Princeton nor the Navy nor NASA had trained him for that: what alliances to strike, which ones *not* to strike, who might be plotting behind his back because they were pissed off some rocket jock came in from the outside and leapfrogged five guys to become their boss. And for God's sake, one never, ever spoke what was *really* on his mind.

The pilot hadn't learned this set of procedures, this pattern of thinking. Pete Conrad couldn't do anything *but* speak his mind. Strategic alliances? Spreadsheets? Quarterly reports? Corporate politics? This was what a chief operations officer did in the corner office with a cute secretary, a view, and an expense account?

He lived for the few hours a week he actually got to do "operations": looking at schematics, talking with engineers, visiting with the boys in the field dropping wire into a brand-new neighborhood, flying—oh, Lord, yes, *flying!*— Bill to Washington to lobby some congressman or FCC boy who wanted Pete to do nothing *but* speak his mind all night long over shooters, if he would (and he would). But those hours were so few. The rest were traded for that ridiculous sum of money, doing something he wasn't trained to do, wasn't great at, and didn't like.

For this he left the astronaut corps?

Pete spoke his mind once too often. When a personality conflict ended the career of his one true friend at ATC other than Bill—with Pete pulling hatchet-man duty because the CEO wouldn't do it himself—it was the last straw. Pete blazed into Monty Rifkin's office and called it like he saw it. Rifkin didn't much care for the dressing-down, especially from a loose cannon whose only qualification was being famous and the friend of the chairman of the board.

The dickens of it was, the SOB was right.

Pete stopped long enough in his office to dictate a resignation letter, throw his things in a cardboard box, and get the hell out of there.

"Never work for the money," his father had taught him. "Be a part of something." The older Pete got, the smarter his old man became.

# FORTY-FOUR

**"P**ete, it's time for you to meet my Pussy." The old man's eyes twinkled in the firelight as his lovely and much-younger wife entered the drawing room, all smiles. Pete gagged on the martini halfway down his gullet, felt the white-hot burn of gin in his nostrils, and called on all his training in physical control under high-stress conditions not to explode in a volcano of laughter.

The old man was James S. "Old Mac" McDonnell, founder, chairman, and *boss* of McDonnell Douglas Aircraft. North of seventy now, Old Mac came from an era when "Pussy" was a fine and appropriate pet name for Priscilla, the lovely wife who extended her hand.

"Pete Conrad. It's a pleasure to meet you . . . Pussy." *Thank God Gordon and Bean-o aren't here*, he thought.

Old Mac was smitten with the young man sitting on his couch here in the biggest mansion in Saint Louis, but not because of the NASA track record. It didn't hurt him any, but Pete was a pilot and an engineer. He knew airplanes. He loved airplanes. He *lived* airplanes. Just as Old Mac had for most of his seventy-plus years.

"I saw you were up for the FAA job."

"Yes, sir. But I didn't get to first base with the Senate."

It was true. Pete was a personal favorite of new President Gerald Ford's to take the helm of the agency in late 1974, and no one was more qualified to do so. But a majority-Democrat Congress was still in a combative mood after Nixon's fall from grace, and decided Pete's military career worked against the interests of a civilian bureaucracy.

"That's typical government. You're perfect for the job, so of course you didn't get it." Pussy poured more martinis.

Pete liked this guy too, an old Scotsman who loved his company, loved flying, loved that bottom line. He personally ran the largest aircraft company in the world—eighty thousand employees, a full executive force, but every buck, every decision ultimately ended with him. He could sure as hell speak *his* mind. "So what can you do, Pete Conrad?"

"Well, sir, frankly . . . I'm not much of an executive. I like people. I like airplanes. And I *love* to fly."

Perfect. He didn't play the astronaut card, didn't puff himself up, didn't bullshit him. The old man smiled, trusting his own gut meter, which was pegged in the green.

"I've got just the job for you."

**D**id he ever. Pete took over international commercial sales after learning the ropes of the company, and learning their aircraft inside and out. Jobs didn't get much better. Already rated in multiengines, Pete checked out in the DC-10, and suddenly found himself flying around the world, demonstrating the aircraft, taking transportation ministers and even heads of state for rides, then telling them stories over steaks and highballs till the wee hours in whatever time zone he found himself in. He never tired of it, never had to hard-sell anybody.

It really wasn't fair to the other international sales guys. Who would you rather sit down with? Bob the great guy, business-school grad with a sales and marketing background, who could write a smoking contract? Or one of twelve men in history who'd walked on the Moon? And a guy who'd be happy to take you up in a DC-10, flying the damn thing himself, and hand you the controls if you wanted to "get a feel for it."

It was like shooting fish in a barrel. The DC-10 was *the* wide-body jet in the seventies, and now, in the eyes of the world's commercial aircraft community, came with the seal of approval of one of America's finest, a real pilot and an astronaut—not some guy paid to sell it.

Sales went through the roof. The company's stock was soaring, and Pete was enjoying a "paid vacation," as he called it, even in the presence of Old Mac himself, who couldn't pay him too much.

On one particular sales call, Pete stepped out of an elevator in Taiwan, paying a visit to China Airlines, and almost had a heart attack—seeing thirty employees applauding and bowing to him, a WELCOME, CAPTAIN CONARD (yes, they mispelled his name) banner hung high and proud across the lobby.

And in the handshakes, and bows, autographs, and glasses of sake as they celebrated a new contract with a genuine American hero, a strange coldness began to creep into that hero's soul.

Something didn't feel right.


**F**ame is a drug. Some crave it, some run from it, but there's no disputing the fact: It changes everything. Things feel staged. Performed. Life itself becomes less real when you know an entire room is looking at you, recognizing you, whispering about you.

It's not like it was new to Pete. The astronauts really had been rock stars in the Mercury, Gemini, and Apollo days, with every—yes, *every*—favor offered to them that was offered to the Rolling Stones. People want to be with celebrities, be seen with celebrities, sleep with celebrities. It's as old as dirt.

But for an astronaut, fame was a distraction, albeit a fun one, sometimes. It wasn't so damn bad, getting a free Corvette just because a Florida Chevy dealer wanted to give you one. Signing autographs wasn't the worst thing in the world; neither was meeting countless people who just wanted to meet—to maybe touch—a guy who'd done what man has dreamed of since he looked up from the first campfire.

It was part of the job. But it wasn't *the* job. An astronaut's eyes and heart and mind were focused on the mission. Fame and groupies and all of it were just the extras that came with it, and something for the guys to laugh about when they were alone together, which was most of the time.

But Pete wasn't alone with the guys anymore. He was truly alone in this Taiwan hotel room, staring at some woman's phone number on a matchbook. He wasn't an astronaut anymore. He was an *ex*-astronaut. And he wasn't so sure those executives and ministers and heads of state weren't spending their nation's money on the DC-10 because it was a great plane, but just to rub up next to a guy who'd set foot on the Moon.

Did he dial this woman's number or not? Half a world away were Jane and his boys; only Christopher was living at home now. They felt as far away as when he was looking down on them from the Moon. And it was nobody's fault but his own.

The hero. The astronaut. The number one sales guy in the company. All alone in a hotel room.

He lifted the phone.

# FORTY-FIVE

On May 25, 1979, American Airlines Flight 191—a DC-10—lost an engine, literally, and fell out of the sky departing Chicago's O'Hare airport, killing all 271 people on board, plus two more on the ground.

And all hell broke loose.

Suddenly the much-vaunted DC-10 was "unsafe at any speed," which had been Ralph Nader's line about the rear-engined Chevrolet Corvair in the early 1960s. The press speculation was out of control, saying that McDonnell Douglas had supposedly "boondoggled" American Airlines and Continental and a host of other carriers into buying fleets of them, and the company engaged in "reckless cost cutting" and "unfair labor practices" that made an accident like this "inevitable." Some articles even hinted at company sabotage and plain incompetence. In one afternoon, the DC-10 went from the pinnacle of aerospace achievement to the symbol of corporate greed and recklessness.

Echoes of the Apollo fire and NASA in 1967.

Old Mac was deeply disturbed by the crash, and completely unprepared for this sandbag from the media. He summoned Pete into his office after hours, the twinkle gone from his eyes. He was morose, exhausted, and worried.

"Pete, you've investigated this sort of . . . thing before?" He didn't even want to use the word *crash*.

"Mr. Mac," Pete answered, "you've been in this business a lot longer than I have. You know it. You can't engineer out the risk. It's awful. But it happens."

"But a bolt? A goddamn bolt fails, and an engine falls off? What happened?!" he roared back.

"That's preliminary. And I don't buy it."

"Yeah, but the papers do. And the networks."

"That's their thing."

"I want you to jump into this, Pete. I don't care who you piss off; I want you in the middle of it. I need some answers from somebody I trust. Don't tell me what I want to hear; tell me the truth."

"Okay, Mr. Mac. I will."

And the engineer went to work. As an investigator and an employee of McDonnell Douglas, Pete was met with a boatload of suspicion from American, the FAA, and the National Transportation Safety Board. He had to fight to get a look at the physical evidence, which he knew would tell the tale. And after years of bluster and speculation and the grounding of every DC-10 in the United States, the official findings of the NTSB were the same that Pete reported to Old Mac scarcely a month after the crash: It was a lot more than a bolt; it was a system failure. And the failure did not originate with McDonnell Douglas.

The one definitive photograph of Flight 191 showed the jet horrifically rolling over onto its back just before hitting a field a mile from O'Hare and disintegrating. The 13,500-pound engine was already gone; eyewitnesses had seen it actually separate entirely from the left wing, taking most of the leading edge with it. It flew ahead of the jet with a massive thrust before bouncing down the end of Runway 32-R. That told Pete the engine hadn't just dropped off; the entire mounting pylon had given way to the thrust.

Next, Pete was able to convince the NTSB guys to let him listen to the cockpit recordings from the "black box." Nothing unusual: The pilots, unable to see what was happening on that left wing—which was the only design flaw Pete ever saw in the DC-10—believed they had an engine failure just as the plane rotated skyward, something that ordinarily would not have been a catastrophe. But even if they could see what had actually happened, there was nothing they could have done. Pilot error was ruled out, surprising no one.

Pete's gut told him the problem originated in the garage. And when he was allowed to view the subpoenaed maintenance records, his gut was proved accurate as ever.

It isn't easy or cheap to service an airplane's engine. In the case of the DC-10, it took removing the entire pylon structure with the engine, a delicate and very time-consuming task. And just like in any business, time is money. Some maintenance crews were cutting the two hundred man-hours by more than half by lifting the things off—pylon and engine together—*with a forklift*. Something clearly not recommended by the manufacturer.

This was Pete's "aha" moment. The service records of aircraft N110AA looked correct enough—to someone who didn't know how to look deeper. The conclusion the NTSB took a year to form took Pete one evening in a Chicago hotel room, after reviewing not the maintenance schedules and procedure summaries themselves, but the billable man-hours for engine servicing. There weren't enough of them. The only way the airline's maintenance guys in Tulsa could have done the work on these service records in the time they billed for was by following the "forklift" procedure, causing metal fatigue and structural damage.

Sure enough, during the grounding, four more American and two Continental DC-10s were found to have the same structural conditions in the mounting pylons that caused the engine to fall off N110AA. And the billable hours for servicing their engines were virtually identical.

McDonnell Douglas had strongly cautioned against this practice, but with no enforcement powers and little or no inspection access once the planes were in service, their warnings went unheeded, and even ignored. Now 273 people were dead. And Pete Conrad, concluding his first real accident investigation, knew why. It wasn't shoddy engineering or workmanship, it wasn't cover-ups and corruption, and it certainly wasn't sabotage. It was all about cutting corners to save money.

But "the bolt" was a better story. Easy to tell, easy to understand. And the more it got repeated, the truer it got in the public's mind. And suddenly everybody was an aviation expert. The DC-10 was aging; they should ground every one of them permanently and launch a formal investigation into McDonnell Douglas.

"We're not gonna take this lying down, Mister Mac," declared Pete. "We're gonna do the same thing we did at NASA—take the fight to them. We gotta get our message out."

What McDonnell Douglas needed in this perfect PR storm was a spokesman, a credible face and voice to speak for this company and the aircraft itself. Someone people trusted and would listen to. They looked at E. G. Marshall, Charlton Heston, Ronald Reagan. They even considered Bo Derek, the "perfect ten" herself.

But the obvious choice was working away in his office right next to Old Mac's at the company's Saint Louis headquarters: Pete Conrad.

Pete was a straight shooter, not a Hollywood guy. He knew the company because he worked there, and knew the DC-10 because he'd flown it. Who wouldn't listen to a NASA astronaut? He wasn't a household name anymore, but people knew who he was. Besides, Pete was comfortable on camera, unlike some of his fellow astronauts. He'd done commercials for Pepsi, Avis, Days Inn. His "Do you know me?" American Express spot was still running after being on the air for six or seven years.

Every salesman or pitchman in the world will tell you that half the battle is believing in what you're selling; then you tell it like it is. Pete told it like it was—no more, no less. He believed in McDonnell Douglas, believed in the DC-10, and he sure as hell believed in flying.

Americans remembered Pete's face when they saw it on television and in the magazines and newspapers as he took a good company's fight to the people. His message was simple: We grieve the loss, but don't blame the plane.

This wasn't an actor or a paid spokesman or a PR guy. This was somebody Americans trusted, and in the post-Watergate era, that was a short list indeed in the political and business communities. Give people time, and they filter out the noise and hysteria, the drumbeat of reporters and talking heads with their own agenda, and think matters through for themselves.

By the time the National Transportation and Safety Board issued its findings on the cause of the crash, Pete's conclusions had been accepted as fact. Investigators and aviation people noticed; Pete Conrad became an expert witness and consultant in scores of accident investigations in the coming years. The company recovered and moved on.

But things were never the same. The DC-10 was on her way out. As was Old Mac. After a series of strokes, he died a few months later.


Pete's "paid vacation" at the company seemed to end the next workweek.

The DC-10 incident was another one of those instantaneous catalysts for change. Overnight the culture inside the company went from bold and visionary to outright cautious and "corporate." Regardless that the company had been exonerated for any wrongdoing in the accident, and regardless of Pete's public relations success, the damage was done. And as the last of the wide-bodies was mothballed or sold to a foreign carrier or the occasional Saudi prince, everybody associated with the DC-10 was subtly marginalized.

Cocktail-napkin ideas Pete and the old man or some like-minded engineers would draw up over drinks or in the breakroom now had to go through "proper channels." Legal review. Correct proposal format and language. And God help him if every vice president worldwide wasn't cc'ed on every document he generated.

Which had never been his strong suit anyway. Old Mac had hired Pete because he was a people guy, a pilot, and a straight shooter. Suddenly those didn't seem to be assets in the MBA-worshiping corporate climate of the eighties. Old Mac was gone, and Pete Conrad wasn't flying their jets much anymore. He was pushing paper around a desk.


And as if Pete needed another symbol that his dream ride was coming to an end in the summer of 1979, *Skylab* came crashing back to Earth in July— after only three missions, and barely a year of manned service. She could have supported a hundred missions. Could have launched a space habitat, a lunar colony, a permanent orbiting base so the human race could do what we are wired to do—reach higher.

But NASA had left her dark, cold, and alone up there. Left to die by an agency out of money and a public that didn't care anymore. And Johnny Carson had 'em rolling in the aisles with joke after joke about it. Pete's baby, falling to pieces like Patsy Cline over western Australia. All by herself, no direction anymore, forgotten.

# FORTY-SIX

**"M**idlife crisis," the woman sneered derisively to her friend, nodding her head at the gap-toothed middle-ager swinging a leather-chapped leg over his Harley-Davidson. *What the hell,* Pete thought. *She's probably right.* He fired up a Marlboro, kick-started the bike, and headed out of the parking lot of the Kwik-Sak, off for a cold afternoon spin in January of 1986, for no other reason than to *ride*.

It was new to him, riding just to ride. He'd never really done that, not since he was a boy. They all had a purpose, a destination, a job. Fighter aircraft, centrifuges, Corvettes to work, Formula Cars, the *Saturn* 5 to space . . . hell, even down at the ranch, which he had bought from the family after Jane's mother passed away, if Pete was on the back of a horse, it was to *do* something.

But not today. The space shuttle *Challenger* had just gone down. Pete watched the replay at his McDonnell Douglas office, and wept like the rest of us. Not so much for the crash, though he certainly grieved the loss of seven astronauts; it was as much for his beloved NASA family, how the dream had spun out of control on them and blown into a million pieces today. And how they might not recover from it for a long, long time.

Pete wouldn't need Richard Feynman and the *Challenger* Commission to tell him how and why it had happened. With an ultratight budget, a hurried schedule, pressure from inside and out to launch *on* that schedule, a predictable culture of fear among controllers and engineers whose careers were on the line, and seven people locked onto an SRB that blew because a rubber O-ring froze and failed because it was too goddamn cold to launch, but they did anyway . . . ?

*Save the money,* Pete thought. *Give me a call.*

He let the bike stretch out and roar on a lonely highway going nowhere. It seemed like this was the only place he could really think anymore—on the bike. There was a lot of sorting out to do. The coldness he'd felt creeping across his life had just about swallowed him up now. The news today was one more drink from the same bitter cup.

What had gone wrong? And how the hell could he fix it? Like, *now.*


Jane was still beautiful, the perfect wife and mother. But one rare morning when he was actually home, Pete watched her sleeping and wondered who in the world she was. He didn't know this woman anymore. He wasn't sure he ever had. They were kids—twenty-three!—when they got married. He was in Pensacola for sixteen weeks right after the honeymoon, calling only on the weekends. Then deployed with the fleet. Then flight test. Gemini. Apollo. *Skylab.* When were they even together to have kids?

Married more than thirty years, and they were just going through the motions—acting their parts, reading the lines. He couldn't even remember the last time he'd had a deeper conversation than household accounting or their schedule for the next month. He never seemed to be home anymore, jetting back and forth between Saint Louis and Long Beach and Houston and Denver and God knew where the hell else. Just to keep moving. Keep busy. And the hell of it was, he knew it all fell on him ultimately.

Big life, big price.

Peter, Andy, and Tom Conrad were men now, pursuing careers and families. Even Christopher had graduated from college, wanted to be a vet.

*When did this happen?*

Could twenty years have really passed since the NASA hero was taking them out to Ellington AFB to watch the jets come in, feeling like only a father can, seeing their worshipful eyes as he strapped into a hissing, screaming jet and dropped the canopy, and waved so long? He took them on trips to the Cape. He even got them into the Oval Office with Gordo's kids. God, LBJ was a nervous wreck after Christopher picked up the red phone and sang "Row Row Row Your Boat" to somebody in the Kremlin. The boy could have started the big one right there and then.

They were grown and gone now. He wasn't a father anymore. Had he ever been?

An astronaut's day was not nine to five—that was for damn sure. As checklist- and procedure-oriented as that work was, Pete's life had never known routine. Not really.

From Pax River all the way through *Skylab,* he was home only on weekends . . . some weekends anyway. He'd show up at a parent-teacher conference, or the occasional ball game or school play, and people would nod approvingly at the astronaut father who'd somehow made the time to keep his priorities straight.

Right. Pete remembered the look in Andy's eyes as he delivered some overdue discipline one weekend, trying to cram a year's worth of parenting into one lecture. And he'd heard the hollowness of his own words.

First grader Peter had introduced his father at a show-and-tell appearance as an Indian chief who was a secret agent in the CIA. As hysterical as that story became in the Conrad family lore, Pete felt the sting of knowing that as little as that child saw of his daddy, it might just as well be true.

Some hero. That very morning he had stared at the den wall and the refrigerator: pictures of birthdays, ball games, milestones that marked a family's passage through time. Even a passing smile on an average day. And Dad had missed most of them.

He wondered if he hadn't missed the whole damn thing.

\*　　\*　　\*

**D**ownshift. He yanked the throttle back, nodding blankly at the silver fox in a Lincoln, probably headed out to the golf course, as he blew by him. Couldn't miss the disapproving look that practically shouted at him over the roaring motor: *Act your age!*

Okay, call it a midlife crisis. Call it transition, empty-nest syndrome. They could call it any damn thing they wanted; he wasn't listening.

Pete was fighting like hell not to fall into the "ex-astronaut" trap. Some of the guys had trouble when the program was over, especially the Apollo astronauts. It was well documented. People knew it. There was depression, trouble coping with everyday nonspaceflight life, shady business deals cashing in on the astronaut thing, alcoholism. . . .

That one scared him, frankly. Father never really beat it. Pete remembered being distracted during suit-up on his first Gemini flight, worried about Charles in the visitors' gallery. It ran in the blood, just like the wild hair. And Pete liked the evening shooter as much as the next guy. . . .

*Oh, my God,* he laughed to himself. *I'm a talk show.*

He pulled into his driveway as dusk became dark, and shut the bike down.

Okay, so there wasn't a "something bigger than himself" anymore. Old Mac was dead. The dream down at the Cape and Houston was over; hell, NASA would be grounded indefinitely now that a shuttle had gone down. The kids were gone, Jane was on every social committee and charity board from here to eternity, had a hundred friends keeping her well occupied, and why not? Her husband sure wasn't around.

*Suck it up,* Pete told himself. *Circumstances don't make the man; they define him.* He may not have liked putting on a tie every day instead of a flight suit, but it sure as hell beat sitting in a rocking chair, watching the rest of the world go by, thinking about the glory days. He'd just as soon go out on this Hog as rot to death.

No. He'd pull out of this stall. And the first place he'd start would be with his boys.

# FORTY-SEVEN

"**P**ete?" Jane was on the phone. Her voice was tight, choked with emotion. "Get home."

"What is it?"

"Just get home. Now."

Christopher Conrad had been living down at the Ranch in Uvalde, taking care of the horses and the herd, and feeding any stray that came his way, mending wings and paws every day. Connecting with the animals. It was a strange and wonderful gift the DNA gave him. Pete loved animals too, as had Father. He'd just been so busy flying for thirty years that he'd nearly forgotten.

Christopher had been feeling lousy for about a month. Headaches had given way to nausea, then dizziness. He'd sleep till noon and take a nap at three. He finally got a friend to take him to the doctor, who referred him to another, who sent him for tests at the University of Texas Medical Center in Austin.

It was lymphoma. Advanced, acute, and aggressive.

Pete arrived in commander mode, ready to do something. Anything. He immediately got on the phone with "Cruncher," his old flight surgeon Chuck Ross from the Nixon–Brezhnev adventure. "Chuck, I want your eyes on this."

"Okay, Pete, but I'm an osteopath. These are the best cancer guys in the business."

"I just want you in there, Cruncher. Tell me what you see, and tell me straight." He heard himself echoing Old Mac's words.

It was awful, was what it was. Chuck looked at the same test results the UT doctors did, and gasped at the numbers. They were off the charts. Christopher was ravaged with cancer; the best the doctors could do was slow it down.

He fought tears as he dialed the Conrads.

"Pete . . . I saw the results. It's malignant. Definitely advanced."

"Okay. So what do we do?"

"Well . . . there's radiation to start. Then chemotherapy. Transfusions."

"Let's get started right away."

"Yeah. I'm sure his doctors have."

"What kind of time frame are we looking at . . . you know, for recovery?"

*Oh, God,* Chuck thought. *He doesn't get it. Or more likely, he doesn't want to get it.* There'd be no recovery. Temporary remission, maybe, but this would take the youngest Conrad. And it wouldn't be long.

It wasn't. Christopher died in April of 1990 at the age of twenty-eight.


It was like coming out of a trance. Waking from a bad dream, only to realize it wasn't a dream. It was real.

Pete found himself at Cape Kennedy a few days after the funeral of his youngest son, with virtually no memory of how he'd gotten there. The entire week had swirled together as Christopher passed away; Pete found himself at the burial of his child, surrounded by sad cries and loving hugs and cards and casseroles and encouraging words.

Somehow he'd found his way to Ellington Field. He hopped a ride over to Cape Kennedy like it was the old days, and now here he stood. Like a satellite settling into geostationary orbit—for the first time in all his fifty-nine years, it seemed—Pete Conrad stood still.

At Launch Complex 19, where it had all begun as an astronaut for Pete, a lifetime ago.

Silent now, overgrown with weeds, the pad and gantry were rusting in the moist Florida air, paint peeling. Pad 19 had long since used up its usefulness, giving way to Complex 39, which launched Apollo, *Skylab,* the shuttle, and a host of other missiles. Now Pad 19 just sat quietly, decaying in the wind and rain and sun, time leaving it behind. Just a relic of history now, without even a plaque commemorating the Mercury and Gemini flights that left from this very spot. How long till all of this was gone? It would become a nice little gated community of cul-de-sacs, greenbelts, and overpriced seaside homes, whose occupants would live their own dreams, having no clue what had happened here a few generations back.

Pete remembered walking another Florida beach with his father as a five-year-old, Charles patiently explaining the meaning of the phrase *footprints in the sands of time.* The boy watched in awe when the smartest man in the world was proved right yet again, as a gulf wave broke gently over their footprints, carrying them out with the tide.

Charles's footprints were as gone as this launch pad's now. As would be the astronaut's who stood here this humid Florida evening, the echoes of a roaring *Titan II* rocket rattling around in his memory.

As were Christopher's.

*Oh, dear God.* The sight of his child lying still, the life having gone from him. That wasn't him lying there, Pete's mind kept repeating. *Christopher is on his path, on his way now, out of pain.*

*Unlike me.*

The weeded asphalt blurred together with his tears. *Hold it together,* he told himself. He went down this checklist he'd made, subconsciously anticipating this day, despite his denial that it would actually come. Good memories, laughs, even things that made Pete crazy, like the boy's messy room. *Focus on the good. Focus on . . . Oh, hell, what does it matter? Any of it?*

He slid to the ground, straining to hear his son's voice far off in his memory, remembering the smell of his tiny head as a baby. Remembering also the pang of regret the astronaut hero had felt, watching him sleep, knowing he'd be gone again by the time he awoke. The touch of that tiny hand holding his, asking his daddy to take him with him to the moon.

And all the memories he didn't have.

"Oh, Christopher," he whispered to his boy, squeezing his eyes shut, trying to beat back the flood. "I'm so sorry. So . . . *sorry.*"

And all alone on Pad 19 at Cape Kennedy, with a rising Moon looking down coldly, Christopher Conrad's daddy buried his head in his hands, and cried like a baby.

**February 14, 1996**
**Learjet N10BD**
**Approaching Yuzhno-Sakhalinsk, Russia**
**0012 Zulu**

Same Moon. The astronaut looked out at it from the backseat with no emotion. Dan was up flying, Mark in the copilot's seat. Paul was still buried in his paperback.

"Must be one hell of a good book, Paul." Pete groaned, pulling himself off the floor.

Thayer smiled and shrugged sheepishly, wordlessly acknowledging to the other senior on board that this newfangled bird might be one trick too many to teach an old fighter-pilot dog. Pete smiled back, patting him on the shoulder. He'd had thousands of hours in jets, a bunch in this one these last six weeks. But only now was he feeling comfortable with her.

They were all tired, with six thousand miles and two stops to go. They were downbeat, too. The winds weren't nearly what they'd been forecast. At their present rate, even at maximum cruising speed, they'd come into Denver two hours off the record.

They hurried on the ground in Yuzhno-Sakhalinsk, but it was really just going through the motions. The temperature was hovering around zero at the end of this short, gray day. The Russians were quiet and respectful, neither friendly nor unfriendly. Two soldiers stood blankly by, looking the same to Pete as they did in the coldest days of the Cold War. It was curious that these people had once been our most dreaded enemies. Here, in the middle of Siberia, these somber folks didn't look like they could have ever threatened anyone.

"Mr. Conrad," asked the head of the American Consul here, "I know you gentlemen are pressed for time, but there's a woman here who's been waiting for six hours just to meet you." She nodded at a frail, dignified older woman shivering in the cold, apart from the quiet assembled onlookers. Not a day under eighty. "If you could just give her a moment of your time."

Pete glanced at Mark. Mark looked at his watch and sighed. What was he gonna say, *no?*

"Of course I can," answered Pete.

He stepped over and took the woman's tiny gloved hand. "I'm Pete Conrad. It's very nice to meet you."

"I am Irina," she whispered in thickly accented English, clearly fighting emotion.

"Thank you for waiting. I'm sorry we're late."

"My son is cosmonaut," she declared proudly. "You do not know, but he knows you."

"Really. What is his name?"

"His name . . ." She was struggling, "Viktor Patsayev. He . . . he . . ." Her eyes welled with tears. Pete recognized the name and softened, instantly taking her other hand.

"I know who he is." He took her in his arms, hugging her as she sobbed quietly. "We don't forget."

She composed herself, again the picture of old-world dignity. She kissed the astronaut's hand, then disappeared into the crowd.

"Who was he?" Mark asked, sealing the cabin door.

"*Soyuz Eleven.* They held the record for long duration in space till we broke it on *Skylab.*"

"Wow. That's pretty cool."

"Yeah. But their cabin depressurized on the way back in. When the recovery guys opened the hatch, all three of them were dead."

"Her son . . ."

"Yup." Pete belted himself in as Dan powered the Lear up for the runway.

Somewhere over the North Pacific, Mark screwed on his courage. He was in the back right seat, failing miserably at his attempt at a nap. He could see the dim glow from the cockpit lighting Pete's tired, craggy face as he looked out the window, somewhere in his thoughts. And where in the world might this guy's thoughts be . . . ?

This was the opportunity of a lifetime, spending two days in an airplane with one of the men who'd walked on the Moon, and Mark had been afraid to ask him one single question about it. *What the heck?* he thought. *I'll never have this chance again.*

"Pete, can I ask you something?"

"Sure, Mark."

"What do you think about when you look at the Moon?"

"Probably not what you think," Pete answered, looking back out the window. "I guess it makes me sad, mostly."

*"Sad?"* Mark couldn't believe it.

"Yeah. Kinda that 'what might have been' thing, you know. Hell, you'd think we'd never gotten there, looking at where we are today. We'd have been on Mars ten years ago if we'd just kept going."

"Why didn't we?"

"Money."

"Why does it always come down to that?"

"Because it does. It's not a bad thing. Money got us there, and it'll get us back." The astronaut smiled. "Sooner than you think."

# FORTY-EIGHT

**P**ilots, engineers and certainly astronauts are trained to recognize patterns. It's a way of thinking. It's problem solving, thinking past limitations. And it ultimately becomes how they see the world, from history to the present to the road ahead.

When Pete was flying for NASA, the patterns he was concerned with were procedures, checklists, and flight plans. Thinking in patterns, which he'd learned as a student pilot, was how he'd overcome one of the biggest limitations in his own life—*dyslexia*.

Now that Pete was in business, he applied the same method of thinking to the big picture of space—beyond NASA.

As unprecedented and quantum-leap fast as the achievements of the space program may appear, to Pete, the son of an investor, the whole thing followed a historical pattern, just on a much accelerated scale: Need begets innovation. Innovation begets achievement. And achievement begets *value*.

When some brave soul got the nerve to put a dug-out tree in the water a few thousand years ago, it was because he needed to get from point A to point B, and water was in his way. But the boat was powered by him. It didn't go fast and it didn't go far. And never would he take it out of sight of land—how would he get back?

Then the Phoenicians or the Chinese or the Africans noticed that a flat piece of cloth held tight in the wind would make the boat move a lot faster and a lot farther, and the cloth never got tired or homesick.

Then the really brave ones took a boat out of sight of land, and used the stars to guide them from place to place and home again. They crossed the ocean, then sailed around the world, even though "it couldn't be done."

The explorers changed history, helped build empires, even discovered a New World.

And, oh, yeah, made lots of money for their sponsors.

The pattern repeated itself with flight. For all of human history, it was common sense that man was not meant to fly—thinking otherwise in the Middle Ages might get you pressed to death or burned at the stake as a heretic and a sorcerer.

But the specter of a horrible death didn't stop Leonardo da Vinci from thinking about it. He even drew up some very advanced engineering specs for a winged glider and a helicopter. He just didn't have the technology in the sixteenth century to get them off the page and into the air.

Three centuries later, Wilbur and Orville Wright slapped an internal-combustion engine onto an airframe. Orville sprinted off Kill Devil Hill near Kitty Hawk, North Carolina, in 1903, and turned common sense on its head when his kitelike flying machine flew under its own power for a few seconds.

Man *could* fly. And by the time the twentieth century was over, millions were crossing oceans every year in jet aircraft, generating hundreds of billions of dollars in business worldwide.

Need begets innovation begets achievement begets *value*.

But what about space?

Overcoming the limitations of water and the ground were one thing. Escaping the confines of this planet's gravity and atmosphere was another thing altogether. It had taken two nations perceiving a threat to each other's very existence to get into space, then the resolve of this nation to meet JFK's outlandish goal, and millions of man- and woman-hours of America's best and brightest focused on that one outcome.

It had also taken an enormous sum of money.

Apollo had been the climax of the American space program. NASA had been created in a frenzy of activity surrounding Sputnik, and got its mission statement to land a man on the Moon and bring him home safely. And they did it in less than ten years. Neil Armstrong, Buzz Aldrin, Pete Conrad, Al Bean, and eight others were the walking reminders of a job very, very well done.

But when the crew of the *Yankee Clipper* turned to each other as they began their journey home from the Moon, and asked, "Is that all there is?" they might just as well have asked, *So what?*

It was the greatest human achievement of all time, no doubt about it. But other than landing on the Moon itself, some breakthrough technologies, nice pictures, and a few bags of rocks, what had the space program really yielded? What would be the return on an investment of nearly a trillion 1960s dollars? What value had NASA ultimately gotten us? And what value might space really bring as the pattern shifted into its next logical phase?

The answer to these questions would ultimately determine the future of man in space.

# FORTY-NINE

The Soviets didn't go away. The Cold War didn't come to an end just because the first flag planted on the Moon was an American one. The USSR refocused its space efforts on the Soyuz craft and the Mir space station, and built a prototype shuttle much like our own. And its military never missed a beat deploying spy satellites and building more and more nuclear missiles, pointing them right at us. When the USSR rolled into Afghanistan in 1979, they removed all doubt that they were any less formidable and hostile than they'd ever been. Ronald Reagan was elected President the next year, largely on a platform of a stronger national defense and a promise to stop this growing menace before it went any further.

In the mid-eighties, Reagan announced his Strategic Defense Initiative, also known as Star Wars. Best known for missile-killing lasers and super-smart satellites—largely dismissed as pure fantasy by skeptics—the program also called for the development of a National Aerospace Plane, an air-breathing vehicle that could leave the atmosphere, enter Earth orbit, and provide rapid point-to-point deployment of American military personnel.

This idea was *not* pure fantasy. Max Hunter and Phil Bono at Douglas Aircraft had studied the same concept for the Marines in the early 1960s. The Air Force had sponsored numerous studies on supersecret single-stage-to-orbit (SSTO) rocket planes, and many a hopeful UFO watcher was fooled by their late-night high-altitude testing in the Nevada desert.

Still, after years of trial and error, the thing hadn't quite gotten solved. So the Reagan and the first Bush administrations decided to let the private sector have a crack at it.

**"H**ey, Pete. Do you know anything about spaceflight?" McDonnell Douglas executive Bill Gaubatz asked with a completely straight face as he breezed into Conrad's office one day in 1990.

"Don't know jack, Bill." Pete never looked up from some boring-ass quarterly report he was slogging through.

"So you probably wouldn't be interested in this." Gaubatz tossed him a request for proposal from the Strategic Defense Initiative Office, and flopped down on Pete's sofa. SDIO was looking for a better idea for getting a vehicle into space and back, and doing it cheaply.

Pete read the proposal, and before he finished the first page, he knew that the dark curtain that had fallen on his life for ten years was finally lifting.

"I'm in."

**P**ete and Gaubatz agreed that an air-breathing space plane was a flawed idea. It was too complicated and expensive, and if the Air Force couldn't nail it with thirty years and bottomless Black Program funding behind it, chances were pretty good they wouldn't, either. A rocket was a far simpler—and far cheaper—vehicle to build and fly.

Gaubatz had assembled a study team of engineers and visionaries within the company, and they conceived of an SSTO rocket that would take off and land vertically; ironically, it was the stuff of old science-fiction stories and movies. In the tradition of McDonnell Douglas success stories past, they designated the rocket with the old DC prefix (as in DC-10), and suffixed it with an X, as experimental, reminiscent of the X planes that moved us into the supersonic age in the late 1940s.

The key to McDonnell Douglas's proposal was the approach and under-standing of the need to introduce aircraftlike operations into the design of the rocket from the very beginning. They wanted to build a vehicle that could be operated, serviced, fueled, and turned quickly. And the key to that was to have the experience and guidance of someone who'd worked—*and flown!*— in commercial flight, military flight, test flight, and outer space.

There were probably only five people in the world who fit that bill, and one of them helped plan and write the final proposal. The contract was awarded to McDonnell Douglas in 1991, and the DC-X rocket was born.

Sixty-one-year-old Pete Conrad was *re*born; feeling what he'd feared he never would again: being part of something bigger than himself.

# FIFTY

**P**ete's marriage to Jane was all over but for the paperwork by 1988. Both had separate lives now. The truth was, it had been that way for ten years. Once the boys had grown and gone, there didn't seem to be much reason in continuing, beyond the fact that both of them were uncomfortable with the idea of divorce.

But to Pete, divorce meant failure. Abandoning ship. A divorce would have ended his NASA flights at the beginning, when image was everything and divorce was still a rarity in America. It reminded him of his own parents' dissolution, and the pain of living through that every day, and then the aftermath. It was easier to travel, to immerse himself in some great and important work and avoid the matter altogether than to just deal with it head-on.

But now, with no children in the house to stay together for, no image to worry about, Pete realized the greater sin was in living a lie. He did love Jane—too much to make her live that lie with him—and he sincerely wanted her to have what he'd been too duty-absorbed, career-absorbed, hell, *self-*absorbed to give her.

Even so, he just wished she'd do it first.

**N**ot surprisingly, the father of cable television had a spectacular house in Denver. Like any great house, it needed a name, and with typical Bill Daniels subtlety, he'd christened it CableLand. It fit. It was hard not to feel like you were in a fairy tale when you set foot in the place.

Descending from the foyer into the great room, with its soaring ceilings, you were immediately transported into a world of opulent style. The plaster, reflective ceiling featured tiered, multilevel lighting, interspersed with skylights, generating a contemporary feel while softening the room's scale. On a raised platform, a pink Weber baby grand piano sat beside a podium controlling a way-before-its-time networked closed-circuit television system. Bill hosted countless charity and fundraising events. His home theater and network made them interactive technology showcases.

The multilevel main room featured four hospitality centers, each establishing an intimate environment distinguished by shapes and textures. A semicircular bar sat invitingly in a corner beneath an enormous overhead TV screen visible throughout the room—one of CableLand's *eighty-eight* televisions.

Beneath a grand crystal chandelier, the dining room provided ample space for several immense tables, easily seating thirty-two, and of course contained another TV, concealed behind a decorative sculptured wall. Food for all CableLand functions was prepared in an adjacent catering kitchen by some of the best chefs in the world.

Ceiling-to-floor windows permitted guests to overlook the outdoor pool, encircled by terraced landscaping and fountains that mimicked indoor shapes and angles. A bathhouse, decorated in a lush, tropical motif, included a guest lounging area and dressing rooms. A covered patio, stylish service bar, and separate guest house were just off the pool area.

Near Bill's private quarters, there was a health spa and a home theater with a bank of sixty-four TVs, each tuned to a different cable channel, surrounding the ninety-six-inch master screen, rivaling most theaters for video and sound quality.

Generous to a fault, Bill had envisioned and built the place with others in mind. It was the scene of hundreds of charity and philanthropic events that raised untold millions of dollars.

But on this June night, Bill was a nervous wreck, pacing the well-appointed living room, smoking another in an endless series of More cigarettes. He was waiting on a woman—two women, as a matter of fact.

"Bill, relax," Pete said with a laugh. "It's just a dinner." Bill kept pacing, and Pete stopped laughing. "I thought you said this wasn't a blind date."

"It isn't, but . . . Oh, God, Pete, what was I thinking?"

"Hell, I knew it." Pete downed his drink, feeling nervous himself suddenly. "Make me another."

Their friendship had never flagged a bit, even after Pete bolted from ATC, leaving a lot of Bill's money on the table. He and Bill still agreed on the "important things." They still raced cars together, flew together, and found the best steak and single-malt Scotch wherever they happened to meet up . . . but only Pete drank the Scotch. Bill gave it up in 1985.

Bill shared in Pete's heartaches, too. And there had been plenty of those the last few years. He knew Pete's marriage was ending. And that the most popular guy he'd ever known was actually very lonely.

Bill's girlfriend, Karen, had the same kind of friendship with Denverite Nancy Crane, who'd just ended her own marriage. After twenty-two years, Nancy realized *she* was living an unfulfilled life, and with her own kids grown and out of the house, she decided on an extreme makeover, rapidly going from bored housewife and mother to interior designer, artist's representative, and writer.


**P**ete was electric that night. The stories poured out of him, but not the remember-when, macho-bravo stuff of somebody who lived in his past. Nancy found herself speechless that someone had been on such an amazing ride, and marveled at the people, places and things it had brought. She knew this guy was different when he genuinely brushed off Bill's repeated boasts that Pete was the best pilot of them all.

"Not even close, Bill. I was at the right place at the right time with *all* the best pilots." And he meant it.

Bill and Karen faded away at some point. Nancy and Pete continued to talk about the truly important things—dreams, happiness, living every day like it was your last, and being a part of something. Pete was the first guy she'd ever met who didn't need to have her multiple project load explained to him.

"You're following your passion." He toasted her. "That's the secret of life."

*Who knows?* Nancy thought, as both went their separate, slightly less lonely ways. *If the timing had been a little different . . .*

Her phone rang the next day. "Ms. Crane, it's Mr. Conrad, on the way to the airport, talking to you on the shoe phone." Mobile phones were still a good size eleven in the late eighties—and Pete had adored *Get Smart*, even telling his boys the character Maxwell Smart was based on him. "You know, there's this roast for Bill coming up in a couple weeks."

"Yes. I'm going."

"Well, I think you should go with me."

"Sounds fun."

"Really? Uh, I mean . . . great." A pause. "Okay then. Be safe. And remember: There are no aliens in outer space. They're all right here in Denver, and they come out right about now. That's why I'm heading back to Saint Louis."

"Thank you, Mr. Conrad. Have a nice trip."

The shoe-phone bills would be outrageous as they began a long-distance friendship that, over the course of a few months, would grow closer and closer. Pete found more and more reasons to come visit Bill in Denver. They were two peas in a pod, both voraciously curious, high-energy, doing a hundred things at the same time . . . and falling in love. When Nancy's divorce became final, Pete quietly filed a new flight plan for his life.

*   *   *

Nancy looked up from the window seat in the coach section of the Continental flight. Pete was leaving first class, heading her way. Grinning.

"Sorry about the reservations."

"You really know how to treat a girl, Conrad. Take her on a trip and throw her in coach while you sip champagne in first." He'd promised to get her switched, but clearly hadn't succeeded in his mission. There was a man engrossed in a *Sports Illustrated* in the seat next to her.

"Excuse me, sir. I have a first class seat, where the food is a hell of a lot better and the drinks are free. It's all yours if you want it."

He did. He was gone in a heartbeat.

"The champagne was lousy, anyway," Pete muttered as he settled into the seat. "So I had this crazy idea for when you meet Al." They were headed to Houston, and one of their must-stops would be visiting Al Bean, his *Apollo 12* mate.

"Oh, yeah? What's that?"

"Let's tell him that we're getting married." And he removed a ring from his pocket. "I don't want to waste another day, love."

Captain Bean was the first to know, and he welcomed Nancy into the fold with open arms. Pete had been Al's confidant during his own divorce a few years back, so Al was happy to give her his blessing, seeing how happy Pete obviously was. He even toured Nancy through his studio, where he was working on another in a series of lunar paintings, this one featuring Pete. No judgment or attitude, Al was genuinely happy that the two of them had found love. It was the nicest wedding present Nancy could have hoped for—acceptance by one of her husband's oldest friends.

Pete and Nancy were married in the spring of 1990, and moved to Huntington Beach, where Pete would begin working on the DC-X rocket.

They were married in San Francisco, whisked there aboard Bill Daniels's Learjet, the *Cablevision Tool*. And Pete being Pete . . . he couldn't resist the temptation, as Nancy flipped through a magazine en route, to step forward and politely ask Bill's newly hired pilot if he could fly a little on the way. The pilot smiled. He certainly knew who his passenger was, and undoubtedly had been tipped by his boss that there wasn't a chance in hell the old jet-jock groom *wouldn't* ask.

"Mr. Conrad, it would be an honor, sir."

"I didn't get your name."

"Calkins," the pilot said, extending his hand. "Mark Calkins."

# FIFTY-ONE

Nancy had no intention of giving up her life. She liked what she did and was successful at it. It was fun. But it wasn't as fun as being with Pete. Marrying this man was like jumping on a moving train.

The guy went everywhere, going Mach-something. He flew all over the world for McDonnell Douglas, did speaking engagements, showed up at astronaut reunions, and always seemed to be entered in a race of some sort in a machine that rolled or flew. Washington D.C., New York, California, Europe, Asia, the former Soviet Union, even a helicopter trip from Arizona to Venezuela. *Wanna go?* Well, yes, she did. Everywhere. They renamed themselves Boris and Natasha, after Pete's two favorite characters from the Bullwinkle cartoon—international spies, working for no one. And everywhere he went, everybody knew him.

"Boris, how do you know so many people?"

"I do not know, Natasha. I just do."

Nancy found herself in the jungle of Panama, laughing herself silly as her new husband was embraced like a long-lost son by the tribal chief celebrating his seventy-fifth birthday in a loincloth and body paint—and the guy looked pretty darn good for seventy-five. Turns out the chief had trained the Apollo boys in jungle survival back in '65, and he'd put Pete at the top of the invitation list, after family and neighboring tribal chiefs. Happily, Pete kept his pants on through the celebration.

This man defied stereotypes, to put it mildly. Nancy would have been forgiven that first date at Bill's had she expected a slightly arrogant, macho, Type A *uber*-achiever in Pete. What would anyone expect from a Fortune 500 executive, a former Navy test pilot, and an astronaut who'd been to the Moon?

What she *got* was a guy who loved to laugh. A lot. A month into their marriage, Nancy walked into the den to find her husband doubled over in pain, tears streaming down his cheeks. Her momentary panic gave way to relief as he exhaled a huge belly laugh; O.J. Simpson had just plunged down a flight of stadium stairs in a wheelchair, having been neglected by his caretaker Leslie Nielsen in *The Naked Gun*, playing in the VCR.

That night, they were both doubled over in laughter as he sat in front of their hotel room mirror just before a five-star astronaut reunion event. A towel was draped over his French-cuffed shirt, and he nervously awaited his wife's practiced hands and a pair of eyebrow scissors.

"My goodness, Boris. These are without a doubt the longest eyebrows in human history." And she may have been right. A few of the stragglers reached an inch or two in length.

"It's true, honey. My hair is actually sucked off my head, through my brain, down to my forehead."

He'd never cared, never noticed. No hair transplants for this guy, no fixing his gap teeth. Not even platform shoes. What had drawn Nancy to Pete was the man's comfort with himself, flaws and all, and his willingness to share those flaws. The best memories she would have of their marriage were not the grand adventures and the legions of government leaders, movie stars, and captains of industry that seemed to know and love Pete Conrad, but the long walks and talks the two of them shared.

Nancy hadn't married a Type A *uber*-achiever. She'd married a soft and vulnerable, flesh and blood man who never wanted anything more than to love and to be loved. Pete shared his failings with her as easily as his triumphs. And defying another stereotype, he listened patiently to hers. No instinctual male *fixing* everything or overanalyzing with his considerable scientific and logical side. He just listened.

# FIFTY-TWO

The DC-X, now dubbed the Delta Clipper, was fueled up, sitting on the pad at White Sands Missile Range in New Mexico one August morning in 1993, waiting to take her maiden flight. The sun was just coming up, its first rays touching the conical rocket with four gangly legs, similar to the ones on the *Apollo* lunar module. Weather was clear, not a cloud in the sky, no measurable winds. Couldn't be a more perfect launch day.

Flight manager Pete Conrad barked status reports and orders from the launch operations trailer a half mile away, watching the clock out of one eye, the monitor screen out of the other as the fueling lines were removed and the truck pulled away. McDonnell Douglas engineer Tom Ingersoll, one of Bill Gaubatz's first picks for this program along with Pete, served as deputy director, hammering away at his laptop, talking a mile a minute with the rest of the personnel downrange. Gaubatz, his work done, could now only gulp coffee and worry like an expectant father.

Like always, the last hours were the craziest. Three years of work and sweat and trial and error were coming down to the wire in less than a minute. The flight would last less than two, and Pete was way more nervous than he'd been when he was sitting in the cockpit of *Apollo 12* in the final seconds.

"Okay, here we go. T-minus seven, six, five, four, three, two, one . . ." Pete barked into the communicator from their command center. "Let's rock and roll!"

The engine fired right on program. The four-legged Clipper rose easily from the pad, looking like a fifties sci-fi drawing come to life, rising steadily and gracefully. "One hundred . . . two hundred . . . three hundred . . . all systems checking out super here, gang . . . and we are at five hundred!"

This was the Clipper's ceiling this morning, and she paused five hundred feet over the desert floor.

"V-one-zero, begin lateral," Pete continued, focused on the monitor in front of him. "Looks good, looks good."

The Clipper hovered still, like a helicopter, as the thrusters changed angles. And the ship began to move laterally to the east, steady, slow, and controlled, like a boat floating gently toward her dock.

"Thrust good, stabilization right on the money; here comes three hundred, four hundred . . . Come on, baby, a little farther . . ."

The Clipper came to an airborne stop again, hovering easily, rocket steady.

"Okay, descent sequence begin in three, two, one. . . ."

She lurched just a bit, then slowly started heading down. "Four-eighty, four-sixty, four-fifty." Pete called altitudes as Al had for him as they dropped to the Moon's surface. The flight was right on program. She picked up a little too much speed for Pete's liking at two hundred feet, but righted herself, descending easily.

"Here we come, fifty, forty, thirty, twenty, ten . . . a little flare, and you are home free, baby! Main engine shut down! The Clipper flies, boys and girls!"

Victory cries in the headsets as the rocket engine shut down. It worked exactly as they'd designed. Pete turned to Gaubatz and Ingersoll, high-fived, and celebrated being part of something bigger than himself again.

# FIFTY-THREE

Pete and Nancy loved Las Cruces—so much so that they bought a little house and four acres, with the thought of someday retiring there.

"Yeah, right," said Nancy. "Like Pete Conrad would ever retire."

"Okay, then. Boris and Natasha's desert retreat," Pete countered. "It's a hell of a lot more fun than Palm Springs."

What it was in the DC-X flight test days was Camp Conrad, the meeting and eating place and occasional flophouse for engineers, flight managers, and company VIPs who wandered out to the desert to see if this thing really worked. At least three nights a week Nancy cooked up a vat of spaghetti and filled the bar with more *vino* and Mexican beer. The boys would descend on the place, eat, and drink till the wee hours and talk about—what else?—space and the vehicles that would get them up there.

"Half a billion dollars?" gasped Tom Ingersoll one night. "For one shuttle flight?"

"Yeah, roughly." Pete nodded, getting Tom another Coke. "It's one hundred fifty mil just for preps, fuel, and consumables."

"Man, that is ridiculous."

"That's what I'm saying. I think the whole thing could be done for fifty. Not now. But soon."


**S**uddenly Pete wasn't sleeping. It wasn't from worry or fear or guilt or any of the other usual suspects; it was because of an idea. A very simple idea, actually. But like nothing since Apollo, the idea was lighting his candle.

What it was, was the wild hair. Pete Conrad was going back into space. Only this time it wouldn't be as an explorer. It would be as an *entrepreneur*.


**B**oeing makes airplanes. From the engines to the wings to the avionics to the seats, Boeing designs, subcontracts, and assembles aircraft. What it doesn't do is *operate* them. That's for United, Southwest, American, and the other host of airlines that buy and lease Boeing's planes. That's all an airline is, an operations company.

Like Boeing, McDonnell Douglas was also a manufacturer. MD was building the DC-X rocket in 1993, but it was also the operations company, something that wasn't a core competency for the company. It doubled the staff's workload, which made them less efficient. Which cost MD money. The entire DC-X launch complex the company designed had cost a fortune in dollars and time. What if MD just subbed it all out, and concentrated on building and improving its vehicle?

The company had not yet won this new space race. Its contract was to build a reusable launch-vehicle prototype, but the end game was to get a *manufacturing* contract, worth possibly hundreds of billions. Lockheed Martin and Rockwell were going after the same thing. What McDonnell Douglas Aerospace needed was a competitive advantage.

Pete envisioned a separate operations company giving them just that. MD would build the vehicle, and his new company would operate it, from rollout to launch to recovery and even global satellite communication. McDonnell Douglas cautiously approved the concept, Pete and Nancy and Tom Ingersoll got to work writing a business plan for it, and chairman Pete christened it Universal Space Lines.

Now they had to find the funding to get operational. Pete had never been one to ask for money, but he knew that he wasn't going to shoestring an operation this ambitious. Pete talked the idea over with his pal Bill Daniels. Investor John Mecom attended the tests for DC-X-7, and saw the basis of the operation in action. Impressed, Mecom took the idea to a venture capital group with Saudi investors who were very keen on the idea of private-sector space. And with the Apollo astronauts still considered space gods, the Saudis wanted to meet with Pete as soon as possible in Riyadh. This thing was moving into high gear fast.

Pete wanted to keep it all aboveboard and transparent with McDonnell Douglas, as he and Tom Ingersoll and Bill Gaubatz were still employees. The company's lawyers didn't see a problem. Pete sent Gaubatz to MD's headquarters to brief the president and CFO of the company, Herb Lanese, on the possible Saudi investment. Only the meeting never took place. Gaubatz was intercepted by a hostile vice president in strategic development who went through the roof upon hearing this plan.

And all hell broke loose. The lawyers suddenly changed their minds, and just as suddenly USL wasn't an MD competitive advantage; it was just a *competitor*. Pete, Gaubatz and Ingersoll were placed on administrative leave while the company investigated the matter. Gaubatz and Ingersoll were threatened with losing their jobs. Pete was asked to sign documents stating that he would cease and desist from pursuing USL.

It achieved the exact opposite of the desired effect. It pissed the old fighter pilot off. "Are you *serious?*" he roared at the certified letter from the company's legal counsel. "I'm trying to *make* you money!" He wadded it up and tossed it in the trash. Then he turned to Nancy. "Let's go walk."

Four thirty was the Conrads' golden hour. Unless they were traveling or buried under a deadline, Pete and Nancy would cease the day's activities and hit Huntington Beach a block away, to Rollerblade, bike, or swim—but mostly just to walk. And talk.

Pete wasn't doing much talking that day, though. He was deep in thought, staring into the sand. Nancy finally broke the silence, in her best Natasha accent.

"So what is it Boris is thinking?"

"Boris is thinking this company has its head up its—"

"Other than that."

"I was thinking I should have seen this coming all along. It's been like this since Old Mac died. I was just too jazzed with this project to notice it anymore."

"I've never seen you this happy," Nancy said. They walked on. "So what do you want to do?"

"Oh, hell, I'm gonna quit."

"After twenty years, just like that?"

"I work in blocks of twenty. Twenty years here, twenty in the Navy and NASA. It's just time for the next twenty." He grinned, then turned serious. "I'm worried about Tom, though. He's got that young family, plus one in the oven to think about."

"And USL?" she asked. "You want to keep it going?"

"I want to expand it. Form at least two more companies. A worldwide real-time satellite network, and the software to bring it right to the companies' PCs."

Now Nancy laughed. "They shouldn't have messed with Boris."

"No, they shouldn't have."

Ingersoll and Gaubatz resigned from McDonnell Douglas, along with Pete not long after. Universal Space Lines got its first round of capital from individual investors, and immediately launched Universal Space Networks in Horsham, Pennsylvania, and Universal SpaceWare in Denver to construct the tracking network and design the software that Pete envisioned.

And USL's first customer? McDonnell Douglas. Only Pete and Tom had the first clue how to make the DC-X fly.

# FIFTY-FOUR

"**N**o, Pete. It won't work."

"T.K., I'm telling you it will. It's a simple matter of availability."

"And I'm telling you it's market size."

"Availability."

"Market."

"Availability!"

"*Market!*"

It was two A.M., Pete and T.K. were in the short driveway, continuing a "discussion" that started five hours, two bottles of wine, a bucket of pasta, and a pot of coffee ago. They probably wouldn't get this settled tonight.

T. K. Mattingly was one of the ground heroes of the rescue of *Apollo 13*. A backup crew member and newcomer to the astronaut corps in 1966,

Mattingly was one of the thousand NASA engineers who didn't go to bed for a week, solving the crisis on the chalkboard and workbench, talking 13 through it, and bringing the crew home alive. He flew the command module in *Apollo 16,* and commanded two shuttle missions. Candidly, T.K. thought Conrad was an asshole back in those early days.

Which was why Pete loved him and trusted him. T.K. was honest. He was a maddeningly thorough detail man, and more stubborn than Pete, once he'd made up his very capable mind. He'd call it exactly the way he saw it.

And the way he saw it tonight, Pete's newest idea was destined to crash and burn. *Because of the market, Pete!*

The crown jewel in Pete's vision was the fourth entity, the one he'd invited Mattingly aboard to run: Rocket Development Company. To close the loop and make USL a truly full-service operation, they would need their own vehicles.

A funny thing had happened since the government opened up R-and-D funding to the private sector for a reusable launch vehicle: The Soviet Union had fallen. From a military standpoint, the demand for such a vehicle had faded temporarily. But Pandora's box had been opened, as had the eyes of many of Pete's kindred spirits when they saw a privately funded and operated rocket could actually *work.*

The 1990s had hit their economic stride, and investment money was beginning to flow into private space ventures. But it wasn't just Internet zillionaires and movie stars burning up dough for a thrill ride now; it was *investors* looking for an investment—one that would eventually make them money.

Bill Gates was getting into the game with Craig McCaw with a satellite venture called Teledisc. As was Burt Rutan, who would partner up with Paul Allen and win the X Prize in 2004, building and flying their own reusable vehicle out of the atmosphere twice in two weeks. Kelly Space & Technology, Astrolink, Galaxy/Spaceway, Globalstar Telecommunications, Kistler Aerospace—these and a host of new start-ups were challenging the old way of thinking, not relying on the government or NASA but building their own reusable vehicles and providing space services to the business world.

Pete ultimately saw Universal Space Lines delivering a box of raspberries from New York to Rome in an hour. Lunch in Paris, back at your Chicago office by four thirty to take meetings. A weekend camping trip with the kids in

Australia, home in time to make their lunch for school Monday morning. Making space travel as quick, dependable, and profitable as FedEx or Southwest Airlines. Just like the first ships crossing the Atlantic. The first airplanes crossing the continent. NASA had opened the door, and now the pattern was entering that final and most important phase: Making money. Creating *value.*

"Pete, if we learned anything in Apollo, it was *moving step by step.*"

"If we learned anything in Apollo, it was *eyes on the prize.*"

What drove Mattingly craziest about Pete was that he was years ahead of reality. It was the detail guys like him who had to do the math—and throw cold water on visions sometimes.

"Pete, we're at least five years away from a reusable launch vehicle. We'll have to start with an expendable."

"I know that, T.K. We're going with your design. Didn't you see the business plan?"

"I saw the business plan." He was silent a moment, then: "A hundred million won't do it. We need three."

"*Three hundred*?" It was a gut shot. It might mean the end of this dream, actually. Pete had already begun talking with investors about the lower figure, based on a preliminary study. "Oh, hell . . ."

"You wanted the truth, Pete. That's the truth."

Pete sighed, knowing T.K.'s finest quality beside his mind was his honesty. "Okay. If you say it's three hundred, it's three hundred."

"How are you gonna raise that?"

"I have no idea," Pete admitted. "But there's always a way. Always."

He watched T.K. drive away, wondering how the hell he would pull this rabbit out of his hat. But just like at NASA, when Kennedy challenged them with getting to the Moon before they'd even mastered orbital flight and rendezvous . . .

Pete had no doubt that he would. He just needed a little time, that's all.

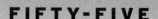

# FIFTY-FIVE

**February 14, 1996**
**Learjet N10BD**
**Somewhere over the North Pacific**
**0501 Zulu**

**B**lack water, black sky. Seemed like this entire flight was at night. Mark Calkins brought his eyes back into the cockpit and to the flight computer in his lap, and shook his head.

"We're toast," Dan Miller had announced to the crew, after running the numbers on wind, fuel, and speed. The numbers didn't lie. Mark checked them twice. They were gonna miss the record by an hour. Maybe more, with this next stop, in the middle of the night in King Salmon, Alaska.

And that was that. The whole thing had been for nothing. Nothing but a hundred sleepless nights, eight poster exchanges, a lot of Bill Daniels's money, and a healthy plate of crow to eat in front of every news camera in Denver, which would undoubtedly be at the field to capture their failure-screaming arrival.

"Crap," Mark muttered, and pulled out of the copilot's seat to let Dan fly alone for a while. He went to look for something to eat in the rear cabin. Pete was already there, also rummaging. He smiled, as disappointed as all of them, and patted Mark on the back.

"I was too optimistic about the winds, Pete. And Saint Kitts killed us."

"Yeah, but India was fun."

The fuel stop at Varanasi, India, had been like something out of a Charlie Chaplin movie. The tower sent them to the wrong terminal, and the correct terminal was a mob scene of utter chaos, with opposing customs officials erupting in a Hindi-shrieking turf war and blizzard of paperwork and pounding of rubber stamps. And of course the local muckety-mucks jockeyed for a photo op with Pete, all while a throng of locals strained to get in on the act somewhere. Still, amidst the hubbub, the ground crew got the Cablevision Tool turned in a blistering thirty-two minutes.

Mark smiled sadly. "I'm sorry about it, Pete. Really I am."

"Sorry about what, Mark?"

Mark just shook his head and slid his back down the extra fuel tank to the floor. Pete slid down alongside him.

"I don't mind it so much for me, really. But you guys . . . you worked so hard. And Bill . . . he really wanted this."

"Bill also knows you busted your ass, Mark. You can't control the wind. Can't control any airport or a ground crew that barely speaks English." He nodded at the Moon going down over the southwest. "We didn't nail that on the first shot, either. We got our asses kicked a few times. You get as old and broken-down as me and Bill, you'll get yours kicked, too." He patted Mark's shoe. "It's just a ride, my boy. Remember that. It's all just one big ride."

"Thanks, Pete."

Pete creaked and groaned, then pulled his tired body up off the floor. "And when you're ready to try again, give me a call. Just let me sleep a couple days, okay?"

## Approaching King Salmon, Alaska
## One hour later

"Wait a minute." Pete looked up from his spiral notebook, full of his chicken-scratch notes. He'd spent the last hour reentering every single calculation since they'd departed Denver, and doing the math by hand. He checked the flight computer again. "This is wrong, Dan."

Miller didn't even look away from the controls. "Not according to the computer," he answered dismissively. "I checked it three times; so did Mark."

"The computer's fine. It's the input. Look. Here on line forty-two. Somebody missed a zero."

Miller looked at the spiral, squinting at Pete's calculations. "Holy shit . . ."

"Yeah, holy shit. Changes everything." He grinned. "I'm gonna wake up Mark."

## Crossing into the Continental United States

"Adding power." Pete was flying now, watching the turbine temperature guages.

"That's the redline, Pete. That's all she's got at this altitude." Mark checked the GPS again. No wind on their tail still.

"Portland's out there at two o'clock. It's gonna be close."

"Come on, wind. Come on."

It had been a quick reunion celebration for Mark in King Salmon. He'd spent a few years in Alaska, flying people and cargo up and down the ice and bush. His best friend was waiting with a stack of pizzas and the best turnaround crew in the state, working way into overtime to help the guys out with a fast turn. Mark reached into a secret compartment in the Lear, where Bill had insisted he hide a stack of hundred-dollar bills—a thousand of them, just in case—and peeled off a healthy stack in grateful thanks. He hugged his pal, then slammed the door.

"Let's rock and roll!" Pete shouted as they rotated airborne one last time, and pegged the throttle for home.

The GPS still showed a flat tailwind. "Dammit, where is it?" Pete shouted at the screen. The Jeppesen Dataplan forecast had promised a healthy wind at their back as they pushed southeast, but they'd yet to see it. "You're a religious guy, Mark. Pray or sing or something."

That instant the Lear hit a thermal crossing the lower Cascade Range and pogoed, just like a *Saturn* 5. Right on cue, either making Jeppesen or the Big Guy Himself look awfully good, the wind started—a big blast, directly on their tail. Airspeed jumped ten knots.

It got stronger as they crossed Oregon, Nevada, and Utah. They whooped and high-fived at every bump, especially when Mark announced there was nearly one hundred knots of wind at their back as they crossed into Colorado airspace, making their ground speed just shy of Mach 1.

"We're crushing it!" Pete exclaimed. "We are kicking this record's—"

"—*ass*, Pete!" The very religious, unprofane Mark Calkins finished for him, slapping the pilot's hand for the tenth time and exhaling a huge, "Yesssss!" Pete unbuckled his seat belt and pushed the autopilot.

"She's all yours, Captain."

"No, no. Bill insisted you either take us off or bring us in. I agreed to that. I know what a favor you were doing us. Besides, it's your rotation."

"Thanks anyway. It's your *flight*."

Mark smiled, and didn't offer another round. Of course he was itching to bring her in. This flight had absolutely consumed his and his family's life for nearly half a year. The least he could have was the final touchdown— especially when the record was theirs. Pete chuckled as Mark slid over like a kid getting to drive for the first time, then assuming the ship's command as naturally as Al Bean had, blasting the lunar module off the Ocean of Storms.

Pete grabbed the VHF. "And Denver Center, Learjet Ten Bravo Delta is with you now."

"Roger, Bravo Delta." Ahh, the good old USA and her instantaneous air-traffic-control communications. "We have you, and there's a few excited people waiting on the ground outside. Something about a record . . . ?" The guy was clearly joking.

"Roger. Something like that. We have the field in sight." Pete flashed a mischievous grin at Mark. "And requesting a low-pass flyover, Denver?"

"Say again, Bravo Delta."

"Bravo Delta is requesting a low-pass flyover, please." What the hell? It was nearly four A.M., and there was zero traffic in the area—what could it possibly hurt? Besides, it was the astronaut making the request.

"They'll never allow that," said Mark. "They're really by-the-book here—"

"Bravo Delta," interrupted the tower. "You are cleared for landing on Runway Three-Five right." Pause. "And affirmative on flyover. Congratulations, guys."

And that was just what Mark did—brought her in fifty feet off the deck over the runway at 350 knots, dipping his wings in salute to the tower, Denver, the crowd, and anybody awake out there. It looked for all the world like Pete Conrad buzzing his beer-drinking naval-aviator pals at the El Centro shoot-out forty years before.

And at 4:28:42 A.M. local time, Learjet N10BD's wheels touched her home ground of Denver, Colorado, USA, once again—forty-nine hours, twenty-one minutes, and eight seconds after Mark pulled the nose up, traveling round the world at an average speed of 468 miles per hour. Kicking the pants off the previous record by thirty-nine minutes.

"Ten Bravo Delta, welcome home. Contact ground on one-one-two-point-eight-five."

"Ten Bravo Delta. Have a nice day."

# FIFTY-SIX

**B**ruce Springsteen's chainsaw guitar and gravelly voice boomed out of the kitchen, wafting toward the tables: "Time slips away, and leaves you with nothing, mister, but boring stories of . . . glory days."

*Isn't that the truth?* Pete thought as he sipped his coffee. Glory days, indeed. But there he'd been, twelve hours earlier, at yet another black-tie fundraiser at some swanky hotel in L.A., featuring him and all the other Mercury, Gemini, and Apollo boys. These things were all the same—"thirty years ago" this, "thirty-five" that. And they'd tell the same stories for the thousandth time to make the guys in the black ties dig a little deeper for whatever charity this one was for.

What the hell. He loved those guys. And Pete Conrad was nothing if he wasn't loyal. *What a ride NASA gave me,* he'd think when he got the invitation, and then check the little box saying yes, he'd be in attendance. Then he'd sit on that panel, trade a few war stories of his own, and get right back to the here and now. And beyond that.

*God, I look old,* he thought, seeing his reflection in the IHOP mirror. With just a dash of his hair left, and a craggy and weathered face, the only truly recognizable feature left of that spit-shined, NASA-polished prototype of a Russian-beating rocket jock was the twinkle in those eyes, and that signature gap-toothed grin, which he summoned as always when he looked up, and saw a man about his age standing there with a young girl hiding bashfully behind him.

"Excuse me. Aren't you one of the astronauts?"

"Yes, I am, thank you."

"You see," the man said to the child. "This is the man. The man they made that movie about!"

The waitress pulled the coffeepot up, just before pouring. "What movie?"

"The one about the Apollo capsule they had to bring back," the old guy continued, excited and proud of the knowledge he kept. "You remember, 'Houston, we have a problem.' They never say that, you know, unless it's really bad. Isn't that right?"

The waitress gasped. "You mean *Apollo Thirteen*? You were in *Apollo Thirteen*?"

"No, he wasn't *in* it. It was him. They made the movie about *him.*"

Her eyes filled with wonder and awe suddenly. "Can I ask you . . . I'm an actress—*of course you are*—what is Tom Hanks really like? Is he as nice as they say?"

Pete laughed softly as he motioned for her to keep pouring. It wasn't the first time. He liked the movie well enough. Lovell was a lifelong friend. But one little thing he couldn't quite square: *Ten perfect flights, six lunar landings, and they make a movie about the one that failed?*

"I wouldn't know, sweetheart. I flew *Apollo Twelve*. We made it there and back just fine."

"Oh . . ." She smiled politely, pulled the check out of her apron, and hurried off. Pete took a sip of the coffee. The man took a paper place mat from the girl, and stammered, "W-would it be too much trouble if . . . I just, you know, I want her to know what all you guys did and . . . she's so young, and it's important, and I can't believe we're not up there right now, and—"

Pete smiled and held up his hand, getting it. "You'd like me to sign it?"

"I sure would," he answered. "For her, of course."

"What's your name, sweetheart?"

"Emily. Did you really walk on the Moon, mister?"

"I really did, Emily."

"My teacher said you all faked it, that it was all just a movie set in the desert."

"Emily!" The older man was horrified.

Pete laughed, pulling a shiny stainless-steel pen out of his jacket. He'd heard that one a few times. "Tell your teacher to give me a call sometime. I'll set him straight."

"What else did you do?"

"Well, I did lots of things. Mostly just sat on top of rockets and waited for somebody to come light 'em."

"So you're a . . . rocketman?"

Pete stopped writing. *Rocketman.* He laughed again, liking *that.* "I guess I am, darling. So what would you like to do with your life?"

"I don't know. I'm just a kid."

"Me too, Emily. Me too." Pete signed the inscription, folded the paper, and slid out of the booth, tossing down a ten. "You ever see a pen from outer space?" He held up the one he'd just used. "We had to invent them because regular pens don't work out there. This one was mine. Now it's yours. So long."

He tousled the girl's hair, patted the old boy on the shoulder, and walked out of the IHOP toward the Harley waiting outside. Unfolding the place mat, the little girl read:

> To Emily,
> Keep your feet on the Moon, and keep reaching for the stars.
> Your pal,
> The Rocketman

He'd never tired of the sound. After all these years riding every machine he could get started, there was still nothing quite like a wall of wind over a roaring motor. Pete loved this part of the ride. Northbound Pacific Coast

Highway, just past Trancas. No traffic and no stoplights till Ventura. Just him, the ocean, and a Harley stretching her legs under him, settling down into her groaning song.

Pete had woken up with a cold this morning. Probably stress from funding the companies, having to dial for dollars. God, he hated that. Hated that it wasn't just obvious what they were doing and why it had to be done.

He probably should have just stayed in bed. Nancy didn't want him to go; she worried, hearing him sniffle and cough at five thirty. He would have scrubbed the mission if he didn't have a gang of pals waiting for him up ahead.

"I'll beat it, love. Don't worry. I always beat it." He popped a couple Advils and kissed her back to sleep.

He was feeling better already. The salt air, gas and oil, leather jacket. He could almost smell them now. This ride was better than chicken soup. This was the real Pete, anyway. No black-tie affairs, no boring stories of glory days. Just being out for a ride.

Road construction. *Damn.* He slowed the bike to a stop, dropping his boots to the pavement. He was the only guy out here, north or south. The sun was burning through the fog now. The half-Moon hadn't set. He looked up at it. Thirty seconds later the flagman waved the once-famous rider on, with not a clue as to who he was.

Pete turned onto Highway 150, a quick cut-over to Ojai. He pulled the throttle back, and the bike happily obliged. It was a good ride today.

Fourth gear. He'd seen a restored Indian motorcycle at a classic-car show a few weeks back, and just about flipped. The guy must have thrown fifty grand into that beauty, and damn, did she shine. He never loved any ride quite like that old oil-dripping Indian. It had broken his heart to sell it—for three hundred bucks in 1952. He wondered where she went from there. Wouldn't it be funny if she were still out there somewhere?

He glanced back up at that Moon. She was giving one last shine before dipping down till she came back around tonight. He'd talked to Dick Gordon and Al Bean last week, making plans to go to some Apollo thirty-year shindig coming up. Wow. Thirty years ago, he and Al had been stomping around on that rock.

He hadn't talked much to either of them since he'd gotten so busy with the four new companies. Al was his usual pragmatic self: "Pete, I think you're biting off more than you can chew." Maybe he was right.

Gordon laughed, like he always did at Pete's latest adventure. After all these years, the old pilot could still sound like a kid going to Disneyland when he was onto something new. And by God, if anybody could pull off a space airline, it would be Pete Conrad. Still the best of friends, Dick and Pete had been at the top of the world together, and at the bottom as well. Dick had lost his own boy to an automobile accident.

He squeezed his friend's hand the last time he saw him. "Give me a call when you get that thing built. I'll fly it with you."

Gordon was right too. It was so Pete, still blowin' and goin' at sixty-nine. Old Squarewave didn't know *how* to slow down, and didn't much care to learn. There were too many rides to take.

The ocean mist was fading now, the morning sun breaking through. It was gonna be a hot one, but the warmer dry air felt wonderful on his face.

*Man, this is a great ride today!*

He roared past a strawberry field, downshifted up a rise, came over the top, and damn if there wasn't a guy in a red Stearman biplane on his right, spinning up for his takeoff roll on a dirt runway, looking for all the world like that mystery-man aviator at Paoli Field fifty-something years ago, when Pete swore he'd grow up to be him.

A little shorter, and Pete couldn't get his mustache to grow like his, but he'd grown up to be a pretty decent driver himself. Still couldn't fathom how that SOB had made that impossible landing that day.

*This is perfect,* he thought. A biplane bouncing down the runway on his right, his old pal the Moon still hanging in there on his left. And him hauling ass on a Harley right in the middle. "*Rocketman,*" Pete Conrad repeated his new name given him by his new friend back at the IHOP.

He laughed out loud. *Yeah. This is a good ride today. The Rocketman has had sixty-nine years of good rides, Emily. And they're a long way from done.*

He'd get those raspberries to Rome some damn way. He'd find his way back out of this atmosphere, maybe even hitch a ride on the shuttle like Glenn in eight years when he was old enough.

And the great-great-great-grandson of Thones Kunders, the bearer of the Conrad wild hair himself, the jet jockey, the Moonwalking, Harley-riding Rocketman felt the wind whistle through that gap-toothed grin one last time as he downshifted into the curve on a damn fine ride.

It was the last curve of the last ride of his life.

# EPILOGUE

No one knows for sure what happened on that last curve on Highway 150, just outside of Ojai. Pete wasn't going very fast; there was no collision. One of the riders he'd joined up with saw him lean into his turn, then straighten up suddenly, heading for the shoulder. The gravel and dirt gave way instantly to a ditch; no way he could have seen it. The bike went down. He wrangled the Harley back up like it was his favorite horse at the ranch, but he was hurt. The bike went left, he went right, landing hard on his chest.

Why did he turn out? Did he need to pull over to rest? Was he swerving to avoid something? Maybe he just wanted to look over the magnificent valley of Ojai, the Native American word for Moon.

Only he knows.

Pete was taken to a small community hospital, fully conscious, with what appeared to be a minor chest injury. That was the first mistake. He should have gone to a trauma center. He had to wait and wait for treatment, which caused him to deteriorate fast. By the time attending physicians realized the seriousness of the situation, it was too late. When Nancy arrived at three o'clock, he was in grave condition. He died on the operating table two hours later.

Charles "Pete" Conrad Jr. was buried with full military honors at Arlington National Cemetery. Thousands came to pay their respects, from senators and Hollywood types to corporate heads, children, teachers, and blue-collar workers. Neil Armstrong spoke, as did Dick Gordon, Jim Lovell, Al Bean, NASA administrator Dan Goldin, and Congressman Dana Rohrbacher. Willie Nelson, singer and songwriter of Pete's favorite country tunes, interrupted his tour and drove his bus down from Maine to sing "Amazing Grace."

Pete's headstone reads, simply, "An Original."

Bill Daniels died eight months later after a long illness. Mark Calkins sat with him at his bedside, reading from the Psalms as he left this life. Bill deeded his magnificent home CableLand to the city of Denver, and it now serves as the mayor's residence. His billion-dollar fortune went to the Daniels Fund, which provides full academic scholarships, including room, board, books, and tuition to needy children in the four-state area. It also funds programs for the homeless as well as help for victims of drug abuse. Bill's ashes were sprinkled over the Pacific near his home in Del Mar, released from Learjet 10BD, Mark at the controls.

Learjet 10BD broke the world's record for circumnavigating the globe in a business-class jet on February 14, 1996. Its time of forty-nine hours, twenty-one minutes, and eight seconds still stands unchallenged as of this writing. The shell of the *Cablevision Tool* hangs proudly over Concourse C in Denver International Airport, dedicated June 25, 2003. Its interior was dismantled and sold, the money donated to the Daniels Fund.

Pete had given Bill a number of pieces from his space collection, and they are on display at the Daniels Fund headquarters. The hands-down favorite among visitors is the photo of Pete standing in front of the NASA surveyor on the surface of the Moon. The inscription reads, "Sorry I didn't make it to the Board meeting. I was out of town on business."

Mark Calkins left Daniels Communications in 2001. He flies for Alaska Airlines and lives in Murieta, California, with his wife, Deb. Mark is also the proud owner of Pete's Harley-Davidson, now lovingly restored. The bike had been given to Pete by Bill Daniels in appreciation for his old friend's help in breaking the Round the World mark. In Nancy's eyes, Mark was the perfect person to have it.

Dan Miller flies for Southwest Airlines and lives in Salida, Colorado.

Paul Thayer lives in Dallas.

Jane Conrad has remarried and lives in San Antonio.

Peter Conrad works for Sierra Industries, a company that refurbishes airplanes. He is married and has two sons, Christopher and Brad. He lives in Uvalde, not far from his grandfather Winn DuBose's beloved ranch.

Thomas Conrad lives in Denver and works for Price Waterhouse in their software division. He is married and has three children, Christopher, Nicholas, and Thomas.

Andrew Conrad flies for United Airlines. He lives in Denver, is married, and has two children, Christa and Andrew.

Astronaut Alan Bean lives in Houston, Texas. Alan continues to paint pictures of his adventures in space, showing at galleries around the world. One of his favorites, *The Best Astronaut*, is a portrait of Pete on the Moon.

Richard (aka "Dickie Dickie") Gordon lives in Prescott, Arizona.

Jim Lovell lives in Chicago.

Dr. Joe Kerwin continues his work in Life Sciences in Houston. His office is a mile away from Johnson Space Center.

Paul Weitz lives in Prescott, Arizona. After *Skylab*, he went on to command STS-6 in 1983, the maiden flight of Space Shuttle *Challenger*.

Gordo Cooper died in 2004.

Stockton Rush, Pete's lifelong friend from the Main Line, enjoyed a long and prosperous career in business. He spoke movingly at Pete's funeral, never knowing he himself was ravaged with cancer. He was gone six months later.

Nancy Conrad devotes her time and energies to the issue of patient safety on a global scale. "My husband spent a lifetime working in high-risk environments, and yet died a preventable death in a place where safety should have been a given—a hospital."

Nancy has partnered with Dr. Chuck Denham, who spearheads a Safe Practices Program for the Leapfrog Group, a consortium of Fortune 500 companies and organizations appalled by the staggering loss of life due to medical error and working toward a sea change in the world's health care systems. According to the *New England Journal of Medicine*, one out of five of you reading this will experience a medical error in your family at some time resulting in death, disability, or serious harm.

The Rocketman used to say, "When life hands you lemons, you make champagne." In true Conrad fashion, Nancy has dedicated her life to using Pete's unnecessary and preventable death to bring about fundamental change in the hope that this might never happen again.

Which is precisely how the Rocketman would have it. "Life's too short, Natasha," he would always say. "Press on. Don't look back."

Likewise, Pete's business colleagues have indeed pressed on. Universal Space Ware was folded into Universal Space Network no "s" in Newport Beach, California, and appears on the Deloitte and Touche Fast Company 500's list of North American companies to watch. Tom Ingersoll heads the operation as CEO, former NASA associate administrator for space flight Joe Rothenberg is president, and T.K. Mattingly is chairman of the board.

NASA's current vision statement includes the establishment of a lunar base by 2020, employing it for, among other things, a launch platform to Mars. Exactly as Commander Conrad had advised as the Apollo Program was coming to an end . . . *in 1972.*

Echoes of Pete also rang over the California desert skies in September 2004 as Burt Rutan and Paul Allen claimed the X Prize, sending their piloted reusable Launch Vehicle into space and back twice in two weeks. Private sector space travel: It's here, just as the Rocketman foresaw and was working feverishly toward with the now-dormant Universal Space Lines and Rocket Development Company when he left this planet for the last time.

Like a comet streaking by, so went the sixty-nine-year ride that was the life and times of Charles "Pete" Conrad Jr. And like a star in the evening sky, his vision for the future still beckons to us steady, strong, and bright as ever.

"If you can't be good, be colorful." Pete Conrad was both. And it's fun to think, looking at the night sky, that somewhere out there, the good and colorful Rocketman's ride goes on. . . .

# ACKNOWLEDGMENTS

This book began long before Pete Conrad left the planet for the last time. Pete and I talked so many times about his story, we had recorded hours of microcassette tapes, and had begun looking for a cowriter. We had just finished cataloguing and filing the last of the papers, photos, and stuff—this guy kept everything—when the accident happened.

I felt an enormous sense of responsibility to see to it that Pete's story saw the light of day. I knew it had the power to inspire, and so I continued to interview writers. I hadn't found the right combo: a guy who knew space and could understand the colorful character I was so blessed to call my husband. I had just about given up when my colleagues in our health-care foundation suggested I chat with Howie Klausner. They explained to me that Howie was the screenwriter for *Space Cowboys*. I loved the movie and thought it might be interesting to check him out. The minute Howie walked in the door, I knew he was the right one.

It has been an extraordinary collaborative relationship . . . no doubt, made in heaven. Not only is Howie a fine writer but he is an outstanding individual. I have immense admiration for his skills, his fine mind, his compassion, and his unfailing dedication to this project. Without him this book could not exist. I am so blessed to have had the opportunity to work with him. A special thank-you to Chuck and Betsy Denham for connecting us.

My heartfelt gratitude to Lynda Ruffo for suggesting we take the project to Steven Beer, and to Steven for his support; to Gil Amelio and Bill Simon for connecting us to our terrific agent, Bill Gladstone; to Doug Grad, our editor and a superb guy with wisdom and vision, who not only "gets it" but has a wonderful heart; to Tracy Bernstein, who stepped in, stepped up, and could not have been more fantastic; and Kara Welsh at New American Library for her insights. My gratitude beyond measure goes to Pete's sister and twin flame, Patty Moss, and to Gertrude Houston for her assistance. This book would not exist without dear "Aunt Patty."

I bow deeply to the many classmates and friends, each of whom, in a variety of ways, helped us to tell Pete's story: Mario Andretti, Neil Armstrong, Secretary James Baker, Dick Barzin, Alan Bean, Dick Behrendt, Harvey Brandt, Barb Buckner, Bill Bailey, Mark Calkins, Bill Close, Mark Collins, Jayme Coplin, Jack Crosthwaithe, Tim Cutler, Val Gianinni, Richard Gordon, Andy Granatelli, Evan Gray, Gerry Griffin, Dr. Bill Gaubatz, Senator John Glenn, Carl Haas, Jim Hartz, Professor David Hazen, Barry Hey, Nick Heineger, Dick Hobson, Bob Hoover, Herb Hudnut, Tom Ingersoll, Larry Joline, Morgan Jones, Parnelli Jones, Dr. Joe Kerwin, Chris Kraft, Gene Kranz, Jim Lovell, Skip Madden, T.K. Mattingly, Bruce McCaw, John Mecom, Joe Moorer, Tom Parke, Peter Paul, Jim Rathmann, Lloyd Ruby, Monty Rifkin, Dr. Chuck "Cruncher" Ross, Tommy Rowan, Secretary Donald Rumsfeld, Johnny Rutherford, Wally Schirra, Hazel Sekac (Banks), Gardner Smith, Al Taddeo, Bob Taylor, John Tierney, Dave West, and Nancy Wolf.

A special thank-you to Neil Armstrong, for his wisdom, and to the "Dream Team": John Aaron, Dick Gordon, Gerry Griffin, Joe Kerwin, T.K. Mattingly, and Paul Weitz. Your friendship and support during this project was amazing and incredibly heartwarming.

Humble and deep thanks go also to Buzz Aldrin. Since Pete's passing, you and Lois have been especially warm and supportive, and you have reminded me how fortunate Pete and I were to have you as friends. Thank you.

I am grateful for the support and information from former NASA administrator Sean O'Keefe; Sheree Stoval Alexander, Laura Rochan, General Deke Howell, James Brandenburg, Gary Lofgren, and Mike Gentry from NASA; Michael Pablo of the National Aeronautics Administration; and space photographer Roger Ressmeyer. Many thanks to our publicist Janet Donovan of Creative Enterprises International for her outstanding expertise.

Finally, I am indebted beyond words to my family and friends who have been so gracious, patient, and supportive: Judy Beard, Vicki Bagley, Dollie Cole, Bill Daniels, who is in heaven with Pete, TheLea (Karen) Gray, Gwen Griffin, and Bob and Toni Kramer; my aunt, Rosella Wandel; my parents, Jan Lubbin and Seymour Fortner; my brother Tom Fortner; and my dear sons, Dan and Jeff Crane.

Nancy Conrad

I was at Warner Brothers on the set of *Space Cowboys* when word came that Pete Conrad had died in an accident. We had broken for lunch, and I remember looking over at Tommy Lee Jones, playing the part of Hawk, who might as well have been called Pete. He paused in his own moment of silence, as we all did.

I remembered coming on board the film. The studio had a comedy about "old guys in space," but it was slightly preposterous. Still, you knew it could work if you believed, and liked the characters. "You know a lot about pilots and space stuff, right?" my cowriter Ken Kaufman had asked me. Yeah, I guess I did.

Like most every boy in the sixties, I either wanted to be the fifth Beatle or one of the astronauts when I grew up. One of the proudest days of my life was when I read my first book—a giant print "story in pictures" on the original *Mercury* 7. For show and tell, I recited all their names.

I read every astronaut thing I could get my hands on, growing up: Mercury, Gemini, and Apollo. I was too young to remember where I was when

JFK was shot (I was probably in my playpen), but I damn sure remember when we landed on the Moon in '69. G.I. Joe in Outer Space was sitting right next to me in his Mylar suit and space helmet when those grainy images came back live that Sunday night in Nashville.

Sure, I knew who Pete Conrad was. Not only did I crank my channel-changer back and forth between all three networks covering the flight of *Apollo 12*, even if they did lose the TV picture, I read everything I could on the *Skylab* mission, too—Conrad commanded that thing. He'd actually logged more time in space than all of the original guys combined.

Still, when Nancy Conrad contacted me about this project, I was slightly skeptical. I felt I'd kinda done my "astronaut thing" and I wasn't sure I could really bring anything to the party; nothing that hadn't been said or done already.

Curiosity got the better of me, though. I'd met a couple of the original astronauts and a whole crop of the current ones while making the movie, but none had walked on the Moon. Meeting the widow of one of the twelve who had was the next best thing, I thought. So I agreed to have lunch at her home in Huntington Beach, listen to some stories, see some pictures, meet the wife of a real American hero. Humor her, I guess.

"Well," she began, "as you know, he was tossed from the Mercury Program because he had an attitude problem . . ."

No, I didn't know. Or I'd forgotten. It had been a long time since I'd read *The Right Stuff*, and what I did know about Conrad was pretty much the sanitized, NASA-approved PR version of his life. That was the first of many consciousness shifters that day—like the fact that the Moon didn't mean all that much to Pete. Not compared to *Skylab*, and the commercialization of space, the thing both he and Nancy were working on at the leading edge when he died.

This lady was a dynamo. As full of "beans" as Conrad, and though clearly grieving her loss, Nancy was hell-bent on telling this amazing story. "Lunch" turned out to be a five-hour meeting.

I have a simple test before I choose to write anything—do I like the character? Is this person interesting to me? Can I relate to his journey? The triumphs *and* the times he got his ass kicked? And can I even *do* it?

I had to think about this one. Did I really want to spend the next couple years of my life with this man? Besides, I'm just a lowly screenwriter. Even if I did know a lot about "pilots and space stuff," a screenplay is one thing; a book is quite another. I spent a minute alone in Pete's office, thanked Nancy for lunch, told her I'd call her when I got back to Orcas Island, fairly sure I would decline her offer, deferring to a more seasoned "biographer."

As the sun's going down, I'm driving south on the Pacific Coast Highway out of Huntington. Classic rock station on the radio. Elton John's "Rocketman" comes on. I pull over next to the cliffs, watch the sunset and the surfers and listen to the words of that song—

*"I'm not the man they think I am at home—oh no, no, no. I'm the Rocketman."*

I'd been reverently following astronauts my whole life, but this was the first one I thought I could sit and have a beer with, and not feel like a quivering mass of underachieving human Jell-O. He was the best damn pilot anybody ever saw, and flew in space more than all of them, but he was first and foremost, *a guy*; a guy with a warm heart, a quick smile, and always a great joke. A guy who'd gotten his ass kicked by life more than once, but kept coming back. Smiling. And as I would come to know, a guy who left an indelible impression on every soul he encountered in this life.

And listening to that song, I wondered who was choosing whom. Besides, I already had the title.

Like Pete, I am fortunate to be surrounded, guided and mentored in this life by strong and determined women. That started, and continues, with my mother, Mary Neal Kennedy.

I especially want to acknowledge and thank Nancy, whose indomitable, tenacious, never-say-die spirit made this project come alive, and pushed me beyond myself in writing it. I am forever grateful she brought "the Captain" into my life, and I remain in awe at her ability to just get things done. You are a great friend, Rocket Chick.

Thank you, Betsy Ross Denham, for connecting us.

My wife and best friend, Heather Niblo Klausner, has shown otherworldly patience with me, not only in this journey but in my entire meandering writing career. That comes from being a gifted artist herself, and though a terrifically talented photographer, her true gift is the most important one of all—mothering three more strong and determined young women: Kate, Caroline, and Camille, who you better believe are already guiding their daddy.

I also humbly acknowledge all the contributors mentioned by Nancy. It is true that this book could not have been written without them. Special thanks and admiration go to Doug Grad, our editor, who, like a great coach, knows when to hang back and when to push. And "Rocketbabe" Tracy Bernstein, who stepped in like a champ.

And of course there is the Rocketman himself. I was not even remotely prepared for the profound impact Pete Conrad would have on the way I think and see my own life. With all the Right Stuff, achievements, and records that are rightly his, it was his flaws and simple humanity that gave him that irrepressible heart and spirit; and I agree with Dan Goldin that those were the greatest of all his contributions. What a ride you had, Pete. I just hope to have that beer with you somehow, some way. And hear these stories firsthand.

Finally, I give thanks to our Heavenly Father, who brings us together in this life in the most amazing and ironic ways and teaches us constantly that perhaps the finest of His gifts is the gift of each other.

Howie Klausner

# APPENDIX

## Pete Conrad's Navy/NASA Career

### Navy

22 January 1949      Charles Conrad Jr. applied for Naval Officer Candidate Training.

29 March 1949      Charles Conrad Jr. accepted for enrollment in Naval Reserve Officers' Training Corps, fall 1949.

1 July 1953      Ensign Charles Conrad Jr. reported Naval Air Station, Pensacola, Florida, Flight Basic Training Unit.

11 August 1954      Ensign Charles Conrad Jr. activated flying status Fighter Squadron 43.

| | |
|---|---|
| 15 October 1954 | Ensign Charles Conrad Jr. reported to Commander Fleet Air, Jacksonville, Florida. |
| 25 April 1956 | Lt. Charles Conrad Jr. recommended for retention as permanent officer in the Navy. |
| 5 August 1957 | Lt. JG Charles Conrad Jr. recommended for Test Pilot Training. |
| 1 August 1958 | Lt. Charles Conrad Jr. reported to U.S. Naval Test Pilot School, Patuxent River, Maryland. Upon completing course of instruction, was assigned as project test pilot in armaments test division. Also served at Patuxent as flight instructor and performance engineer at the Test Pilot School. Logged more than 6,500 hours flying time, with more than 5,000 hours in jet aircraft. |
| 22 September 1961 | Lt. Charles Conrad Jr. reported 22 September 1961 for flying status Fighter Squadron 96,142, Miramar, California. |
| 27 September 1962 | Lt. Charles Conrad Jr. reported NASA Manned Space Center, Houston, Texas. |
| 23 April 1963 | Lt. Charles Conrad Jr. appointed Lieutenant Commander. |
| 4 September 1965 | Lt. Commander Charles Conrad Jr. appointed Commander by President Lyndon Johnson. |
| 14 September 1965 | Charles Conrad Jr. appointed captain, U.S. Navy. |
| 31 December 1973 | Charles Conrad Jr. retires, U.S. Navy/NASA. |

## NASA Flights

### Gemini 5
21–29 August 1965
Gordon Cooper and Pete Conrad
Titan II rocket

- Distance with Earth orbit: 5,331,752 km (3,312,997 miles)
- Duration with Earth orbit: 190 hrs, 55 min, 14 sec

## Gemini 11
12–15 September 1966
Pete Conrad and Dick Gordon
Titan II rocket
- Altitude with Earth orbit: 1,369 km (850.65 miles)

## Apollo 12
14–24 November 1969
Pete Conrad, Dick Gordon, and Alan Bean
Saturn 5 rocket
- Duration of stay outside spacecraft: 7 hrs, 37 min, 52 sec (Conrad only)
- Duration of a lunar mission: 244 hrs, 36 min, 25 sec
- Duration in lunar orbit: 88 hrs, 56 min, 1 sec
- Duration of stay on the lunar surface: 31 hrs, 31 min, 12 sec
- Duration of continuous time on the lunar surface outside the spacecraft: 3 hrs, 52 min, 6 sec (Conrad only)
- Duration of accumulated stay of all crew members on the lunar surface outside the spacecraft: 14 hrs, 2 min, 25 sec
- Greatest mass lifted into lunar orbit from the surface of the moon: 2705.9 kilograms (5965.6 pounds)

## Skylab II
25 May–22 June 1973
Pete Conrad, Paul Weitz, and Joe Kerwin
Saturn 5 manned rocket
- Distance: 18,536,731 km (11,518,190 miles)
- Duration: 28 days, 0 hrs, 49 min, 49 sec
- Total time in space: 49 days, 3 hrs, 38 min, 36 sec (Conrad only)
- Duration with spacecraft linked: 27 days, 6 hrs, 48 min, 7 sec
- Distance with spacecraft linked: 18,059,391 km (11,221,585 miles)

- Greatest mass of spacecraft linked: 88,054 kg (194,127 pounds)
- Total time in space in orbital flight: 38 days, 23 hrs, 2 min, 11 sec (Conrad only)

## DC-X and DC-X/A

- Flew in less than two years from ATP (also a continuing resolution hiatus) for only $65 million
- Completed all twelve flights successfully
- First reusable vertical-takeoff and vertical-landing rocket
- Demonstrated first intact abort of a rocket
- First time a flight-damaged rocket was repaired and flown again
- Demonstrated first twenty-six-hour flight turnaround of a rocket (touchdown to ready-to-fly status in eight hours)
- First powered vertical rocket landed on multiple surfaces, including concrete, a metal grid over a trench, and unprepared and "prepared" gypsum
- Demonstrated routine small crew operations, sometimes under stressing locale/weather conditions
- Proved in-field flight critical hardware changes possible including computer and isolators
- Flew at speeds of 300 fps forward, 230 fps backward, 110 fps sideways
- Flew high angle-of-attack rotation maneuvers
- Flew a composite hydrogen tank, valve, and feed lines in flight
- Flew a Russian-built AL-Li LOX tank in flight
- Demonstrated blended differential throttling (engine EMA-controlled valves) plus engine gimbaling
- Demonstrated an all-propulsive control capability in flight
- Demonstrated a GH2/GO2 RCS system in flight
- Demonstrated free venting of LH2 and LOX
- Demonstrated GPS INS-aiding in the horizontal channel
- Demonstrated differential GPS aiding in the horizontal and vertical channels
- Retargeted a landing to the pad corner—with complete S/W verification—in four hours

- Survived a helium bubble in propellant lines on Flight 3 liftoff— vehicle recovered control
- Survived the radar altimeter erroneously indicating zero altitude for 1 second at 5,000 feet
- Had the vehicle catch on fire—destroy a flap—but fly the next flight on schedule
- Small operational crew—two-person flight control and ten-person ground crew

## Honors

- Congressional Space Medal of Honor (awarded October 1978)
- Two NASA Distinguished Service Medals
- Two NASA Exceptional Service Medals
- The Navy Astronaut Wings
- Two Navy Distinguished Service Medals
- Two Distinguished Flying Crosses
- Princeton's Distinguished Alumnus Award for 1965
- The U.S. Jaycee's Ten Outstanding Young Men Award in 1965
- American Astronautical Society Flight Achievement Award for 1966
- Pennsylvania's Award for Excellence in Science and Technology in 1967 and 1969
- The Rear Admiral William S. Parsons Award for Scientific and Technical Progress in 1970
- Godfrey L. Cabot Award in 1970
- Silver Medal of the Union League of Philadelphia in 1970
- The FAI Yuri Gagarin Gold Space Medal
- The De La Vaulx Medal in 1970 for *Apollo 12*
- National Academy of Television Arts and Sciences Special Trustees Award in 1970
- Federal Aviation Agency's Space Mechanic Technician Award in 1973
- The Collier Trophy in 1973

- FAI Gold Medal and the De La Vaulx Medal in 1974 for *Skylab I*
- The AIAA Haley Astronautics Award in 1974 for *Skylab I*
- The Harmon Trophy in 1974
- Enshrined in the Aviation Hall of Fame in 1980

## Technical Specifications

### Titan II GLV (Gemini Launch Vehicle)

- Height: 109 feet
- Diameter: 10 feet
- Weight: 340,000 pounds
- Fuel: A 50/50 mix of hydrazine and unsymmetrical dimethylhy-drazine (also known as "Aerozine-50"), with nitrogen tetroxide ($N_2O_4$) as an oxidizer.
- Propulsion: First stage: two Aerojet LR-87-7 rocket engines; Second stage: one LR-91-7 rocket engine
  First stage: Thrust: 430,000 pounds
  Second stage: Thrust 100,000 pounds
- Guidance: Radio-inertial
- Reentry vehicle: Two-man command module with an ablative heat shield
- Cost: $3,160,000 each, in 1965 dollars
- Production quantity: Twelve, built by Martin Marietta

### Saturn 5

- Height: 363 feet
- Diameter: 33 feet (Stage I and II)
- Weight: 6.1 million pounds

- Fuel: First stage—RP1 (kerosene) and LOX (liquid oxygen); second stage—LOX and LH$_2$ (liquid hydrogen); Third stage—LOX and LH$_2$
- Propulsion: First stage—five liquid fueled Rocketdyne F-1 engines; Second stage, five liquid fueled Rocketdyne J-2 engines; Third stage, one J-1 engine.

    First stage: Thrust: 7,680,982 pounds

    Duration: 161 seconds

    Impulse: 1,3000,000,000 lb-sec

    NAR designation: 5 × AC 6,700,000

    Second stage: Thrust: 1,163,854 pounds

    Duration: 390 seconds

    Impulse: 270,000,000 lb-sec (1,200,000,000 N-sec)

    NAR designation: 5 × AB 890,000

    Third stage: Thrust: 203,615 pounds

    Duration: 475 seconds

    Impulse: 100,000,000 lb-sec

    NAR designation: AC 890,000

- Guidance: Inertial
- Reentry vehicle: Three-man command module with an ablative heat shield
- Cost: Development cost $7,439,600,000 in 1966 average dollars. Launch price: $431,000,000 in 1967 dollars
- Production quantity: Sixteen (thirteen were launched, three are on display). Primary contractors were Rocketdyne, North American and Douglas Aircraft

## Saturn IB

- Height: approximately 139 feet
- Diameter: approximately 21.5 feet
- Fuel: first stage—RP1 and LOX; second stage—LOX and LH$_2$.
- Propulsion: first stage—eight Rocketdyne H-1B liquid bipropellant

and four outboard engines gimballed for steering; second stage, one gimbaled liquid fueled Rocketdyne J-2 engine.

First Stage: Thrust: 1,500,000 pounds
Burn time: 150 seconds
Second Stage: Thrust: 200,000 pounds
Burn time: 475 seconds

- Guidance: Inertial
- Reentry vehicle:
- Cost: $101,800,000
- Production quantity: Twelve (nine were launched; one converted to Skylab space station). Primary contractor was Chrysler Corporation

SOURCE: DR. WILLIAM GAUBATZ

## DC-X and DC-X/A

- Height: 39 feet
- Diameter: 13 feet at base (conical-shaped vehicle with a L/D >2.0)
- Weight: 41,630 pounds (fueled)
- Fuel: LOX and $LH_2$
- Range: 20,000 feet
- Propulsion: Control blended aero and propulsion—main engines were gimbaled as well as gaseous hydrogen and oxygen auxiliary side thrusters—aero control by four body flaps with a split windward flap
- Thrust: 4 Pratt & Whitney RL-10A-5 engines, 58,240 pounds total
- Stages: One (DC-X was a demonstrator for a single-stage-to-orbit rocket)
- Fuel Tanks: DC-X used aluminum tanks, DC-XA used a composite liquid hydrogen tank (first of its kind) and a lithium-aluminum liquid oxygen tank (first of its kind)
- Top speed: Mach 0.3
- Guidance, navigation, and control avionics: Advanced 32 bit, 4.5 mips computer, F-15 Navigation System with ring laser gyros. F/A-18

accelerometer and rate gyro package. Global Positioning Satellite P(Y) code receiver. Digital data telemetry system. Radar altimeter.

- Reentry vehicle: n/a
- Cost: $58,900,000 in 1991 dollars
- Main contractor/builder: McDonnell Douglas. Components built by McDonnell Douglas Space Systems Company, Douglas Aircraft Co., McDonnell Aircraft Co., McDonnell Douglas Electronic Systems Co., McDonnell Douglas Missile Systems Co., McDonnell Douglas Research Laboratories, Pratt and Whitney Government Engines and Space Division, Scaled Composites, Aerojet Propulsion Division, Allied Signal Aerospace Co., General Connector, Eagle Engineering, Harris Aerospace Corp., Honeywell, Martin Marietta, Messerschmitt-Bolkow-Blohm/Deutsche Aerospace, Fluor Daniel, Process Fabrication, Inc., Integrated Systems, Chicago Bridge and Iron Services, Inc., SpaceGuild
- Production quantity: One

The DC-X was a pre-prototype experimental demonstrator of a single-stage-to-orbit rocket. Its primary objective was to demonstrate that a rocketship could be made to be totally reusable and be operated with the safety, simplicity and cost effectiveness of an airplane. The focus of the demonstrations was on the operations and safety and the vehicle was not designed to go to space or even reach supersonic speeds. All test and demonstration objectives were met. Had the program continued, the next step was to scale-up the design (DC-Y) to achieve suborbital (300,000 feet) altitudes and flight speeds up to Mach 8. Following these demonstrations the design would be scaled-up (DC-1) to go to orbit and return carrying up to 20,000 pounds of useful payload to orbit or fifteen passengers and a crew of three.

# INDEX